the
About.com guide to
BABY
CARE

A Complete Resource for Your Baby's Health,
Development, and Happiness

Robin Elise Weiss, LCCE

Adams Media
Avon, Massachusetts

About **About**..com

About.com is a powerful network of more than 500 Guides—smart, passionate, accomplished people who are experts in their fields. About.com Guides live and work in more than twenty countries and celebrate their interests in hundreds of topics. They have written books, appeared on national television programs, and won many awards in their fields. Guides are selected for their ability to provide the most interesting information for users, and for their passion for their subject and the Web. The selection process is rigorous—only 2 percent of those who apply actually become Guides. The following are some of the most important criteria by which they are chosen:

- High level of knowledge/passion for their topic
- Appropriate credentials
- Keen understanding of the Web experience
- Commitment to creating informative, actionable features

Each month more than 29 million people visit About.com. Whether you need home-repair and decorating ideas, recipes, movie trailers, or car-buying tips, About.com Guides can offer practical advice and solutions for everyday life. Wherever you land on About.com, you'll always find content that is relevant to your interests. If you're looking for "how to" advice on refinishing your deck, About.com will also show you the tools you need to get the job done. No matter where you are on About.com, or how you got here, you'll always find exactly what you're looking for!

About Your Guide

 Robin Elise Weiss (BA, ICCE-CPE, CD [DONA], LCCE, FACCE) is a childbirth and postpartum educator, doula, doula trainer, and proud mother of seven beautiful children. She has two passions: pregnancy and writing. A natural fusion of the two allows her to share her knowledge with others using a blend of wit and wisdom in the classroom, through her books, and on the Web.

Since 1989, Robin has attended hundreds of births in a variety of settings and educated couples about pregnancy, birth, and parenting. She is the author of several books, including *The About.com Guide to Having a Baby, The Everything® Pregnancy Fitness Book, The Everything® Getting Pregnant Book,* and *The Everything® Mother's First Year Book.*

Acknowledgments

This book is dedicated to all the moms of the October 97 Group—Only October in Common. I've learned much of what I know about being a good parent from this group of ladies who have often opened my mind to new experiences as a mother. Thank you for the friendship and support, even when we agree to disagree.

To the others who have supported me: Teri Shilling, Pat Predmore, Kim Goldman, Eve Hiatt, Paula and Andy Pepperstone, Elizabeth Pedley, Marci Yesowitch Hopkins, April White, Sharon McKenna, Juliet Diestch, Ashley Benz, Jana Pedowitz, Barb Doyen, Brielle Kay, and Bekki Williams.

To Will the Beast, for showing us what courage and strength through adversity is really all about. We all miss you.

To an amazing father and husband, Kevin. Thanks for agreeing to always back me up and for being my coparent on this wild journey.

ABOUT.COM

CEO & President
Scott Meyer

COO
Andrew Pancer

SVP Content
Michael Daecher

Director, About Operations
Chris Murphy

Senior Web Designer
Jason Napolitano

ADAMS MEDIA

Editorial

Publishing Director
Gary M. Krebs

Managing Editor
Laura M. Daly

Acquisitions Editor
Brielle Kay

Development Editor
Katie McDonough

Marketing

Director of Marketing
Karen Cooper

Assistant Art Director
Frank Rivera

Production

Director of Manufacturing
Susan Beale

Production Project Manager
Michelle Roy Kelly

Senior Book Designer
Colleen Cunningham

Published by Adams Media, an F+W Publications Company
57 Littlefield Street
Avon, MA 02322
www.adamsmedia.com

ISBN 10: 1-59869-274-7
ISBN 13: 978-1-59869-274-7

Printed in China.

J I H G F E D C B A

Library of Congress Cataloging-in-Publication Data
is available from the publisher.

This publication is designed to provide accurate and authoritative information with regard to the subject matter covered. It is sold with the understanding that the publisher is not engaged in rendering legal, accounting, or other professional advice. If legal advice or other expert assistance is required, the services of a competent professional person should be sought.

—From a *Declaration of Principles* jointly adopted by a Committee of the American Bar Association and a Committee of Publishers and Associations

Many of the designations used by manufacturers and sellers to distinguish their product are claimed as trademarks. Where those designations appear in this book and Adams Media was aware of a trademark claim, the designations have been printed with initial capital letters.

This book is available at quantity discounts for bulk purchases. For information, please call 1-800-289-0963.

How to Use This Book

Each About.com book is written by an About.com Guide—an expert with experiential knowledge of his or her subject. While the book can stand on its own as a helpful resource, it can also be coupled with the corresponding About.com site for even more tips, tools, and advice. Each book will not only refer you back to About.com, but it will also direct you to other useful Internet locations and print resources.

All About.com books include a special section at the end of each chapter called Get Linked. Here you'll find a few links back to the About.com site for even more great information on the topics discussed in that chapter. Depending on the topic, you could find links to such resources as photos, sheet music, quizzes, recipes, or product reviews.

About.com books also include four types of sidebars:

- **Ask Your Guide:** Detailed information in a question-and-answer format
- **Tools You Need:** Advice about researching, purchasing, and using a variety of tools for your projects
- **Elsewhere on the Web:** References to other useful Internet locations
- **What's Hot:** All you need to know about the hottest trends and tips out there

Each About.com book will take you on a personal tour of a certain topic, give you reliable advice, and leave you with the knowledge you need to achieve your goals.

CONTENTS

CONTENTS . . . *continued*

Introduction from Your Guide

What a brilliant moment in your life, being handed your new baby! There's only one problem: Now that he's here, you haven't got much of a clue about what to do with him. You have the vague sense that he needs feeding, clothing, and to have his diapers changed, but beyond that you're feeling pretty alone in this parenting thing.

The truth is that society perpetuates that feeling of aloneness for new parents. It's a sink-or-swim kind of world for many parents. You might have the idea that you already ought to know all of this stuff about babies and parenting, but at the same time it's stuff that no one has ever taught you, and if you're like a lot of people, you probably haven't had much experience with babies or small children in your life. Some like to say that it takes a village to raise a child; if that's true, then you've got to live in the right village.

The reality is that all new parents have experienced those feelings of isolation at one point or another along the way. On some days, for instance, I'm on top of the world and everything is going better than I could have hoped—the baby is eating well, being friendly to me, and is generally adorable to snuggle with—but then the tide turns. Suddenly, for no reason I can figure out, the baby seems to cry all the time. I am getting no sleep, and I feel worthless in my role as having primary responsibility for this other, mostly helpless person. Your life as a new parent does not need to be like this.

Sometimes we get the sinking feeling that maybe parenting is just too hard, and we're not up to it. Or we might somehow get the opposite message, that we as parents aren't working hard enough. Day in, day out, we are dealing with some seriously smelly issues, and I'm not even talking about diaper duty. Given all of the decisions that parents have to make, it is no wonder that we're a stressed-out group of people. But parenting does not have to be the gut-wrenching experience that has become the subject of so many tales of woe.

With seven children of my own, I have picked up a trick or two along the path of parenting. One of the things I have managed to learn, which seems to be a well-guarded secret in most parenting circles, is that you can have fun and still be a good parent. This book is filled with information meant to help you see that it is possible to have fun, be silly, and yet maintain the sense of style and dignity a parent must have.

The key to great parenting is to relax. There are some things that are now your permanent responsibility. You are charged with doing them, and eventually you will know how to do them well (and in just that certain way that your baby likes them done). But that doesn't mean you have to give up everything else in your life. Being a parent is not about losing yourself; it is about finding a whole new side of your life that you didn't know existed.

If you are worried that somehow you might not be able to be a great parent, don't be—the fun-loving mommy or daddy in you is there, just waiting to come out. My goal here is to show you how you can enjoy your baby-care activities and see that even the mundane tasks like feeding and diaper changing don't have to be viewed as chores. You will also learn how to make your pediatrician your friend and enjoy baby baths, all while raising a great kid. You'll also find some hints and tips from other great parents, who found them out the hard way, that you can incorporate into your parenting repertoire. These small things can make a huge difference in your daily life and can make you and your baby happier as a family.

I challenge you to learn everything you can and to use your knowledge to make the best decisions you can for your family. Being educated and aware will bring you the power to take on this big responsibility with confidence and calm.

Chapter 1

Bringing Your Baby Home

Your Time in the Birth Center or Hospital

You've been caring for your baby for upwards of nine months now, and the last few weeks of your pregnancy have prepared you to finally hold that baby in your arms. In the minutes, hours, and days after you give birth in the hospital or birthing center, you will be surrounded by a helpful and knowledgeable team whose sole purpose is to help you figure out how to care for this new person you've brought into the world. Immediately or very soon after you give birth, one of your nurses will bring you your baby to hold and nurse. The feeling may be overwhelming, but don't worry.

Take advantage of the professional support that surrounds you. Ask for help whenever you think you need it. Ask any questions that occur to you, regardless of how obvious or silly you think they will sound. One thing most new mothers ask about is the baby swaddle technique. You will notice that the nursery nurses have a knack for swaddling a newborn into a snug, secure, and easy-to-handle little package. It looks easy but takes some practice, so

have them show you how it's done. In a very short time, those kind nurses and other health-care professionals will be sending you on your way home with your little one. Now is the time to take advantage of all their years of experience.

Heading Home

You might have thought that planning for birth was about as complicated as it could get. As it turns out, there wasn't enough on your plate after all, and now you need to plan to bring your little one home. Often, parents take great care writing their birth plans and postpartum care plans, but they neglect to think about what is going to happen when they are discharged from the birth center or hospital. Having some idea of the events that are in store for you is a way to help this part of your life go more smoothly.

Have a plan for getting home. By this I don't mean you should plan the route that you will drive on the way home, though if you live particularly far away from where you are giving birth this can be helpful. I am speaking more of an idea of who will do what and who will go where.

If you gave birth in a hospital, you will need two sets of discharge orders—one for you and one for your baby. This can mean that even after you've seen one doctor and gotten the okay, you're stuck waiting for the doctor to discharge you. When this happens it can leave you in limbo for several hours. Since you now know that it is a possibility, you won't be shocked if this happens.

For instance, even after you have been discharged, you are often allowed to stay in your same room while you wait on the pediatrician's orders to release your baby. The problem here is that after you have been discharged, you will not be given any pain medication, food, or any other support from the nurses or hospital staff. So if this happens, be prepared to have your husband or other family member run and bring you food. You may even want to consider getting your prescriptions filled right away so you can have them if you need them. Once you have received one discharge, ask your nurse about how long you can anticipate the other orders will be in coming. This will give you an idea of what to plan for during this time.

It is rarely a big deal for your baby to be discharged first. This is because newborns do not get the same support services, like pain medication, that a new mother may be getting. You should still be able to have lactation services if you need them.

Once it is time for both you and baby to be discharged, someone will come in and notify you. You might laugh after all the times they've told you to get up and walk, but now they will be bringing in the wheelchair to take you down with your baby. Ask for a cart to help carry any gifts or flowers you may have collected while in the hospital.

In some places, it is a hospital policy for a nurse to accompany you to the car. This is to ensure that your car seat is present and properly installed. Don't laugh—many a frantic parent has gone off and forgotten the car seat.

When I had my first daughter, they actually gave me a car seat at the hospital. Once we had her strapped in it, though, I realized it wasn't very newborn friendly. Her head kept nodding forward. I rode in the back of the car to watch her breathe, and I gently held her head upright with my fingers on her forehead so she wasn't slumped forward.

As we drove along, every single pothole sent me into a tizzy. Every car seemed to be pointed at ours. The world looked completely different and scary to me. I was not prepared for what it felt like to leave the hospital as a new mother. Maybe it was the hormones, or perhaps it was the consciousness that my role in life was shifting, but those three miles to our house were

TOOLS YOU NEED

▶ A baby head-rest insert is a must-have. These small, rounded, padded pieces come with some car seats but not with others. The way they work is to fill up the space between your baby's head and the edge of the car seat. This provides a little added support so her little head doesn't flop around. A similar product is a neck ring, but I'm not a fan of these. They look uncomfortable, and I was always worried that it might choke the baby.

▶ In the first several weeks after coming home with my baby, I liked to keep a nursing book handy so I could find answers to basic questions as they occurred to me. *The Nursing Mother's Companion*, by Kathleen Huggins, is an excellent reference book. Another good resource for information about breast-feeding is *The Breastfeeding Answer Book*, by La Leche League.

horribly long that day. My husband was never so glad to pull into our driveway.

Getting home should feel good.   For me, it was a good feeling to arrive back at home with a new baby, but I was also nervous. Our daughter was in her snowsuit and asleep in her car seat. When we were inside the house, my husband and I put the car seat in the middle of the floor, sat on the couch, and spent an hour trying to decide what to do with her. Should we let her sleep there? Should we take off the snowsuit before she got too hot? Did she need to go to her crib? What if her diaper was dirty? It was a long afternoon. Finally she woke up and told us what we needed to do!

It's important that you try not to panic over every little thing during this time. While people often joke that babies don't come with a user's manual, you will get more guidance from your baby than you can possibly imagine. Your baby will tell you everything she needs you to know. You just have to pay attention.

You will begin to learn what your baby needs and when. You will learn when she is hungry, tired, or wet. Your days—and nights—will find a rhythm that is manageable for your whole family. Just remember that on the days when sleep deprivation seems to be clouding everything.

Your goals for coming home should be simple. Bringing a new baby in can be a very interesting feeling. Your goal should be just to relax and settle in to your home. Resist the urge to run around with the baby and get a lot of things done. If you have a multistory house and you haven't set up diaper-changing areas on each floor, that is a great first project. This is a must if you had a cesarean or other surgery.

The diaper changing areas need not be a big deal. You don't need a changing table on every floor; what you're doing is creating a convenience for yourself, something to keep you from running up and down the stairs during the day every time the baby needs a change. Here's what you need for a changing area:

- Diaper pad
- Diapers
- Wipes
- Hand sanitizer
- Spare outfits

I would also recommend setting up a feeding station. Make a small pile of pillows by your favorite chair. Put a book or magazine nearby and perhaps the remote controls. You might even put your favorite nursing book there.

The first few days at home are fun and exciting, even if they do feel a bit strange. After all those months of pregnancy and then the drama of having the baby, it is almost anti-climactic just to be resting at home. It's a good time to finally try out all of that baby stuff you've accumulated over the months. Here is where you get to find out if your baby really looks good in the outfits you selected or if the crib really works. Remember, not all of the new gadgets on the market are good for small babies.

You will also probably do a lot of new parenting things for the first time. These things are basic but important, like bathing your baby, caring for your baby's umbilical cord, and other tasks that go along with having a newborn. Don't be intimidated. Your baby is not going to know if you accidentally skip a cord-cleaning session or a diaper change at 4 A.M.

Practice caring for your baby right away. This is the best way you can build the confidence you need in your parenting skills. This is not the time to let your mother or mother-in-law take care of your baby's basic needs as a way to try to help either you or your husband. If you have help around the house, remind your helper that you need assistance with the housework and not the baby.

There are several rules to having a new baby. And while some are clichés, they are important to remember:

- Sleep when the baby sleeps. (It really does make a difference.)
- Try to get a shower or bath every day, even if you can't manage it until three in the afternoon.
- Eat well; don't let fast and easy food win out over nutrition.
- Say please and thank you to your spouse and other helpers.
- The house will wait. Don't be tempted to choose chores over sleep.

Above all, remember to enjoy your baby. Time will begin to go by faster and faster, and newborns don't stay teeny-tiny for long. Both you and your spouse should take plenty of time each day just to look at and love your baby. It's never too early to start bonding.

If You're Already a Mom

There is something very special about your first pregnancy. Everyone is very quick to tell you about that feeling. Subsequent pregnancies are also special, of course, but they have a different feel. Pregnancy when you're already a parent is special because it comes with something extra. Not only are you experiencing the happiness that comes with having a new baby, but you also get the joy of watching your older child (or children) become a sibling. This is an amazing transformation!

When should you tell your child or children about your pregnancy? You're probably very excited and ready to spread the news, and you should be! It's thrilling to share the joys of preparing for a new baby with the child who was your first baby. This was always the thrill of a subsequent pregnancy for me—watching each of my children become an older sibling.

No matter how excited you are, though, I do not recommend telling your children about your new baby until after the first trimester, at least. As difficult as a long-term project like pregnancy is to explain to a child, pregnancy loss is a much harder concept for a young person to grasp. My husband and I made this mistake once when our first two children were five and three. It was not horrible or disastrous, just painful to watch our little ones grieve. Besides the risk of pregnancy loss, nine months is forever away to a young child.

What and when you tell your children should be based upon their ages. The longer you wait to tell them, the less time they have to be impatient about the baby. And when you do tell them, try to make the time seem more concrete to them. While you want to avoid saying specific dates, you can say things like "Mommy is going to give birth near Thanksgiving." Or perhaps you can say, "Mommy will have the baby around the time you go back to school in August."

Be sure you do not tell your child that you are expecting a baby until you are ready for the world to know. They will tell everyone, and I do mean everyone. Our older daughter liked to make songs up about mommy having a new baby and sing them at the top of her lungs everywhere we went. Another mom I've talked with said her son went around telling everyone that she was going to have a baby come out of her vagina.

The one thing I would certainly recommend is that you tell your children about your pregnancy before they figure it out on

▶ Check out your local hospital or birth center to see if they offer classes for new siblings. If the place where you are planning on giving birth offers one, it can be a helpful way to prepare your child in terms of what to expect and on the logistics of where you will be when the baby comes. If you are having a home birth, the classes can still be helpful. You will just have to explain to your child the extra information about the process of having the baby at home.

their own. If you wait too long, it can lead to negative thoughts and a feeling that you were trying to keep something from them.

Most children are very excited to hear that a baby is coming. Once you have told your children about the baby, be prepared to talk about it nonstop for a while. There are lots of books available on the subject. I have reviewed many of them on my site, but you may also want to read them through before showing them to your children. Find one that is on your child's level. If you have children of different ages, you may need more than one book.

Consider taking your child with you on a visit to your doctor or midwife. Let him see what happens. He may be thrilled to hear the baby's heartbeat. My midwife was always great about letting the kids play with the measuring tape and helping them measure my growing belly. They also got to practice hearing the baby with a special stethoscope. Ask your doctor or midwife for the same type of attention if you desire this for your kids.

If you are giving birth away from home and without your children, be sure that you tell them ahead of time about what they can expect to happen. Tell them that it is possible that the baby might come at night, and if so, they may wake up and you won't be there. Tell them who will be there and what will happen next.

If your child will be attending the birth, whether at the hospital, birth center, or at home, she also needs additional preparation. She needs to know what birth looks and sounds like and what will happen. Depending on the age of your children, it also works out well to give each child a job. Wiping Mom's brow with a wet washcloth is something even the smallest child can do. Also consider giving your children fun jobs, like announcing if the baby is a boy or a girl, even if you already know.

Introducing your baby to his new siblings is exciting.
We've all heard stories of little kids and their cute remarks upon seeing the newest member of the family, like "Take him back," or "Why is he so wrinkly?"

If your older child will be seeing the baby at birth or right after birth, prepare him for what he will see. Babies are born naked. They are wet. They have an umbilical cord. That cord has no nerves and just like a haircut, it doesn't hurt to cut it.

If your child was not at the birth and will be coming in several hours after the baby has been born, you can skip telling him what brand-new babies look like. You will want to consider how you greet your child, though. Do you want to be holding your new baby, or do you want to greet your child first while someone else holds the baby? There is no single right answer to this question; instead, I would say it largely depends on the older sibling.

As the days go on, you will have many opportunities to describe to your older child how he looked as a newborn. Talk about how you took care of him just the same way you are caring for the new baby. Be sure to give him age-appropriate tasks to help with the new baby, if he wants them. Some children want nothing to do with the new baby, which is fine. You do not want to push a kid into helping if his heart isn't in it.

Be careful that you don't blame the baby for anything in front of your child. Avoid saying that you can't do something because of the baby. This will build resentment in your older child, who might start to believe that his whole life has been ruined by the addition of a sibling. Instead of saying "I have to change the baby before I can make you lunch," try saying, "I will fix your lunch in just a minute."

Siblings will have good days and bad. Even if your little one appears to be rejecting the new baby, it is not a cause for worry. Eventually everything will fall into a new pattern of normal.

ASK YOUR GUIDE

Why does my older child suddenly look so big?

▶ It is a weird phenomenon. Even if your older child is still quite small, he will suddenly look very big to you when you see him next to your new baby. The comparison of the older sibling to the baby really puts it all in perspective. The key is remembering that your older child is not any older—he just looks that way. Don't be tempted to treat him as such.

▶ Kevin Henkes has a marvelous book on sibling rivalry called *Julius, Baby of the World*. It is a great look into the life of one big sister and how the long-awaited addition of a little brother to the family turned out to be not quite as fun as she had hoped. I found this book inspiring in my deepest, darkest sibling moments. The kids at least enjoyed having me read to them.

Here are some rules for siblings and new babies:

- Do not leave your older child alone with the baby.
- Set rules about holding the baby.
- Aggression toward the baby needs to be addressed immediately with appropriate actions.
- If you see your toddler carrying your baby, don't scream! Slowly move toward them so you don't startle them.
- Be sure to spend some alone time, even if it's just a few minutes, with your older child.
- Plan activities your older child enjoys. If you are not up to enjoying these things with him, ask another family member or friend to set aside some special time.

Managing Visitors

The arrival of a new baby is like a magnet for relatives, friends, and other well-meaning acquaintances. Everybody wants to visit, to say hello to you as the new mother and to see the tiny baby. Visits like this may be a welcome thing, or they may be increasingly annoying, depending on your moods and on the particular visitor. Luckily, there are things you can do to help make visits more convenient and welcome and even to make your visitors helpful.

Try the concept of visiting hours. One of my clients handed out little notes at her baby shower and at the hospital after her baby was born. The notes were printed with a poem that spelled out the visiting hours and rules for visitors ahead of time. It was a cute and clever way to get her point across.

Boundaries are what postpartum visiting should be about. It is very important that you take advantage of this time to rest and to bond with your new baby. There will be plenty of time later to chat with friends and show off the new baby to coworkers. Still, it isn't always easy to tell these people that you'd rather have your privacy at a time when everyone seems to want nothing more than to visit with you.

While you are in the hospital, it is a bit easier to set boundaries. In some hospitals and birthing centers, the phone is shut off to incoming calls at certain times, ensuring that you and the baby can count on some uninterrupted time together. There are also posted visiting hours, and you have a whole bevy of nurses to run interference for you. If you need privacy or a period of rest, one of your nurses should be more than happy to post a "No Visitors" sign on your door.

Once you are at home, however, it is a bit more difficult to control who comes to visit you, when they choose to visit, and how long they stay. It is important to have a plan for handling visitors, especially at times when you need privacy, and for letting people know when a visit has gone on long enough. This is not a time to worry about being rude or to wonder whether you're hurting other people's feelings. The days after you come home with a new baby are hectic and difficult; it is the best interest of your new baby, your family, and yourself to channel your energy as productively as possible. Here are a few suggestions for handling visitors.

Enlist the help of a close friend, and ask her to spread the word regarding your willingness to see visitors. Maybe you'd like to set aside one day when anyone who feels like it can drop in. Or maybe you'd like people to call and see whether you feel like a little company. Or maybe you'd prefer to invite a few select people to drop by and just keep the rest of the crowd at a distance for a while. Whatever approach you take to visits, ask your friend to let everyone know. Most people have your best interests at heart and simply want you to know they are thinking of you. They will be happy to comply with your wishes.

Inevitably, there will be some people who just drop by anyway. Don't simply refuse to answer the door. People have a way of knowing when someone is home, and it might worry them if no one answers a knock or the repeated ringing of the doorbell. Instead, post a sign on your door announcing your new arrival, with clear language underneath stating how you want to receive visitors: "Thank you for dropping by! Mom and baby are doing well, but they both need their rest and aren't up for visits quite yet. Please call [you or that close friend] to arrange a visit soon."

Controlling who visits and when is only half the struggle. If you let someone in your house, you may have trouble getting rid of the person when you feel the visit should end. Some suggest answering the door in your bathrobe to get visitors to leave quickly. An old wives' tale has you turning a broom upside down and placing it in the corner. The truth is it is hard to turn well-meaning and often gift-bearing guests out of your house. Here's where that good friend comes in handy once again. When she is calling around to inform people of how you prefer to receive visitors, ask her to be very clear about how long (or brief) you expect those visits to be: "Robin would love to see you any afternoon this week, any time between noon and four, but she's only up for really brief visits, so plan to stay for just fifteen minutes or so." Again, people at this point are mainly interested in letting you know they care about you and your new baby. Feelings will not be hurt if you communicate your wishes clearly and diplomatically.

If you don't have a friend you can count on to act as your social secretary, you will have to handle visitors on your own. If someone calls and says she wants to visit you later, explain when would be a good time for you and the baby. If visitors are wearing you out, try to have several guests at once to minimize the amount of time you have people in your house. I have also found that having multiple guests at once encourages them to leave sooner. This works better if the parties don't know each other, but sometimes even if they do know each other, someone will take the lead and encourage everyone to leave.

It's smart to have a plan for handling guests who have overstayed their welcome. You can take a hard-line approach and just announce that it is time for them to leave. You might also drop hints about needing to go take a nap or leave the house. Though some people won't get the hint. I have also been known to take leave with the baby and leave guests with my husband. That usually got the point across.

If someone offers to help you, say yes. This can be difficult to do but it is important. I always encourage new moms to keep handy a list of chores or errands that they need help with. When someone offers to help, produce the list. This prevents you from having to rely on your memory and allows the person to pick something she is able and willing to do. Examples of items on your list might include the following:

- Pick up something for dinner
- Take an older child to the park
- Fold a load of laundry
- Hold the baby while you take a quick shower
- Drive you to see the pediatrician
- Pick up toilet paper and paper towels at the store

All of these are simple tasks. Most people will be overjoyed to help you in any way. If they are unable to help you, they will say so and you can move on.

Dealing with Family Members and Unwanted Advice

A big, joyous event like the birth of a baby should bring out the best in people—and often it does. Your friends and family will probably turn out in droves to offer help and support. Unfortunately, there are also some people who take such an event as an open invitation into your private life. You are going to be tired, overwhelmed, and unsure of certain things right after you give birth. The last thing you need is for anybody, no matter how well meaning, to be prying for details and pushing opinions on you.

Everyone has an opinion on parenting. It's just a fact. You may be shocked to find that the most opinionated family members and visitors are those who aren't even parents themselves! Be prepared for the random aunt or cousin who thinks you should be doing something differently to speak up quite openly and tell you so. As your baby's parent, however, you should also be prepared to assert yourself.

From how you bathe your baby to where she goes to school, there's always somebody who won't like how you do things or the choices you make. My mother-in-law was terribly upset that we didn't have a crib for our third baby. We were confident in our ability to parent without a crib at that point. She kept dropping hints and telling us scary stories and finally she purchased a bassinette and left it on our doorstep. Though she was trying to be nice, her advice was not welcome.

Remind those around you that you value them and their experiences deeply. Tell them that you will definitely ask if you have questions. Remind them that you are a new mom and that finding your own way comes with the territory. Sometimes this means making small mistakes or big ones. The bottom line is that you are confident in knowing when to ask for their help.

If you have house guests who are staying for a while, your life may not be so simple. Remind them that your goal during the time they stay with you is to either have them help with the house or visit with you and the baby. It is not for them to take care of your baby—that is your job.

Sometimes you have to stand your ground. No matter how well-meaning others are, this is your baby. From feeding methods to sleeping arrangements and everything in between, you and your partner have the final say. While there will always be disagreements over how you care for or raise your child, they will diminish as you grow as a parent. It is almost that as a new mother you are more vulnerable, and therefore people feel like it is open season. Remember that standing your ground is never the wrong path.

Basic differences of opinion are never so pronounced or painful as when there's a new baby in the house. There are some things that are almost certain to give rise to family arguments, like a difference in ethnicity or religion. You and your partner may have seen certain conflicts coming from miles away—perhaps while you were still pregnant. And you may have tried to forestall any problems by coming up with solutions to the big issues ahead of time. No matter how well prepared you were before the fact, actually holding your baby may make you have different feelings than you anticipated.

While it is okay to readdress topics, be sure that it is done appropriately. Don't let anyone browbeat you into doing something you don't want to do. Talk calmly and rationally. If you are having trouble doing this, suggest that a decision be postponed.

You might try speaking politely but firmly to whoever is offering an opinion: "Thank you for caring so deeply about us. I know this is a very important topic to you. My husband and I have discussed it at length. Our decision was not made lightly, and it is our final decision. Please don't keep bringing it up." Something along these lines is diplomatic and respectful while also perfectly clear.

One of my clients said that she was unable to get her husband's family to drop their argument over a religious ceremony and her baby. She finally had to lay down the law in a more forceful way. She had to say that if they couldn't be supportive of her choices, then they were not invited to attend. The key here was the support of her husband.

A Word about Pets and Your Baby

While this might be your first human baby, that doesn't mean you are an inexperienced parent. You might already have a furry baby in your home. Many people love and care for their pets as though they are members of the family. Having a baby doesn't have to change how you feel about your pets. There is room for both pets and babies in your family. Depending on how your pets are allowed to behave in the house, however, it might mean that your pets are in for a big change.

Prepare your pets for the baby's arrival ahead of time. Much as you would prepare any other older sibling for the changes about to come, it is wise to do the same for your pet. For cat lovers, this basically amounts to teaching your kitty that some places in the house are off-limits. For dog lovers, the job is a bit more complex.

If your dog has already encountered young children at the park or at your house, when friends with kids came to visit, you might have an idea of how your dog feels about little people. This test, however, is of limited value when it comes to figuring out how your dog will react to what amounts (in its head, anyway) to an invasion of its turf. Even the calmest and best-trained dogs can have negative reactions to a new baby. It is therefore worthwhile to spend a little time and energy getting your dog ready for the changes to come.

The first change has to do with your dog's idea of dominance. Dogs have a pack mentality, in which they are constantly evaluating their place in the group they belong to to figure out where they are in relation to the leader (you). It is critical that your dog understand that your baby is another dominant human being. Because it will be some years before your child can exert the will to show a dog directly that he or she is dominant, it's up to you to teach your dog its place in the new pack.

If you enjoy training your dog and have had success using positive training techniques, this challenge will be fun for you and your dog. However, if you are short on time, this is a very good time to seek help from a dog-training professional. It is absolutely essential that your dog understand clearly what behaviors you expect and what it can do to be a valued member of the pack. There is nothing worse for you, the baby, or your dog to have a situation in which nothing the dog does is right. Going to a dog trainer now will save you a lot of trouble in the long run.

There are some basic practices and commands that will help you and your dog be successful in the short run. For instance, it is now time to establish very clear boundaries about where your pet is allowed to be in the house. Perhaps you have always allowed your dog to join you on the sofa, or to curl up with you in bed. If so, now might be a good time to teach your dog the "Off" command, so it knows when the furniture is off-limits, or to teach it to stay off the furniture entirely. This will be an especially big relief to you in the days right after you bring your new baby home—your hands will be full enough without having to worry about your pup jumping up to join the fun in your lap.

It is also a good idea to teach your dog to go to a particular spot on your command and to stay there until you release it. This is a good time to introduce a crate or kennel to your dog's routine, if you haven't already. With a baby in the house, it can be a lifesaver to put the dog someplace safe and out of the way (where the dog also feels secure and not punished in any way). Again, this is where a dog trainer can be very helpful.

To keep a cat out of the baby's crib, you might try draping a sheet over that or any other furniture that is off-limits. You can also try keeping a spray bottle filled with water near any furniture you want the cat to stay off of. Spray the cat whenever you find it trespassing—this is a gentle way to teach your cat its new boundaries. Given the way cats feel about water, it's a lesson your cat is also likely to learn fairly quickly.

Your dog should also learn to leave the baby's things alone. According to many experts, that means no sniffing, smelling, slobbering, or chewing on anything that belongs to the baby—clothes, toys, furniture, or other accessories. Dogs sniff and mouth things to learn about them, it's true, but once they've had that brief initial sniff, they should not be allowed to "control" those baby items in any way. For a dog, the power to hold, carry, and chew indicates that the dog is in possession of a particular item—think of how your dog carries a favorite toy or a nice bone. If your dog is permitted to get the idea that it "owns" the baby's things, it will be more likely to have a sense of dominance over the baby, too. A good dog trainer (one who uses positive training techniques) will be able to show you how to introduce your dog to the baby's things without forming that unwanted sense of possession.

It can also be helpful to institute more discipline into your dog's life in general. Teach your dog to stay in a certain spot while you eat dinner, or have your dog sit or lie down a certain number of times before feeding a treat or giving a nice scratch. Dogs thrive on discipline—they want above all else to know that a strong leader is in charge of the pack, and they're happy for that leader to be you.

When the baby comes home, the dog's routine will change drastically, a change that can be upsetting for even the best-tempered pets. Babies are unnerving to almost any dog. They are small, they smell funny, they make startling and sudden movements, and the noises they make sound a lot like the squeaks and cries of creatures that the dog's wild ancestors would consider prey. On top of all that, you have suddenly withdrawn a lot of the attention that once went to your pet and are devoting it to this strange new creature. No wonder so many dogs react badly to the introduction of a baby to the household.

Again, a good dog trainer can help you prepare your dog for the baby invasion so that your dog continues to feel like a valued and successful member of the pack. One thing you can do to get ready for the time you will be away having the baby, and for the baby's introduction to the home, is to put your dog on a predictable schedule far in advance of the baby's arrival. If your dog knows to expect time outside in the morning, for instance, and a walk in the afternoon, it will be less likely to find the other upsets to the household routine unnerving. Therefore, during the time you are gone, it is a good idea to arrange for a friend or a professional pet-sitter to come by and keep your dog on schedule. When you come home with the baby, try to go in alone first to greet your dog and let it smell the baby's scent on you. Then ask your dog to go to its spot, or put it in its crate, before you bring the baby inside. The dog's special spot or crate is a safe spot where the dog is likely to feel most secure. If the dog is allowed to stay there during the tumultuous time of bringing the baby inside for the first time, both you and the dog are likely to find this transition a little more peaceful.

Sometimes there are problems. Most of the time, problems happen when families assume that their wonderful pets (usually dogs) will not be affected by the new baby in any way.

ELSEWHERE ON THE WEB

▶ The Humane Society of the United States offers some great information on introducing your baby to your pets and vice versa. This includes information from animal professionals and videos. You can even print or customize the hints for your own situation. Check out the Humane Society's Web site, at www.hsus.org.

Unfortunately, this almost never works out. If you think about it from the dog's point of view, you can understand why. The pack structure, again, is all-important to the dog, who always knows what members of the family are above it in the pack hierarchy and what members are below it. Placement in the pack determines all kinds of things that we as people hardly think about at all. Suddenly, with a baby in the house, your dog is expected to treat a totally helpless creature with deference. This is unnatural to the dog. Unless you have prepared your dog (again, sorry to be boring here, but preferably with the help of a good dog trainer using positive training techniques), there is likely to be some conflict.

The most important thing to remember is never to leave your baby in a position or place where your dog can exert dominance over him or her. If you want to put the baby on the floor, for instance, be sure the dog is in its crate first. If your baby is asleep in his or her carrier, and you want your dog to have a little free time in the house, put it on a leash and keep it by your side. Never leave your baby alone with your dog, even for a minute. This is hard for people whose dogs are sweet and gentle to understand, but it is vital. A huge number of dog-bite victims are children, and most children who are bitten suffer damage to their faces, which can be devastating. Dogs bite not only out of aggression but out of fear, and while it seems silly in the human way of thinking, babies are scary to a lot of dogs. Innocuous things like a sudden hand movement can startle a dog and cause it to bite.

Aside from the training you have done with your dog prior to bringing your new baby into the family, the best thing you can do to help your dog through this transition time is to set aside special time for fun activities. Take ten minutes while the baby naps to throw a ball or just sit and give your dog a nice scratch. If the weather permits, bring the dog with you on short errands. Put the dog's crate in a central part of the house so that it is still in the middle of things even during crate time. You might even consider hiring a neighborhood child to take your dog on walks or to play in the yard if you can't find the time to do it yourself.

Young children are a challenge to the pet-lover throughout their early years. Once your dog gets used to having a baby in the house, everything will change again as soon as your baby starts to crawl. And toddlers are a challenge to even the best of dogs. Again, just in case you haven't gotten the idea yet, it is best to turn to a professional when it comes to acclimating your dog to the presence of your new baby. The cost, time, and energy you spend now will be well worth it in terms of the continued happy companionship you get from your beloved pet in years to come.

Get Linked

Bringing your baby home and getting into the swing of a new normal in your life is not always easy. Here are some links on my About.com site that can help you ease into your new family life.

UNWANTED ADVICE

Just as your pregnant belly drew strangers who thought it was perfectly permissible to reach out and touch you, a new baby will bring on a flurry of unwanted advice. Here is a practical look at how to take what you need and leave the rest while still enjoying your siblings.

http://about.com/pregnancy/unwantedadvice

TIPS FOR NEW DADS

This is a primer for dads on managing life with a new baby and a new mom. The information you'll find here will definitely give you a great start on staying out of trouble with your spouse and looking like an a-okay guy.

http://about.com/pregnancy/dadtips

FIRSTBORN JEALOUSY

If you have other children, you may wonder how bringing a new sibling into the family will affect them. Here are some secrets to beating firstborn jealousy before it ever gets a chance to start.

http://about.com/pregnancy/jealousy

PREPARING FOR A NEW SIBLING

It's never easy having a baby. But when you have to worry about adding another baby to your life, there are other things to worry about—like your first "baby." Here are some ways to help ease your older child into the transition.

http://about.com/pregnancy/newsiblings

Chapter 2

Getting to Know Your Baby

The Scoop on Bonding

The bond between parent and child is meant to be a strong one. Like iron, the tie between you and your child should be strong enough to weather long, sleepless nights and dirty diapers, the terrible twos, and teen angst. If you listen to other new mothers or read parenting magazines, you might get the idea that bonding is a perfectly wonderful state that happens naturally, all on its own. Still, you might wonder: Just how do you bond with a baby who is seemingly incapable of telling you what she needs?

Bonding doesn't happen in an instant. You probably hear the word *bonding* and imagine a beautiful scene at birth. Your baby emerges, and you immediately fall in love with her serene face and beautiful smile. This isn't always the way it works.

The American Academy of Pediatrics (AAP) recommends that your baby go straight to you at birth for bonding and breastfeeding purposes. This special time is marked by a heightened sense of

WHAT'S HOT

▶ If you or your baby is very ill, and the two of you need to be separated for medical purposes, see if you can send your husband or another family member or close friend who attended your birth with the baby. This will help keep you aware of how the baby is doing. It does not mean that you cannot bond with your baby. Bonding is a process that takes time, not a single moment that once past is gone forever.

alertness on the part of your baby. You are also especially attuned, given the fact your hormones are ripe from labor and birth. Even if you only hold your baby, this taking-in phase is wonderful for most moms.

While there are some moms and dads who report that they fell immediately in love with their baby at birth, many don't report that at all. It is more common to hear mothers and fathers say that they felt relieved or tired or just glad that the baby was here. Labor is an amazing but difficult process that has the potential to leave one feeling quite worn out. This can make the process of bonding slightly more difficult.

Some parents aren't allowed time to bond with their baby because their baby is taken away for routine observation or necessary medical tests. Be sure to tell your practitioners that you want to be able to hold, touch, and stay with your baby in these early first moments of life. This time frame is special, even when you're also feeling tired, overwhelmed, and relieved.

Don't worry about getting it right. There isn't anything you have to do in a certain order or just right to help you bond. Just be there with each other. I would suggest limiting outside distractions. Here is where it's a good idea to put up those boundaries and keep unnecessary visitors out of the room for a while. Cuddle your baby skin-to-skin at the breast, even if your baby isn't currently nursing, and cover you both with a warmed blanket.

Taking your baby in is a great experience. Look at your baby. Stare into her eyes. Talk to her. Tell her whatever comes to your mind. Remember there isn't anything right or wrong here. Have your husband talk to her. She has been hearing both of your voices for months. They will comfort her in her transition because they are familiar to her.

You might have fun chatting with your husband about who the baby looks like. Does she looks like you or your husband did at birth? Does she look like siblings? Maybe your baby has traits you thought she would. My husband and I were shocked to see our twins when they were born. All I could say was, "They've got red hair!" It seemed so strange and funny at that moment, particularly after four blonds.

Another thing to do is simply to restate the obvious about the journey to birth and reliving the details with your baby. I've seen many a mom turn to her baby and ask, "Was that hard for you, too?" The good news about this immediate post-birth bonding is that labor is over. You're not usually thinking about the labor, and you don't feel like you're in pain. Though you may be a bit sore, most moms say they don't even notice that part once their baby is placed in their arms.

Continue this process of snuggling and talking often and frequently throughout your baby's first days and weeks. Eventually you won't even have to think about it. This becomes snuggle time. It is also something that you all will look forward to doing together.

Finally, remember that the way you bond is individual. Just as no two people are alike, even identical twins, no two people will have the same bond. It is just as important for you to bond with the baby as it is for dad to establish his unique relationship with his child. These ways you connect are likely to be very different—think of the way you spend time having fun with friends versus how he spends time together with his friends. They are usually radically different with only slight similarities.

Getting in Sync with Your Baby

Finding your rhythm as a parent means having an idea of what your baby needs and expects of you. It is always helpful to feel that you're doing some things right, at least. It gives you a sense of direction and purpose, even when you're not quite sure what you are

ASK YOUR GUIDE

What if I don't fall in love right away?

▶ Don't be too concerned. If you have a tough pregnancy and/or labor, you'll probably just be exhausted right after the birth. If you've spent a lot of time being worried about getting to this point, you might be in a state of shock or denial that the pregnancy is over. Time will usually cure all. Just be content to be there with your baby and let everything else fall into place. Love at first sight is not a given.

▶ Parenting is a daunting task; even if you've done it before, you've never done it with this baby. You spend a lot of time doubting what you're doing, and you might even worry about doing it wrong. I truly enjoyed Lu Hanessian's book, *Let the Baby Drive*. It was a great reminder that parenting is a fluid process and that I had to learn to trust my baby and myself.

doing or why. Finding your rhythm also is calming because it helps you know what you'll be doing next or gives you a general idea of what to expect, anyway. The key to doing this is to find your baby's natural rhythm and go with it.

Listening to your baby is key. Believe it or not, even a tiny baby has a personality. This was very evident to me when I had my fourth baby. I told my grandmother that I'd come over later, if Lilah wasn't in one of her moods. My grandmother laughed and asked me what I meant. I said that even though Lilah was only three months old, there were certain times when it was simply impossible to get her to do anything happily, like go on a trip outside of the house. I was "reading" my baby.

Being able to read or listen to your baby is a huge help in parenting. It lets you know when and how to help your child. For example, if you have a baby who is cranky, you are going to think twice about going somewhere where you need to be quiet. You will either plan to go at a different time or alter where you are going. This shows respect for your baby's ideas. After all, do you like being dragged to the mall when you're in a foul mood?

This isn't to say that your baby's mood should dictate where you go at all times. Sometimes there is no way around what you need to do, even if your baby's mood says otherwise. But the flexibility and respect that you get from paying attention to your baby's needs are helpful to you both.

Go with the flow, even if that's not your style. That is one of the hardest lessons of new parenthood. You will have to learn to occasionally be late and to feel a bit out of sorts and intermittently discombobulated. It goes with the new parent territory.

Many parents find this early stage terrifying. You might fear that your life is never going to be normal again. The good news is that this does not last. As you find the flow of life—your new normal—you will begin to see clearly again.

You will find the pattern of days and nights that make you, your baby, and your family happy and healthy. This does not look the same for every family. It will vary depending on your general lifestyle, typical schedule, and what kind of structure you and the others around you need.

Feel free to play with what works and what doesn't. For example, if you had your heart set on using cloth diapers but you find that this is just not practical for your family, don't beat yourself up. Go the disposable diaper route. If you thought a crib was the way to go but later decide you want to try co-sleeping, go for it. Every parent learns by doing. This trial and error method will help you find what is best for everyone. It will also help you in dealing with the bumps in the road that are bound to come up.

Talking to Your Baby

Your baby loves your voice. She doesn't care if you don't have the best singing or speaking voice in the world. She just knows your voice and wants to hear it. When you talk to her, it teaches her how people talk and carry on a conversation and how to communicate in general. The sound of your voice is also a great way to strengthen the bond that is already growing between you. Even though she may not seem to be paying attention, you are building her memory of your voice and preparing for the time when she can distinguish sounds and even begin to respond with vocal sounds of her own.

Feel a little funny talking to an infant who can't even understand what you're saying? Don't worry! You have a lot to communicate to your baby, though at times you may feel like you don't know what to say. The easiest way to talk to your baby is just to start.

▶ If you are feeling out of control of your life, try a calendar or journal. Use it to see if there is a pattern that you are missing out of desperation for sleep. Sometimes you figure out a solution to a particular problem and then, in all the turmoil and sleeplessness that is your new life, you forget about it right afterward. A journal is a good way to keep track of all the things you're learning. It may also help you jot down feelings and ideas about getting your life into some semblance of order that makes everyone happy.

If you can't think of anything to say, simply begin to narrate your day. Just tell your baby everything you're doing as you're doing it: "Good morning, Baby. It's time to get up. Oh, it looks like you have a wet diaper. Let's get you changed so you'll feel clean."

You might also try talking about your baby's body or characteristics. "What big blue eyes you have, just like your daddy's eyes." "You're a strong baby! Look at you holding your head up." The great thing is that your baby won't care if you sound a little goofy or trip over your words. She will love the sound of your voice, no matter what you're saying to her.

If even this kind of chatting is hard for you, reading can make a great substitute or at least get you going in the right direction. Snuggle up together in a comfy chair or in bed and get a book to read to your baby. She will learn the natural rhythm of speech. You will also be cluing your baby in on how emotions are conveyed through different tones of voice. After all, the Big Bad Wolf sounds much different from Red Riding Hood.

Singing can be a great form of communication, too. Go ahead and sing any little tune you know. The sound of your voice will soothe your baby, even if you don't consider yourself the best singer. If you're not into singing, you can simply play music for your baby. Lullabies are a great choice, but if that's not your cup of tea don't worry. I have a son who grew up with nothing but the Beatles, and he still loves them to this day. Choose music that you and your baby both seem to like.

You can tell that babies like music by the way they respond. When you're playing upbeat music, your baby will look happy or intrigued. As your baby gets older, she may decide to move to the beat. At first, all she will be able to do is bob her head to the beat or maybe clap her hands. When your baby is more mobile, she may respond to the music with whole body movements, all the way to dancing or spinning.

Slower music will help your baby calm down. This is a good way to transition into naptime or just to spend some peaceful minutes together. While listening to a soothing tune, you may notice that your baby enters a quiet alert state, in which she is awake but lying still and paying attention. You may also find that she drifts off to sleep; this is because she is feeling relaxed.

Reading to Your Baby

Reading is a pleasure that your child will enjoy throughout her life. It's a good habit to instill early, and luckily it's one that you and baby will both have fun doing. All it takes is a comfortable place to sit, a little peace and quiet, and a good book. Babies are never too young to be read to. As your baby gets older, you may find that she is more interested in handling the book than listening to you read. That's all right. As she gets older, you will find that she is eager to climb into your lap with her favorite book and sit while you turn the pages together. It might take a little longer still before she has the patience to listen to you read every word on every page, but the important thing is that she associates books with fun.

Good baby books have a couple of things in common. They are usually sturdy enough to withstand the manhandling a baby can dish out—including teeth. A good baby book will usually have lots of bright, colorful pictures or faces. You will find that even a very young baby can distinguish a face on the printed page and will point to it—especially the eyes. The book should also contain words, though the number of words can vary from a word or two per page to small paragraphs. This won't be very important until the child is older. I generally try to vary the styles and content in the books I pick up for my kids.

TOOLS YOU NEED

▶ You need something on which to play music. The new MP3 players are really great for holding your music and baby's music. I have to admit that "The Hokey Pokey" is in the top-ten-played songs on my iPod. The older kids dance and sing, while the baby claps and enjoys watching the others dance. Best of all it's portable—from the car to the bedroom and even the backyard with portable speakers.

You may find that your baby has a favorite book. Even a young baby can begin to learn what the cover of her favorite book looks like. You will see her eyes light up when she sees it, and as she gets older, you'll hear squeals of joy when it's time to read that book.

When choosing books to read to your baby, don't fret too much. Do not panic about not being able to stand baby or children's books. When my oldest was a newborn, I was finishing up a college-level chemistry class. Every night I would sit down to study with her. I would read the text out loud in various ways to keep her entertained. Who knew that ionic and covalent bonds would be so entertaining to a two-month-old baby? But she was happy, and I got a good grade.

Conveying Love Through Touch

Touch is one of the main ways that human beings show each other how they feel. People may offer a hug to show love, a pat on the back to show approval, and any number of other displays of affection and emotion. With that in mind, it makes sense that babies would need to be touched, too. In fact, babies need a lot more touch than we might think.

If you take a look at all the products that are sold for the specific purpose of holding your baby, you might wonder if your baby needs you to hold her in your arms at all. Think about the products that hold babies: cribs, pack-and-plays, highchairs, car seats, swings, and bouncers. It's true that you might need some or all of these tools for different times in your baby's life, but you should be careful not to rely on any of them too much. Your baby needs and wants to be held and touched by you.

So, how should you hold your baby? Babies like to be held with confidence. They want to be held close to your body. Early on, swaddling is a way to help your baby feel safe and secure. They aren't used to having their arms and legs flailing. After all those months of being tucked up in your womb, freedom of movement is a disconcerting feeling for them. Holding your baby tight or in a swaddle wrap can make her feel much more secure and calm.

Aside from simply holding your baby, there are lots of simple ways to fit touch into your life. When you dress your baby, feed your baby, and play with your baby, you will also be touching your baby. Be sure to use a firm but gentle touch. Try not to tickle her at a young age. Learn what types of touch she enjoys. Just as some grownups enjoy being gently massaged or softly caressed, while others prefer a more firm touch, babies often have a preference about the kind of touch they enjoy. You will be able to tell your baby's preference easily as she will be sure to tell you if you touch her too softly, in a way that tickles, or too firmly, in a way that might be uncomfortable. Your baby will let you know what she enjoys through her calm, relaxed state and eventually her smiles and words.

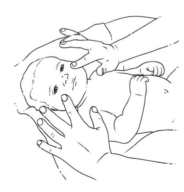

▲ Infant face massage

With our third child, my husband and I took an infant massage class. We learned all sorts of interesting facts about touch and babies. But more important, we learned what Isaac wanted and what he didn't. The instructor was also great about teaching

ELSEWHERE ON THE WEB

▶ The International Association of Infant Massage (IAIM) Web site explains the benefits of infant massage in great detail. The process of giving your baby a healthy, safe massage does good things for the baby, the person giving the massage, and the rest of the family. You can also find local infant massage instructors on the IAIM Web site or purchase products to help you in the infant massage path. Visit www.iaim-us.com.

everyone special "massages" for problems like gas and colic. The class emphasized respect for your baby and how to convey that respect and love through touch.

My husband loved it so much he decided we'd go back with each subsequent child. It really helped him connect with the babies, particularly when he was working and away from them during the day. This gave him his own ritual to do with them—that special bonding time.

What to Do When You Don't Feel Connected

Let's face it: There will definitely be days when you will feel out of sync or disconnected from your baby and maybe even your entire life. Maybe you're overwhelmed, overtired, or trying to do too much. Suddenly that feeling of bliss that you usually get when laying eyes on your baby has been replaced with another feeling—maybe you get a sense of uneasiness, or you feel like crying when faced with the twentieth dirty diaper of the day, or you don't want to sit and cuddle and wish you could just tuck up in bed all by yourself.

Often, new mothers get this sense of not fitting in with their babies when they've been getting a lot of "advice" from well-meaning friends or family, who are also sending the message that the way the mother is doing things is all wrong. Don't panic; this feeling happens to everyone. Typically, it is not a long-term problem, though it is a sign that you need to take action to help you feel better and more connected.

First, figure out why you don't feel connected to your baby. Perhaps you are feeling disconnected because you don't have a lot of time to spend with your baby. There are ways to enhance the time that you do have. Try carrying your baby in a sling when you are around, even if the baby is sleeping. Your baby

TOOLS YOU NEED

▶ Find a good lotion or massage oil to give your baby a massage. Make sure that the oil or lotion you choose is nontoxic in case your baby decides to put a newly massaged hand into his mouth. It doesn't have to be anything fancy or expensive, just something to reduce the friction of a massage. This makes the process more enjoyable for your baby and easier for you to accomplish. We used grapeseed oil that was cold pressed without chemicals.

will be comforted by your presence, and you'll get to learn your baby's rhythm.

If you are feeling like your life has been taken over by stuff or by commitments that seem to multiply without end, try to reclaim it. We all have problems saying no. You're asked to help do something for your neighborhood association or at work. A friend wants to know if you can come to her book club. You promised your mother that you'd visit Aunt Sally this weekend. Oh, and don't forget to cook dinner, finish your chores, deal with your house, play with the baby, and handle everything else in between!

Now, I'm going to share a very special piece of advice: Learn to say no. It can be difficult to do. You want to help, but spending too much energy on things that are not top priority will put a strain on you mentally, emotionally, and physically. It's a real problem that women have today. To take care of yourself and your family, you have to set boundaries, figure out where your time is most valuable, and maintain your sanity.

Every week I try to sit down with my calendar and look at the things I know will be expected of me in the days ahead. I block off those hours, mornings, afternoons, or even whole days when I have obligations and know I will be busy. The areas that are left are my pockets of free time. I choose one of these times (yes, just one!) in which I can add a yes to something I've been asked to do. This means I might say that on Wednesday at 3:00, I can go to the mom's meeting where I've been asked to help with a presentation. If an obligation, request, or favor doesn't fit into one of the pockets of free time that I've identified for a given week, then I'm sorry, I can't do it. I use the other free slots to deal with my life and do what I need or want to do.

So, when you find yourself with a pocket of free time, think of what you'd like to do with it. There are plenty of times when I need a "time out." My kids will sometimes see it before I do and

Can feeling disconnected indicate a real problem?

▶ Feeling disconnected can be a sign of postpartum depression. The key to telling the different between run-of-the-mill blues and actual depression is that depression goes on for more than a few days, doesn't get better no matter what changes you make in your schedule or how much rest you get, or continues to get worse. We often think to worry about mothers who are outwardly saying negative things, but the quiet mother who doesn't say or do anything that looks wrong can also be in great need. Contact your doctor or midwife for a referral if you feel you need help.

say, "Mommy, take a time-out in the tub." Sometimes that short burst of alone time is enough to set me right again.

Other times, a laid-back family activity can rejuvenate you. Cooking a meal together can be a fun diversion. Toddlers and preschool-aged children love to cook, even if they're only dumping already-measured ingredients into a bowl. The point is that if everyone in the family is occupied and happy, you are probably going to be happy as well.

So how does all of this relate to your baby? If the reason you're feeling disconnected from your baby has to do with all the other complications in your life, then you have to acknowledge that fact and do something about it. When I'm in a peaceful frame of mind, I have more energy for my family, my mood is better, and life seems more doable. Don't feel guilty if some alone time is the solution. You'd be surprised what being alone for a few minutes can do. I purposefully get up fifteen minutes before everyone else in my family, just to be alone for a while. It clears my mind and gives my soul a rest.

Take a "babymoon." Technically, a **babymoon** is meant to take place right after your baby is born, but it can be done at any time, even months down the road. All it means is close out the rest of the world for a time. This can be anywhere from an hour or two to several days or longer.

During your babymoon, do nothing but spend time with your baby. I find this works better if you lock yourself in your bedroom without other distractions. Take your baby to bed and simply lie there and look into each other's eyes. This may sound goofy, but it can really help.

You can also try skin-to-skin contact. Undress your baby so that she is wearing just her diaper. Her soft skin will feel nice to the touch and give you the opportunity to open up all of your senses, including your olfactory senses (sense of smell). Babies have their own special smell, from their hair to the way the skin smells at the back of their necks. Investigate your baby to see where she smells nicest to you. Smell is one of the most basic senses a parent has and can really help you reconnect or connect quickly.

Try bathing with your baby. Water can help a baby relax, and the feeling of it might encourage your baby to move around a bit. It is fun to share this experience with your little one and watch her enjoy the feel of the water. Be careful, of course, as a slippery baby and a tubful of water can be a dangerous combination. Just hold your baby firmly while allowing her to move her arms and legs through the water. This can be a magical experience.

Get Linked

Here are some links to my About.com site that will provide you with great ideas on how to get to know your baby. The more you know, the stronger foundation you have to build that trusting relationship you will need to thrive as a parent/child couplet over the course of your lives.

BABY LOVE: BONDING

This link is all about the concept of bonding with your baby at birth. The information you'll find here gives you a look at how to help facilitate bonding and how to make it work for you.

 http://about.com/pregnancy/bonding

BOOKS TO READ TO BABIES

Reading books to your baby is not only a good way to foster intellectual development, it also helps your baby grow attached to you as a caregiver.

 http://about.com/pregnancy/readtobaby

HOW TO HOLD A BABY

Sounds simple, but the way you hold your baby can help you and even improve baby's health—as you might have learned already, holding and carrying a baby can make you weary. Find out which holds work better when.

http://about.com/pregnancy/holdbaby

Chapter 3

Feeding Your Baby

Getting on Track with Breastfeeding

These days, the medical community agrees that breastfeeding is best for you and your baby. Breast milk is the perfect food for your baby, and the act of breastfeeding after your baby is born helps signal your body to recover from labor and delivery, too. But while you'd like to think that breastfeeding is so natural that it just happens without any trouble, this is not always the case. Many mothers and their babies get off to a difficult start with breastfeeding and need some help to work out the kinks.

To prevent you from developing any misconceptions that might lead to breastfeeding problems later on, I usually recommend that people take a breastfeeding class prior to the birth of their baby. This goes for moms, dads, and anyone who will be helping you with the baby. One of the main ingredients to breastfeeding success is a great support system.

The key to great breastfeeding is a good latch. In breastfeeding terms, "latch" refers to the way your baby attaches to your nipple. It can take a little practice (on your part as well as your baby's) to figure out how to position yourselves. Once you have a good latch, everything else will fall into place.

Most books on breastfeeding include illustrations showing how much of the nipple your baby should enclose in his mouth, as well as other details like the angle at which you hold your baby, the hold you use, and how to hold your breast with your free hand while your baby breastfeeds. This all sounds very complicated in theory, but once you and your baby have the hang of things it will all go so smoothly you won't even think about it. Here are a couple of ways to help increase the ability to get a good latch:

- Study up before your baby arrives. Consult books, Web sites, and any other resources you find helpful to get an idea of the basics ahead of time.
- Watch other moms breastfeed. La Leche League meetings are excellent for this purpose.
- Breastfeed early and often. The hospital or birth center where you give birth is likely to have **lactation consultants** on staff; be sure you ask any question that occurs to you. They are there and eager to help.
- Practice with your baby. It's important to stay calm and relaxed as you and your baby figure out how to get together. Though you may need a pointer from a lactation consultant or an experienced nursery nurse, you can rest assured that the two of you will figure everything out.

The American Academy of Pediatrics (AAP) recommends that you breastfeed your baby as soon as possible. Ideally, this means as soon as the baby is born. If you have a vaginal birth, you can expect

▶ One of the things that helped me breastfeed was knowing I wasn't alone. I attended La Leche League meetings and hung out with other moms who shared my infant feeding philosophy, though we each had our own goals and styles. I also enjoyed reading other tales of breastfeeding moms, like *The Breastfeeding Café* (Barbara Behrmann) or *How My Breasts Saved the World* (Lisa Wood Shapiro).

to have your new baby placed on your belly as soon as he arrives, and your doula or the labor and delivery nurses will be ready to help him latch onto you and begin nursing. If you give birth by cesarean section, your doula can help you breastfeed while you are still on the surgery table. If this if not possible, your nurses will bring you your baby as soon as you are in the recovery area, and you can breastfeed there. Starting to breastfeed within the first thirty minutes is optimal. That way, your baby is primed and ready to begin his life outside your womb.

When you get ready to breastfeed your baby, be sure you choose a position that is easy for you to maintain. Most breastfeeding books describe and illustrate the basic positions in which you are most likely to help your baby achieve a good latch without wearing you out at the same time. These holds have been named over time to describe the relative position of mother and baby. You will see them described as the following:

- **The cradle hold:** The key to the **cradle hold** is to make sure that you and the baby are belly to belly and that she is not facing upward. You should also make sure that your baby is not lying at an angle and is perfectly horizontal to your body. If you are feeding from the right breast, you will cradle the baby's head on the forearm portion of your right arm, just before the crook. Use your left hand to form a C shape to hold the breast. This gives you control over the breast without your hand getting in your baby's way.
- **The cross-cradle hold:** The **cross-cradle hold** is very similar to the cradle hold. If you were feeding from the right breast, you would lay the baby on your left arm, using your left hand at the back of his head and neck to help control where he puts his head. You would then form your right

hand in the C position to maneuver your right breast. I like the cross-cradle hold for learning to breastfeed.

- **The clutch or football hold:** The clutch hold is a good one if you've had a cesarean, as it keeps the baby clear of your incision site. In an upright position, choose a side to nurse. Hold the baby bottom first into your side with that same arm. If your baby is very long or large, the baby's legs may go up the back of your bed or chair, or wrap around your back. Use your opposite hand to form a C and maneuver the breast. So if your left arm is holding the baby and managing his head, much like in the cross-cradle hold, your right hand would hold the left breast.

- **The side-lying hold:** The side-lying hold is also good if you have had abdominal surgery. Choose either side to lie on and put a pillow behind your back for support. Turn your baby onto her side as well, facing your body. Her mouth should be slightly lower than your breast (think nipple to nose) so that when she opens wide your nipple points to the roof of her mouth to aid in a better latch. Once your baby is latched, settle in. You may prefer to lie all the way down with your bottom arm extended or wrapped under your head. Other mothers tell me they prefer to lift up on the bottom elbow. Do whatever is most comfortable for you.

After you have established a good breastfeeding rapport with your baby, you may find that the two of you develop a position all your own. In the meantime, be sure you use something to support your baby's weight and keep from straining your arms and back. This is particularly important at the beginning. If your muscles become sore and exhausted, breastfeeding will be difficult and uncomfortable. You can pile up a bunch of soft pillows in the configuration that works best for you. You can also use pillows that are designed specifically to help mothers breastfeed. Two of the most popular brands on the market are the Boppy and My Brest Friend. If you have friends with babies, they will probably have a favorite and be happy to show you how to use these pillows. They do come in handy; in fact, in a recent survey by a parenting magazine, mothers rated their breastfeeding pillows as more necessary to their baby care routines than diapers!

Sore nipples are not a fun part of breastfeeding. They are probably the most dreaded of all breastfeeding experiences. The good news is that you do not have to have sore nipples to success-fully breastfeed.

The most common reason for sore nipples is poor positioning. The most frequent positioning issues I see are very minor things that can easily be corrected. Be sure that your baby's body is turned all the way toward you. If his body is turned slightly away from you even a little, the resulting angle of her head can leave you with sore nipples. The same can happen with a dangling baby, or one whose head or feet are draped off the edge of the supporting pillow. Shift the pillow a little to keep your baby parallel to the floor.

The other big cause of sore nipples is a poor latch. The main reason for a poor latch is that the baby doesn't open her mouth wide enough. Your baby's mouth should close around the aureola rather than the very tip of your nipple. You will have to encourage your baby to open up wide. Believe it or not, leading by example works well here; babies are great imitators. Show your baby how you want her to open her mouth. When she does so, reward her by putting the nipple in her mouth.

When you're putting your nipple into her mouth you need to remember to point it toward the roof of her mouth. Point-ing it straight toward the back of her mouth rarely gets it where

ASK YOUR GUIDE

I've heard that "preparing" your nipples during pregnancy can get you ready for breastfeeding. Is this true?

▶ Preparing your nipples with bizarre torture methods is no longer recommended. I know my mom and grandma tried to tell me I should rough up my nipples with a towel during pregnancy. Other women have shared even scarier stories of ways they were told to make their nipples tougher so that breastfeeding would be more comfortable. Luckily, these methods really don't have any place in modern-day breastfeeding.

▶ I found that a sling was the perfect nursing companion. It helped me learn to nurse in public discreetly so that no one knew what I was doing. The sling also gave me a way to do other things while I was nursing, like read a book, do dishes, or even vacuum. This became particularly handy when I became the mother of more than one child.

you need it. Remember, only the bottom portion of her jaw can move.

Breastfeeding will become a natural part of your life. At first breastfeeding may seem awkward. That is because both you and your baby are learning. As you both get the hang of nursing, which can take a few weeks or more, you will be able to nurse without putting much thought into it.

You will find that one day, without even realizing it, you have learned to breastfeed just about anywhere in any position. Your baby will also become very efficient at nursing. This makes your life so much easier. You can both fall into a rhythm or schedule that works for both of your lives.

Choosing the Right Breast Pump

Not everyone needs a **breast pump**, though most women will use a breast pump at some point in their nursing career. Breast pumps can be used for lots of reasons, and your reason will help you decide which breast pump is right for you.

There are several types of breast pumps. There is not a one-size-fits-all breast pump. Just as mothers have different needs from their breast pumps, there are pumps designed to do what you need.

Manual breast pumps are the least expensive. They use your hand power to create suction. Typically they are only able to pump one breast at a time. They may or may not have multiple settings of suction.

This pump is perfect for the mother who will only be pumping occasionally. Since the manual pump is not designed for power or speed, it is not something you would want to use on a frequent or long-term basis.

The next step up from a manual pump is one that operates on a low power supply. This category would include **battery-operated breast pumps** and small **electric breast pumps**, both of which generally offer the option of pumping two breasts at once. These pumps are also designed for casual use every once in a while, such as when you'll be leaving your baby to enjoy a night out on the town or will be out with your baby in a place or situation where breastfeeding would be uncomfortable or impossible.

The problem with these pumps is that they are not really strong enough to do the job they are designed for. Even if you plan to use your pump only occasionally, it still needs to operate smoothly and offer you a range of suction pressures. These low-power models tend to be less expensive, and the lower cost means that companies producing them cannot include all the necessary functions. Reputable companies that specialize in breast pumps and breast-pump equipment do not tend to produce pumps in this less expensive category, and it is possible that you could injure yourself more easily with one of these models. Be very careful about selecting a breast pump from this category. If you choose this route, make sure you have the advice of a lactation professional who works with breast pumps frequently and not just a casual recommendation.

Electric breast pumps are very hot items today. You can go into any big baby-related store and walk out with a very nice electric breast pump, something you couldn't have dreamed of doing even ten years ago. These breast pumps are designed for everyday use. They are great for moms who work or who have a supply that needs maintaining due to a sick infant or who choose to pump exclusively. These breast pumps can do single or double pumping to maximize your time.

You can plan to spend at least $200 on a new breast pump. These breast pumps are considered single-use items and should not be passed to others or sold after use, even though you can buy

ASK YOUR GUIDE

Is it okay if pumping is painful?

▶ If your breast pump hurts you, something is wrong. While it may feel strange, using a breast pump should never hurt. Try adjusting the settings of your pump for more comfort. More suction does not necessarily equal more breast milk. If you can't find a setting that works, discontinue using that pump or you may damage your nipples. Seek help from a professional to find the right fit for you.

replacement tubing. Some of the newer models also offer two-phase pumping rhythms: stimulation and expression.

Hospital-grade breast pumps are available for rent. These are used to help you build a supply as well as maintain it. Most of these pumps also offer the two-phase suction option. These pumps are perfect for mothers of premature babies or babies who are too sick to nurse. The hospital-grade pumps have all available options so you can use them as much as you'd like without causing discomfort or damage to your nipples. This way, you can build a supply of breast milk to store. Also, the act of pumping regularly will stimulate your body to produce more milk.

You are likely to find a pumping room and system in any **neonatal intensive care unit (NICU)**. This will save you the cost of renting a pump while you are in the hospital. Talk to the nurses to find out where to rent a similar system for your home. I found my hospital-grade pump at a local nursing store that specialized in breastfeeding. I rented one for a year with my daughter. Insurance picked up part of it because of the health benefits of breastfeeding and my flexible spending account took care of the rest.

Most baby stores carry breast pumps. This does not mean that the breast pumps they sell are of good quality. A bad breast pump can actually damage your nipples and breasts. It is always important to go with a good breast pump. If you choose a reputable manual model, quality does not always have to be expensive.

Your choice of breast pump should depend on a couple of factors. Ask yourself the following questions about your needs for a breast pump:

- Will I be using this breast pump every day?
- Will I need to pump breast milk to use as a replacement for breastfeeding?

- Do I need to pump my breasts quickly?
- Will I have access to electricity at times I am most likely to pump?

Once you have made an assessment of your breast pump needs, you can start looking at pumps. The first thing to do, after you've talked to a lactation consultant, if necessary, is to talk to other mothers in similar situations to yours. Ask them what pumps they have used and what they liked and disliked about them. I would also recommend reading online reviews of breast pumps, even if you don't make your purchase over the Internet.

Once you have narrowed your search down to a couple of breast pumps, it is time to compare prices. Some retailers offer specials, like free accessories or baby-weight checks. If you buy online, where you can find some really good prices, be sure to check on shipping costs as well as return policies.

Milk Storage

Once you have your breast milk out, you need to do something with it. Breast milk storage practices vary from mom to mom. Most have found methods that work really well for them. If you talk to other moms who pump and store their milk, you are sure to get some great ideas.

Storing breast milk doesn't have to be complicated. You simply put the milk in a clean, sealable container and store it in the refrigerator or freezer. That said, some containers are easier to store breast milk in than others.

Take into consideration how much space you have available to use for breast milk. Do you have tons of space in your fridge or freezer? Then don't worry about finding room to store your breast milk. If you don't have tons of space, you may want

ASK YOUR GUIDE

Is it okay to only pump breast milk rather than nurse?

▶ Absolutely! Many women either choose to pump exclusively for their babies or are forced to because their babies cannot nurse and pumping is the only way they can provide breast milk. I had a baby with an oral difficulty and I pumped for a year. I had a lot of help and support from the moms at the Pump Moms group at Yahoo! Groups. If you find yourself pumping exclusively, be sure to find other moms who are doing the same thing to help you get the support you need.

▶ The Avent sterilizer for bottles and pump parts saved my sanity! It was the easiest and fastest way to make sure everything was clean and ready. This was particularly true while pumping. I had two of these items—one at work and one at home—though I also used the sterilizing bags from Medela when I traveled. If you pump at all, you really need to try some of these sterilizing products.

to consider pumping a minimal amount of milk ahead of time so you can keep it stored in very small containers. You should also consider how you intend to use the milk. Will it stay in the same container while being used, or will you place it in a different container for feeding?

Some moms choose to store breast milk that will be used within a few days in bottles that can be warmed and used right away. If you intend to freeze your milk and you have limited amounts of space, this might not be a good option for you. I used plastic storage bags for milk. I think I tried every brand. In the end, I learned that storing them by laying them flat was the most economical space-wise.

You need to know the basics of how to use stored breast milk. The first thing to know is how long you can safely store your breast milk and where. Your breast milk is good for several hours at room temperature, for up to eight days in the refrigerator, and for up to six months in the freezer compartment of your refrigerator.

You can put your freshly **expressed** breast milk in the refrigerator in any clean, sealable container. You may choose to pump directly into the bottle that you will feed from, or you may prefer to refrigerate your expressed milk in other, larger containers. I recommend that you do not store your breast milk in the door of the refrigerator. This area is a bit warmer and more exposed with each opening of the door. I usually pushed my milk to the back of the top shelf in my side-by-side refrigerator.

If you are freezing your milk in the freezer compartment of your refrigerator, you should store your milk on a shelf rather than in the door of the unit. It's also a good idea to rotate your stored milk supply by putting the newest milk in the bottom of the stack. Then, when you need milk, you take it from the top of the stack.

This way you are sure you are using all your stored milk well within that six-month safety period.

If you have a lot of milk or need long-term storage, you can store milk in a self-contained freezer (that is, an upright or chest freezer that is not part of a refrigerator) for up to a year. Because they are dedicated freezers, these appliances are better able to maintain a safe cold temperature. Also, they are not opened as much as the freezer compartments of the fridge, so the cold temperature stays more constant.

When you are ready to use breast milk that has been frozen, you can put it in the refrigerator and leave it there for up to twenty-four hours to begin the thawing process. The key to breast milk storage is to remember that you can always go colder, but once you have warmed the milk, you cannot chill it again. So you move freshly expressed milk from the fridge to the freezer, but once you have warmed the milk once, you cannot put it back into the refrigerator. Once it is warm, you need to use it or throw it away.

Breast milk should not be placed in the microwave. Not only does the microwave kill off some of the good qualities of the breast milk, heating milk this way can also create hot spots that even shaking won't resolve. This can lead to your baby being scalded by the hot milk.

The way I found it easiest to heat frozen milk was to use the hot water method. I took a big plastic cup, filled it with hot water, and placed my packet of breast milk inside it. I left the hot water on a trickle and let it slowly warm up that way over the course of a few minutes. You can also buy warmers that essentially do the same thing.

Dealing with Feeding Problems

Feeding your baby seems like a very natural thing, right? Well, it is, but that doesn't mean that all your feeding efforts will go smoothly.

WHAT'S HOT

▶ There are several breast-milk storage systems on the market today. Most of these are designed to help you label your milk so you know when you pumped it, and they have some organizing feature to ensure you can use your milk efficiently and within the safety period. Some of these systems are sold mostly for short-term use, and others are for long-term use. This kind of focus helps make sure you keep good track of your stored breast milk.

▶ A nursing bra can really make a difference. These bras have special flaps that allow you to leave your bra on but expose your nipple. This means that you can quickly, easily, and discreetly feed your baby anywhere you need to feed him. Nowadays you can also find specially designed nursing clothes, like tops and even dresses, that are attractive and stylish. You can find these at maternity stores as well as at online stores like www.mother wear.com.

Whether you're breastfeeding, pumping, bottle feeding, or doing a combination, problems will arise either for you or your baby at one time or another. The most important thing to know is that there are solutions to your problems.

Some families worry that if they don't introduce a bottle early on that the baby will never take a bottle. This is absolutely false. In fact, offering a bottle too soon can actually jeopardize breastfeeding.

Offering a bottle too soon can cause what is called **nipple confusion**. In this situation, the baby grows to actually prefer the bottle to the breast. This happens because bottle feeding is easy to do. The baby simply depresses the plastic nipple, and milk flows. The work of breastfeeding, the suckling, is more difficult. It is important work, though, that actually helps develop your baby's facial muscles and promotes healthy jaw development.

If you're having trouble breastfeeding your baby, your pediatrician will probably help you consider an alternative. If your baby cannot latch on properly or is having trouble suckling from the breast, you can help teach your baby with the use of a cup, spoon, or other specially designed infant-feeding device. There are several items available, and your pediatrician will know the pros and cons associated with all of them.

Nursing clothes can be your best friend. I went for years just wearing two-piece outfits and button-down shirts, but when I actually tried a nursing top, I was sold. I didn't have to pull up my shirt any longer! Nursing tops are designed in three main styles:

● A single slit in the center of the top, allowing you to reach in from either side to unsnap your nursing bra and feed, usually concealed under another flap of fabric

- Slits on both sides of the top, usually near the underarm area, allowing you to reach in from the side—these are also hidden under flaps or layers of fabric
- A double-layered top, with the bottom layer slit either in the center or on the sides, and the top layer attached only at the top, making it easy to lift

My advice to you is that which style to choose really centers around your breasts. If you have small breasts, the center opening may be difficult for you to use. I'm a fan of the double-sided style, myself. Both work well and come in many fashion styles including casual, dressy, and work clothes.

You don't have to own every single piece of clothing as nursing clothing. I started with a few basics. I enjoyed a couple of T-shirts, a dress, and a nice shirt. You can mix and match pants and outerwear like sweaters and jackets to create different looks.

Bringing Your Baby to the Table

The American Academy of Pediatrics (AAP) says that you can start introducing other foods (besides breast milk or artificial breast milk) to your baby when he is about six months of age. This is a fun time of exploration—for you and your baby. Be prepared for some mess, some thrills, and some misses.

Starting solids is a gradual process. It's not like the day your baby turns six months old, you will suddenly plunk him down in front of a full plate of food. Eating solids is a new adventure for a baby. Yours will want to investigate the sight, smell, and feel of the solids you put in front of him. It might take a long time before you feel you're getting more food into his mouth than ends up on his front or all over the floor.

▶ I love my baby-food grinder! It makes feeding my babies so easy. I simply throw a bit of dinner in and grind it up. I don't have to worry about canned foods, and I get to decide what consistency my baby needs. If you have any desire to make your baby's foods, a grinder will help ease your food preparations.

As you're making this transition, remember that breast milk is very easily digested and other foods are not. Introducing new foods raises the possibility that your child will have an allergic reaction to something he eats. This means that his immune system reacts to a food as though it is harmful or toxic. In order to reduce the possibility of food allergies, it is recommended that you introduce foods one at a time, waiting about four days before you try your baby on a new food. This way, if your child has an allergic reaction, you will be able to tell easily what food he reacted to.

I used a small calendar so I could mark the day on which I started a new food. I would then offer that food every day for five to seven days without introducing any other new food. During that time period, watch your baby for signs of irritation, from skin rashes to runny noses. If everything checks out, you can safely add another food and go through the same process again.

There is a lot of controversy over the order in which you should introduce solid foods to your baby. Most people start with a single-grain cereal, like rice cereal, and add a bit of breast milk to it. No one really questions this step. However, the debate over whether to introduce fruits or vegetables next is hotly contested. Some claim that if you start with sweet fruits, you'll never get your baby to eat vegetables, though many mothers find no such trouble. The key is to do the allergy testing; the rest is personal preference.

Spices and flavorings are also a new concept. You have to remember that your baby is able to taste the spices you've been eating through your breast milk—garlic, curry, everything. This means your baby has been exposed to these flavors before. Certainly babies in other cultures eat foods that are native to their areas. So the reasoning goes that you should not be too fearful of feeding your baby some spice.

In our family, once the baby has been tested for allergies through a slow introduction of one new food at a time, we go straight to table food. Usually, we grind up the baby's meals for a while first using a baby-food grinder. Eventually, the baby joins us at the table and enjoys the same foods we do.

You may choose to use canned foods out of the single-serving jars available at the grocery store because they are very convenient, particularly in the early months. If you do, be sure to read the labels. Most baby foods are numbered to indicate their smoothness, with number one being the thinnest and smoothest and therefore a beginning food. The higher the number, the older your baby should be, as the higher numbers indicate a thicker food that may require chewing.

Baby foods come in a variety of styles and flavors. These days you can even choose from a variety of organic foods. This might be very important to you, particularly with meats. Be sure to read the ingredient list printed on all labels. I've been tricked into thinking a jar labeled "Mango" was just fruit when in reality it was full of sugar and meant to be served as dessert. If you are avoiding dairy products or other particular ingredients, you should also keep an eye on the label.

Weaning your baby is a gradual process. The American Academy of Pediatrics (AAP) recommends that you nurse your baby for at least a year and as long after as you both desire. What most people fail to realize about nursing that long is that it is nothing like nursing a newborn. Nor is it the sip of milk and bite of cookie that others think it may become. The older your baby is, and the further into toddlerhood, the less frequently he will nurse.

Most babies begin decreasing the number of times a day that they nurse at around four months. With the addition of solid foods, beginning at about six months, you will see fewer feedings as well. Eventually it becomes a game of how many feedings you do versus how many solids. Some babies are only nursing early in the morning and then again at bedtime by the age of one year.

▶ *The Nursing Mother's Guide to Weaning*, by Kathleen Huggins, is an excellent resource for any nursing mother. It talks a great deal about weaning with love and includes all the helpful tips and hints that you might need. It even addresses some common problems with weaning and how to avoid them.

The weaning process is meant to be gradual, starting from when you begin to offer solid foods. If you wean too suddenly, you may actually cause yourself to get **mastitis**, a breast infection from plugged ducts. You are supposed to cut down slowly, by just one feeding a week.

Some babies wean very easily, taking the opportunity to breast-feed when it arises and eating solid foods when they are offered. Other babies are a little more uncomfortable with the change in their feeding routines. They may refuse solid foods. Alternately, they may have **nursing strikes** or periods of time where they refuse to nurse.

As you reduce the number of times your baby nurses, you may find that your milk supply doesn't slow down commensurately. If you have to go someplace for an extended period, be sure to bring a breast pump to handle your milk supply, even if you think it will not be a problem. I had a friend who had to leave town for an unexpected funeral and thought her one-year-old daughter nursed infrequently enough that she wouldn't need a pump. She called me in tears and I talked her through how to hand-express her milk.

No matter when or how you choose to wean, it should be a process of love. Breastfeeding is not purely about nourishment. It is about feeding your baby with love. You will need to find extra ways to get snuggles in and to provide them with lap time and other opportunities to be near you.

Get Linked

My About.com site is a great place to find more advice and resources about feeding your baby. Check out these links to learn even more about breastfeeding, pumping, and other feeding topics and techniques.

FEEDING YOUR BABY

One of the main jobs you have as a parent is that of nourishing your baby. Here is everything you need to know in one spot, from breast-feeding to using bottles, weaning, and introducing solids.

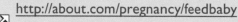
http://about.com/pregnancy/feedbaby

BREASTFEEDING QUIZ

Take this fun breastfeeding quiz to test your knowledge and learn interesting facts about breastfeeding.

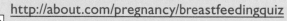
http://about.com/pregnancy/breastfeedingquiz

HOW TO BREASTFEED

This quick how-to on breastfeeding will help you learn the basics step by step.

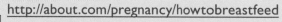
http://about.com/pregnancy/howtobreastfeed

BEFORE YOU BUY A BREAST PUMP

Choosing the right breast pump is very important. These tips will help you save money and ensure that you have the right pump.

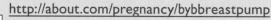
http://about.com/pregnancy/bybbreastpump

ONLINE BREASTFEEDING CLASS

This six-week e-mail course is designed to help you get all the in-formation you need to breastfeed your baby, from the benefits and first few feedings to managing breastfeeding with your life.

http://about.com/pregnancy/breastfeedingclass

Chapter 4

Diapering: The Dirty Deed

Preparing for Diapering

Everyone who enters the parenthood phase of life should expect to be faced with a few dirty diapers. Since your baby will use between eight and twelve diapers a day in the beginning, you will soon become an expert on diapering. What you may not realize as a new parent is that a lot of choices go along with diapers. From what type of diapers to how long to use them, you have many decisions to make.

The debate between proponents of cloth and disposable diapers is a hot one. Some parents actually combine methods. This allows them the best of both worlds. You might hear stories about families who use **cloth diapers**, but only at home. They use disposables for travel and day care. They may also use disposables at night if their baby urinates in large volumes.

While you may think you will just go to the grocery and pick up a package of diapers and go from there, I highly recommend you give diapering a little extra thought. It is not simply about covering

your baby's bottom for pottying. Diapering has an impact on your life as a parent in terms of how you and baby deal with diapers, the financial outlay involved, ease of use, and so on.

There are multiple factors to consider when it comes to choosing which diapers to use. Regardless of whether you choose cloth or disposables, there are a lot of diaper choices available to you these days. A quick tour of the Internet will show you a greater variety of cloth diapers than you ever thought possible, and a trip to the grocery store will show you that disposables also come in a great range of prices. Some parents forego this decision completely and choose instead to go the diaper-free route! (See page 65 for more info on this method.)

There are some basic questions that you will have to answer as you make the decision about what type of diapers you choose to use. It's a good idea to give this some thought before your baby is born. Here are some of the things you need to think about when it comes to diapers:

- Initial costs
- Long-term costs
- Availability of a diaper service
- Availability of a washer/dryer or clothesline
- Your lifestyle and preference, if any, for natural products
- Whether your baby will be in day care

After your baby is born, you will have other factors to add to the list. This can be more important for some babies or parents than others. These factors might include:

- Baby's weight
- Baby's skin sensitivity

- Amount your baby urinates at one time
- How often your baby urinates
- How often your baby has bowel movements

When you take all of these factors into consideration, you will have a good idea of where to start. For example, if you have a baby who is prone to skin irritation, and you can afford a larger initial cost, cloth diapers are probably easier for you. If you are planning on using a day-care center or other formalized child care, you may be forced to use disposables at least during the days that your child is in their care.

Whatever you choose, stock up now. Take advantage of the time you have before your baby is born and make preparations for diapering. Look for sales in stores or on Web sites for the diapers you want to use most.

Some might advise against stocking up on diapers. This is because what you choose now, before your baby gets here, may not be what actually works for your baby. Or it may be that you wind up not really liking a particular brand of disposables or that your baby's size is radically different, larger or smaller than you had previously expected, including how quickly he grows after birth. While this is an important consideration, diapers that are unused can usually be donated, returned, or at least traded for different diapers.

Some mothers choose to register for diapers for their baby showers. Most cloth diapers are sold over the Internet, either by baby-care stores or by work-at-home moms who have designed and marketed their own particular diaper brands. Either way, it may be possible to register for cloth diapers online, depending on the retailers' preferences. You can also register for disposables if you set up your registry at a store that sells them. Choose a few small

TOOLS YOU NEED

▶ A good diaper bag is a must for any parent. Wait to buy your diaper bag until you have decided on the kind of diaper you will use. The type of inserts and size of bag you need may be altered by the types of diapers you choose for your baby. Or you can be like me and have several diaper bags. Which bag I use depends on where I'm going.

▶ Diaper services were very popular and prevalent in generations past. This service can be a boon to the mom who chooses to use cloth diapers—the service picks up dirty diapers and drops off a new supply, clean and folded and ready to use. Though they may be hard to find today, these businesses seem to be making a comeback. If you are considering cloth diapering, be sure to check out local diaper services and what they offer. You may find that the price is competitive, compared to what you would spend to wash your own cloth diapers, though this can vary from place to place.

cloth diapers or a few packs of disposables in the smaller sizes, and then select the medium sizes, where your baby is likely to stay for a longer period of time.

Cloth Diapers: Not Just for Environmentalists

From what you may have heard about them, you may have deduced that cloth diapers are just a hassle. You might also have memories of bulky cloth diapers with long, sharp diaper pins—a pretty unsettling image. Luckily, those days of cloth diapers are gone. There are lots of much better options available for cloth diapers these days, and despite the extra energy and cost this choice requires, many parents do choose it and make it work. If you have any interest at all in using cloth diapers, it's worth it for you at least to investigate the options before making your decision.

There are numerous types of cloth diapers available. Today's diapers include **prefolds** of all varieties, **all-in-ones**, **pocket diapers**, and more. The style you choose will depend on your preference.

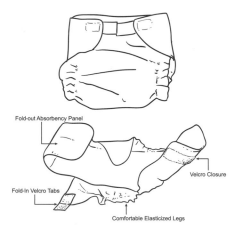

Fold-out Absorbency Panel

Velcro Closure

Fold-In Velcro Tabs

Comfortable Elasticized Legs

▲ Anatomy of a cloth diaper

Cloth diapers tend to be a significant expenditure, at least initially, but using cloth diapers can save your family hundreds of dollars in the long run. This is because you get more than one use out of each cloth diaper. After we figured out what brand and style of diaper we preferred, my husband and I figured out we needed to use each diaper about twenty times to make it worth the cost. We figured our baby used them that many times in the first couple of months alone.

Cloth diapers are also easier on your baby's skin. Parents who use cloth diapers report fewer diaper rashes and skin irritations than those who use disposables. This was our main reason for choosing cloth diapers, as our babies had very sensitive skin. The chemicals in some of the disposable diapers just really irritated their bottoms.

Some parents choose cloth diapers for environmental reasons. This is supposedly because landfills are full of disposable diapers that take many years to break down. Since cloth diapers are supposedly teaching your baby the difference between clean and dirty, wet and dry, others choose to use them because they believe that this leads to an easier toilet-training experience. There are many reasons you might choose cloth diapers, and they are all valid for your family as individuals.

With our first two children we considered cloth diapering, but rejected the idea because of a lack of washer and dryer. We also had no **diaper service** in town. We did briefly use a cloth diaper service with our third baby, but then they closed shop. So we started washing our own diapers after already having experienced disposable diapers. I was totally prepared to hate it and was pleasantly surprised.

We chose some cloth diapers and **diaper covers** after reading some online reviews and talking to some friends who used cloth diapers. We have found the whole experience pleasant and the

ELSEWHERE ON THE WEB

▶ If you are looking for a good tutorial on how all the varieties of cloth diapers work, I recommend checking out the Diaper Pin Web site (www.diaperpin.com). In addition to links to a variety of diaper retailers, the site also includes a tutorial that describes how all the various diapers work. This can be a big help in deciding which diaper you want for your baby. You will also find a bunch of user forums on this site, where cloth-diapering parents discuss their problems, triumphs, and favorites. This takes at least some of the guesswork out of buying cloth diapers.

diapers to be very easy to use, even when out in public. That said, we do use disposables occasionally. We used them for the first few days while we were still in the **meconium stools** phase, and we used them when our kids went to stay with someone else, were in child care, or were on vacation.

Washing cloth diapers is simpler than you think. For the most part, you simply throw the diapers in the washer and wash them. When your baby is being breastfed, the diapers with stool in them need no extra care. Once your baby starts solid foods, you can choose to dump out any formed stool in the toilet before placing the diaper in the diaper pail.

The trick is that diapers need to be washed separately from your regular clothes. This means you will need enough cloth diapers to get through more than a few hours without doing a wash; I recommend having between one and two dozen diapers, with about half as many covers (if needed). We chose to go with two dozen cloth diapers and twelve covers, because I did not wish to do laundry every other day.

Some cloth diapers have washing instructions on the label, much like most other items of clothing. We just used regular detergent. Our washer offered an option for two rinse cycles, which was what we selected. If your washer does not offer that, you can manually set it to do two rinses. We did this to ensure all the soap was out of the diaper.

Drying diapers is done a couple of ways: line drying or in the dryer. Either method is fine, or you might try a combination of the two. You might find that the diapers take a long time to dry in the clothes dryer because of how bulky they are. If that's the case, and you find you're using a lot of electricity, you can do some line drying to compensate. Just remember to stay organized about it; you

▶ Our over-the-door hanging diaper pail by Mother of Eden was amazing. It looked so simple and useless, but it worked wonders. I simply would drop a dirty diaper in the bag that connected with snaps over a door knob (the knob was still usable). It was waterproof and did not smell. When I was ready to wash diapers, I emptied the bag into the washer and tossed it in too. You can find them online in different sizes and colors at www.nurtured family.com.

don't want to find yourself in need of a clean diaper but only have damp ones available.

Disposable Diapers

Decades ago, cloth diapers were the only option available, but disposable diapers are now the norm. Over the years, diaper companies have made great strides with improved chemicals and materials to help hold the contents inside and keep your baby drier. Diapers will probably continue to improve in quality and innovation in the years to come as well.

If you're looking for an easy-to-use option for diapering, disposables are probably the right choice for you. Most brands offer stretchable sides with Velcro-like fasteners. This makes it easier to alter the size to fit your baby's legs.

There are many brands of disposable diapers. Each one will tell you why their brand is better, but in essence they are all nearly identical, particularly in their purpose—to keep your baby from having accidents. The brand or style you choose is completely up to you, and you may find it takes some trial and error to find the right one.

Probably the biggest issue with disposables concerns the sizing. While they all sound the same, how each diaper fits your baby is very important. Some brands of diaper will gather better at your baby's legs but may be totally wrong for your best friend's baby. You may have to try a couple of different brands to ensure a good fit. It's important to check the fit around the legs, around your baby's belly, and around his lower back. You want to see if there are any visible gaps anywhere.

If you have a baby who was born prematurely, you will need to purchase special diapers for a while, at least until your baby's weight is equal to that of an average-size newborn—about six or seven pounds. These extra-small diapers can usually be purchased through a hospital, although today you can also find them at some of the larger chains and for sale online. Be sure to shop around for the best price.

Disposable diapers often have special features. Some are adorned with cute characters, while others are plain. There are diapers that have a notch cut out for the umbilical cord, though I found this notch was never really big enough and wound up folding down the diaper more in the front. Some disposable diapers have gatherings at the leg. Talk to other parents to see what works for them and what they like when it comes to diapers. I would even encourage you to borrow a few diapers to try out prior to spending the money on a whole pack of diapers. Hospitals, birth centers, and your doctor or midwife may also have samples of different disposable diapers. Just remember, the highest-priced diaper is not always the best buy for you and your baby.

The little things can mean a lot when it comes to selecting diapers. Some parents I know have switched brands because of issues with gel or residue being left on their baby's bottoms. While it wasn't hazardous, it just didn't sit well with them. I also avoid one particular brand because I don't care for the odor. You will need to see which brands meet all of your needs.

How to Change a Diaper
The first thing you want to do before changing any diaper is to gather up all of your supplies. This prevents you from having to run around with a half-naked baby armed with a full bladder.

The items you should have handy while changing a diaper include the following:

WHAT'S HOT

▶ You can usually tell that it is time to move up a size or to try a new brand when you begin having more leaks with the diapers you are currently using. This signal means your baby has grown or his body's proportions have changed in such a way that the diaper isn't fitting as well. A change in size or brand can usually rectify this situation.

- Diaper of your choice
- Diaper-changing pad
- Baby wipes
- Creams or medications as needed
- Toy to distract older baby

Spread the changing pad on the floor cloth-side up. (Typically one side is shiny and waterproof, and the other side is cloth.) Lay your baby down on top of it. Open the diaper fully. By this I mean undo any flaps that will need to be fastened. You should also open up any gathered sections in the center of the diaper near where your baby's legs will go. This will help the diaper work better.

Open the old diaper. I usually open it and leave it there while I wipe the majority of the mess off the baby. If you are using disposable wipes, leave them in the old diaper. If you are using cloth wipes, set them aside to go in the diaper pail.

Remove the soiled diaper and set it aside. At this point, I generally use another wipe to make sure the baby is clean. Baby girls always need to be wiped front to back to prevent feces from contaminating the vagina and causing an infection. For baby boys, don't be afraid to clean the scrotum well. Sometimes the skin seems to hold onto fecal matter and make it difficult to clean; you can exert a fair amount of pressure to clean the baby without hurting him. Apply any cream or medication needed. (I usually wipe my finger on the front of the new diaper to get off the majority of the excess lotion or cream to prevent me from getting it everywhere.)

Place the clean diaper under your baby and fasten it. Redo your baby's clothing. Hand your baby to someone else or place her in a safe place. Fold up the old diaper and put it in the diaper pail or

ASK YOUR GUIDE

What do you do with dirty diapers while you're out?

▶ I try to carry several plastic bags in my diaper bag. You can use sealable plastic lunch bags or the bags your groceries come in, or you can purchase bags for this purpose. I don't usually throw away disposable diapers while I'm out unless it's very obvious that it is okay. You wouldn't want to leave a smelly mess at the doctor's office or another public place. The bag seals in the odor and allows you to take it home.

throw it away. Finally, wash your hands before handling anything else.

Stuff for Baby Bottoms: Wipes and Creams

Along with diapers come the diaper products. There is a wide array of wipes and creams you can use for cleaning or soothing your baby. How often or how much you use for cleaning your baby will depend on your preferences and the baby's skin. Just as with choosing a brand of diaper, it might take a little time and some trial and error before you find the right diaper products for your baby.

Wipes are used to clean your baby. You use wipes to clean off any stool or urine still on your baby's sensitive skin. You can choose to use disposable wipes or cloth wipes. Most parents also keep a package of wipes handy for cleaning little hands and faces while out and about. (The glove compartment in your car is a good place to store these.)

Most disposable wipes are treated with chemicals to keep them moist. Some of these chemicals can irritate your baby's skin. Try to select wipes that have no alcohol in them to help protect your baby's bottom.

If you choose to use cloth wipes or even a washcloth, you will have more control over what goes onto your baby. You can also use paper towels with a bit of water on them. I've kept a small spray bottle of water to use when I needed it to moisten a wipe. Another mom says that as she's gathering her supplies, she just wets a wash rag specifically for this purpose.

Disposable wipes are very handy to have when traveling. I will use them even if I am using cloth diapers, though I do try to find a more natural brand that has fewer chemicals in it. Then I can also use the wipes to wipe up messy faces, sticky hands, and small spills

▶ I love a product from California Baby called Diaper Area Wash. (In my house, we call it "bottom spritz.") It is a spritz-type cleaner used during diaper changes. It smells great and helps clean off the baby's bottom. It also helps protect that sensitive bottom area. We found it at a local baby store, but it's also available online.

in public places. My toddlers also like them to use when they are helping me clean the house.

Diaper-rash creams are a must. I think it is important to have some diaper-rash cream in the house whenever you have a baby because you don't know when a rash will happen, even if you do everything right. Your baby shouldn't have to suffer while you go out and get the right cream.

There are two types I recommend. One type is a simple water-proof barrier. This is great for skin that is at risk of getting chapped for whatever reason. The most frequent reason I use it is when a baby has very loose or frequent stools. This helps protect her bottom when she stools or urinates. A client of mine also applies this waterproof barrier to her baby's bottom every night before bed, figuring her baby has a greater chance of being in the same diaper for a longer period of time.

The other type of diaper cream is used specifically to treat diaper rash. These creams can contain a variety of effective ingredients. I prefer zinc oxide. This thick, gooey substance will help heal a tender bottom quickly. It also provides that barrier to protect the skin from further assault.

Many of these creams come in tubes. In my opinion, tubes are messy and annoying. I like some of the newer models that provide the ointment in pump form. No matter what type of dispenser you get, your hand will get messy spreading the cream around. Simply wash up after you are done changing the diaper.

Forget the Diapers: Infant Potty Training

Forget the diapers? You might be wondering: "Is this really an option?" Believe it or not, there is something called **elimination**

ASK YOUR GUIDE

How long do diaper creams last?

▶ Diaper creams, like medicine and makeup, actually can go bad. Be sure to check expiration dates prior to buying your diaper creams and lotions. If you have products you only use occasionally, remember to check their dates periodically throughout the year. This can be particularly important to remember if you had a previous child and are just pulling out the diapering equipment from your last child. If the expiration date is long past, simply throw it away, as the product has probably lost its effectiveness.

communication (EC), which is essentially infant potty training. Many parents are using this method to help their child be diaper-free or at least less diaper dependent.

The idea is that you learn to read your baby and understand the signals that mean he has to go to the bathroom. Usually, proponents of this method are always on the lookout and ready to hustle their babies to the bathroom when they see a signal that the child has to go. The most common method is to sit with the child on the toilet and make a sound, such as "Psssss," that the child will eventually associate with the act of eliminating.

Listening to your baby is important. This is a fact whether you are working on infant potty training or not, but it's fundamental when you're using this particular method. Being able to recognize when your baby needs to go to the bathroom is at the heart of elimination communication.

Elimination communication is done by observing your baby's signals. You look for clues that your baby needs to relieve himself. He may have a special noise he makes just before he goes to the bathroom. Maybe he holds his face a certain way. These are the types of signals that you look for in your baby.

These signals start at an early age, from birth in many babies. The belief that babies don't know when they need to potty is outdated. By allowing your baby the chance to tell you, you can help him or her go to the potty. Imagine being able to go without diapers at just a couple of months old!

There are several ways to potty-train your child using elimination communication, though most involve diapers in the beginning. This allows you and your baby some room for growth without too many accidents. Remember, though, if you choose to use this method, that any type of toilet learning will involve accidents, whether it be at three months or three years.

ELSEWHERE ON THE WEB

▶ Going diaper-free can be something that works better when you have the support of other parents who are doing what you are doing or who have been where you are. There are groups and meetings in some cities as well as online groups where parents can share their experiences. You can hook up with these groups and share stories at www.diaperfree baby.org.

Getting started with elimination communication is easy. First you will need to decide how you are going to help your baby potty. There are a couple of different, popular methods. This can be very simple, or it can be complex.

Some parents choose to sit on the toilet and spread their legs enough to allow their baby to sit between them and use the toilet. Other parents choose to use other receptacles, including small potties or even just small buckets held up to the baby. There is not a right answer as to which receptacle you use. Choose whatever works well for you and your baby. You might try a couple of ways to see what works for you. Also know that as your baby ages, your best solution might change.

Once you've spent some time getting to know your baby, you will start to notice his body language and noises when he goes to the bathroom. To do this, you must have the baby fairly unclothed or at least in a cloth diaper without a plastic cover. This is so that you can tell if the baby has wet.

You can then try to offer the potty when you see the signal that means it's potty time for your baby. You simply remove any bottoms on your baby and hold him over the potty receptacle. Then it's a waiting game. For some this is a quick process, and for others there's a wait.

Some practitioners recommend that you have a word or a sound to let your baby know that it is okay to go. For some parents this involves saying "potty" or making "shhh" noises. This becomes your baby's word that he associates with the potty. Eventually your baby needs you less and less as he goes potty.

I have personally seen many families use elimination communication. Most of them would say that it was a huge success for them. One of my friends had a daughter who was diaper-free by eight months. So, if you're interested, look into it. It is a great method for many families.

TOOLS YOU NEED

▶ *Diaper Free! The Gentle Wisdom of Natural Infant Hygiene*, by Ingrid Bauer, is a great resource for those seeking to do elimination communication. The book is broken down into three parts, including a philosophy and research section, a how-to section, and answers to common questions about elimination communication.

Get Linked

Diapering has many more avenues that you probably never thought about. Which type of diapers? How do you choose? How do you diaper? And can you go diaper-free? You'll find more answers and photo tutorials on my About.com site.

HOW TO DIAPER A BABY

Looking for information on how best to diaper your baby without tears for either of you? Check out this link for a step-by-step description of the process.

http://about.com/pregnancy/howtodiaper

NEW BABY DIAPER CHART

Baby diapers are a window into the baby world. The contents of your baby's diaper can tell you how he is eating, what he is eating, and if he is well. This link offers a picture tour of baby diapers.

http://about.com/pregnancy/diaperchart

REASONS TO CLOTH DIAPER

Cloth diapers are becoming very popular again, partly because of their increasing ease of use and partly because of the added savings. This link offers great information.

http://about.com/pregnancy/clothreasons

BEFORE YOU BUY DIAPERS

Trying to figure out what you need to know before you buy diapers for your baby? Check out this link for some factors to take into consideration when buying diapers.

http://about.com/pregnancy/bybdiapers

Chapter 5

Getting the Sleep You Both Need

Solving the Sleep Dilemma

Sleep is the number-one issue in almost any parenting circle you frequent. Pregnant women often fear they will have sleep problems and won't get enough sleep, and new mothers and fathers always complain loudly about these issues. Chances are you've been frightened by stories of how a new baby means you will never sleep through the night again. The good news is that there is help available for parents and babies experiencing sleepless nights.

Your first task is to figure out a sleeping arrangement. There is not a single right answer that meets the needs of every family or every baby. You may even need to experiment with what works for you, your baby, and your family. My husband and I found that each of our babies needed something slightly

▶ Twins and other multiples are often placed together in the same bassinette in the hospital. Studies have shown that this practice of co-bedding has a positive effect on even the smallest of babies in terms of measurable health outcomes. These babies literally breathe more easily and have more relaxed heart rates. Our girls slept together for months before being separated. Now, at almost four years old, they are happily sleeping together again of their own accord.

different from the older siblings. Even our **monozygotic twins** had specific preferences from an early age.

A small, close space seems to work best for most newborns. Some experts think that this is because it simulates a womb-like environment. This can be in your bed, a co-sleeper, cradle, or bassinet. Babies tend to feel out of sorts and lost in a huge crib, away from the warmth of their mothers whom they have always known.

Having your baby close at night also helps you respond more quickly to her needs. This allows you to prevent your baby from getting really worked up from crying. The more quickly you can feed your baby or meet her other needs, the more quickly you can get her back to sleep.

The small, cozy space you create for your baby to sleep in will be a great home for the first few months of your baby's life. Once she can sit up or roll over, you may need to consider another solution. Smaller places like bassinets and cradles can quickly become dangerous for a baby as she becomes more mobile. In order to prevent falls or other injuries, move your baby to a more suitable space when she reaches these milestones.

Many families choose to use a baby crib at this later point. If you choose a crib, be sure to follow the safety guidelines in Chapter 11 for selecting one that is sturdy and safe for your baby. Thousands of injuries and crib-related deaths occur every year. These safety guidelines include avoiding using sleep positioners to hold your baby in one place, having a tight-fitting mattress and sheet, and not placing anything, not even a stuffed animal, in bed with your baby.

You might choose to keep your baby's crib in your room for at least a little while. This will still keep you close enough to respond quickly to your baby when she needs you. If you are trying to decide whether or not to keep your baby's bed in your room, think about the following things:

- How often does your baby awake at night?
- How many times does your baby feed at night?
- How easily are you awakened by your baby?
- How easily does your baby go back to sleep?
- Will others be helping with your baby at nighttime?
- Will a baby monitor provide you with enough noise to help you?
- Will you have other things to worry about, like siblings or room temperature?
- What are your concerns about the crib in your room?
- What are your concerns about the crib in another room?

There is some research that says that parents who sleep with the baby in their room get more sleep than those who choose not to have the baby in their room. This is because you can respond more quickly and thus keep the baby from waking up completely. Also, it enables you to sleep more soundly knowing you will hear your baby should she wake up in the night. Some dads think that keeping the crib in your room will only lead to more interruptions. I'd encourage you to try this arrangement out for at least a couple of nights to see how it works for you. If it does not work for your family, you can always simply put the baby's crib back in the nursery.

If you choose to move the crib out of your room, be prepared to get a bit less sleep. This might just be a short-term problem, but many parents find that, at least for a while, they sleep less well with their baby moved into another room. Just remember it's not a permanent decision. You can also bring your baby back to your room for special situations like illness or for a longer period if you or your baby wasn't ready for the move.

There are rules to co-sleeping. These rules are designed to ensure that you and your baby are safe during sleep. You should

TOOLS YOU NEED

▶ Using a co-sleeper is the middle ground between sleeping with your baby in bed with you and having him sleep separately. Your baby sleeps in a separate unit that is attached your bed. The co-sleeper was a great alternative for our family, particularly when the twins were born. It provided us with the closeness to the babies that both they and we needed and wanted, but with extra space. It also helped if someone wet the bed—I didn't have to change my sheets!

always follow these rules, no matter how old the child or how experienced you are at co-sleeping. After a while the rules just seem natural and you do not really have to think about them. Take a look at this checklist:

- ○ Your baby should sleep on his back.
- ○ Your baby should never sleep on a couch, futon, recliner, or waterbed.
- ○ You should not sleep with your baby if you have taken medications that could make you sleepy.
- ○ You should not sleep with your baby if you have been drinking alcohol.
- ○ You should sleep with the bed pulled away from the wall.
- ○ You should not let pets or other children in the bed with the baby, even when you are there.
- ○ You should always use a firm mattress.
- ○ You should avoiding bulky bed clothing or decorations to the bedding.
- ○ You should not sleep with your baby if you are excessively overweight.

Some mothers accidentally fall asleep with their babies. This is not safe because it is not planned. This means you may not be meeting the safety requirements set up for a safer co-sleeping arrangement. This can be a big problem when you are sleep deprived; it can happen to even experienced parents.

I started co-sleeping when I kept doing it accidentally with my first baby. I figured my baby would be safer if I just planned it that way. It also kept me from waking up startled, wondering where the baby was and what I was doing. That rush of adrenaline kept me awake much longer than I wanted.

▶ You may have heard people say that you can "train" your baby to stop crying and go back to sleep by letting him "cry it out." While some parents might swear by this method, if you're like me, you probably find it unbearable to listen to your baby cry without going to her. If this is how you feel, check out the book *The No-Cry Sleep Solution*, by Elizabeth Pantley. This book offers gentle alternatives to rigid-sleep training methods.

There are many reasons that families choose co-sleeping. My husband and I chose this option as an extension of the other parenting practices that we felt were best for our children. We believed that sharing sleep was a way of listening to our children's needs and being readily available to respond when they needed us. That said, not all of my children liked to co-sleep.

Have a backup plan ready for when you and your baby are both ready to graduate from co-sleeping. Will your baby stay in your room? Will your baby move to a room alone, or will the baby's bed go in with another child? Will your baby sleep in a crib or portable crib, or will you have some other arrangement?

If you decide that sleeping with your baby in your bed is what you want to do, be sure to talk to other parents about how they do it. I have learned many good tips and tricks from discussing co-sleeping with other parents. Do you know people who have co-slept? You do, even if they do not say it out loud at many parties. When you start asking, you'll be surprised at what you learn about who co-sleeps.

Babies Sleep a Lot and Other Myths

You may have read in some baby books that a newborn baby sleeps about twenty out of every twenty-four hours. Sounds like a dream, right? That's because it is a dream! I have never met a mom or dad who had a baby who slept that much, even as a newborn.

It's a myth that babies sleep for long stretches of time. Yes, newborns sleep a lot. The average baby will sleep many hours a day in the beginning, on average about sixteen hours per twenty-four-hour period. But that's not the whole story. The trick is that this sleep takes place in short bursts. The sleep of a new baby is usually broken into bits of time throughout the day and night. Think of this sleep as several naps over a twenty-four-hour period.

During each sleep period or nap, your baby will cycle through each of the following stages of sleep:

1. Drowsiness
2. REM (rapid eye movement) sleep
3. Light sleep
4. Deep sleep
5. Very deep sleep

Typically, a baby won't sleep for more than about three or four hours at a time until he is several weeks old. This can be very frustrating to a new parent who is also desperate to sleep. Try to remember that these short bursts of sleep are only typical of a very young baby. Plan for help and naps accordingly.

Occasionally, you may actually need to wake up your baby to feed. This might feel like it goes against every parenting rule you ever learned; however, you should consider doing so if your baby was premature, had a low birth weight, or is having trouble gaining weight since birth. Waking her up for a feeding will actually help her gain the weight that she needs to get stronger and grow bigger.

It's another myth that babies should sleep through the night soon after birth. This is an old wives' tale. Babies are generally not ready to sleep all the way through what an adult would consider a night until about five or six months. Yes, I know there are babies who do, and if you're lucky one of them was born into your family. But the vast majority of parents do not have a baby like that. If your baby wakes several times throughout the night, it doesn't mean you have done anything wrong, and it is not a result of poor parenting.

ELSEWHERE ON THE WEB

▶ The American Academy of Pediatrics (AAP) recommends that babies sleep near their mothers. The reason for this is so that you can respond quickly and more easily to their needs than if you were in a different room. The AAP say that this helps protect not only your sleep but also your baby. You can read the whole statement at www.aap.org.

There are things that you can try to do to help your baby sleep soundly for longer periods. Try to teach your baby the difference between night and day. Show her that nighttime is sleep time by being quiet and limiting playful activities. If you wake up to go to the bathroom in the middle of the night, you probably do not turn on all the lights and sing or play. You simply go to the bathroom, wash your hands, and get back in bed. By following this same routine with your child, you give her the tools she needs to feel loved, safe, and comfortable. This will go a long way toward helping your little one sleep for longer periods of time.

It's another myth that if you sleep with your baby, she will never leave your bed. Plenty of us crept into bed with our parents, and we're not still there. While there can be safety concerns with sleep for any baby in any location, the biggest sleep-related factor is giving your child the sense of security to sleep where she wants. This includes in your bed.

Bedtime Routines

Bedtime is often pictured as a nightmare of screaming and crying—and that's just the parents. The truth is much fuzzier. Everyone has different beliefs about baby sleep, though there are some common threads that seem to work well for the majority of parents. You need to find a routine that works for your family. By finding what works well in your house, rather than adopting someone else's routine, you can help ease you and your child into the nighttime routine of sleep. These do not have to be elaborate, just ritual.

There are lots of ways to make bedtime go more smoothly. Most babies find a bath very calming and soothing. They enjoy the feel of the warm water surrounding them and enjoy splashing and moving in it. You can either take a quick soak in the

WHAT'S HOT

▶ Sudden infant death syndrome (SIDS) is a very real thing; my nephew died of SIDS in 1992. Having your baby sleep on his back will help reduce the risks of SIDS. There are many ways to reduce those risks, including breastfeeding and not exposing the baby to second-hand smoke. We currently do not know what causes SIDS or how to prevent it from happening altogether—we can just reduce the risks. We do know what SIDS is not: it is not smothering or overlaying on a baby.

▶ Lullabies are so much fun.
In fact, I find them quite
addictive. Though you probably think the lullabies you
know and grew up with are
the best around, I suggest
broadening your horizons
and trying something new. I
truly love the international
flavor of the lullabies available in music stores today.
Try out some different ones,
and you'll find that you stay
in your baby's room for the
music.

tub with your baby, or you can put your baby in a baby bathtub
and give her a more thorough wash. It is nice to have a warm towel
(from the dryer) to wrap her up in afterward.

After the bath, it is a good idea to keep your baby's skin moist
by rubbing down with some lotion or baby oil. This is especially
important if you wash your baby with a soap product, as even the
most gentle formulations of baby soaps do have a tendency to dry
a baby's tender skin.

Since you're using lotion or baby oil anyway, you might also
consider incorporating a massage into the routine at this point to
further promote relaxation. A good massage has a way of calming
you both down. It also is a great way to promote that skin-to-skin
contact that your baby craves. You will find that you love it as well.
My kids have always enjoyed their bedtime massage. When they
were still babies, I could see their eyes light up as they began to
realize that it was the lotion I was pulling out. We all looked forward to this part of the bedtime routine. Now I simply do quick
neck massages with their favorite lotions after we read. They claim
it's a very helpful way to get them ready for bed and sleep.

Bedtime is not the time for being loud or playing fun and silly
games. These types of activities will only serve to stir up your kids
and make it harder for them to get to sleep. This it true whether
they are two weeks, two months, or two years old. Instead, bedtime is the time for calm, quiet activities. One thing that's popular
is the use of a rocker or glider. Many of these are specially designed
to accommodate a parent holding a baby—they are wide enough
to allow you to sit with a nursing pillow on your lap, so your baby's
legs don't dangle over the edge. Some families find that rocking
while reading, making up some stories, or even singing is a good
way to soothe the baby in preparation for bed and sleep.

Once you have found what works for your family, repeat it
daily. Eventually the mere act of starting the routine will help you

and your baby feel like you are ready for bed. This is a very private and special time of day to spend with your child, a quiet sanctuary between wakefulness and slumber. It will always be one of my favorites because of the sweetness of it all.

Your baby will tell you when she's tired. Once you've learned to distinguish the signs that mean she's sleepy, it will be easier to start instituting your bedtime routine. When you see the signs that mean your baby is ready to go to bed, do not delay. By noticing that she is tired and showing her what to do when she feels that way, you can teach her good sleep habits. It is also easier to encourage her to sleep if she only goes to bed when she's actually sleepy. A newborn can rarely stay awake for more than about two hours at a time, and sometimes even less than that. These periods of wakefulness will grow longer with age.

In addition to the unique indications you notice in your own baby, signs that a baby is tired can include the following:

- Yawning
- Rubbing eyes
- Pulling at ears
- Being fussy
- Turning away from activity
- Circles under eyes

When you see these signs or others, depending on your baby, you will know it is time to gather up and head for bed! Each of my children developed a slightly different way of signaling to me that it was time for bed and sleep. At first, this can make it a bit more difficult to tell if that is what your baby is trying to tell you. But once I was able to read each child's body language and understand

ASK YOUR GUIDE

Should babies sleep on their stomachs or on their backs?

▶ Babies should sleep on their backs. The American Academy of Pediatrics (AAP) recommends this, and since parents have begun implementing the practice, the number of SIDS cases has dropped. The shelves of most baby-care stores include items advertised to help babies sleep on their backs. You do not need any special products.

what he or she did when sleepy, bedtime became a lot easier in my house.

Practical Solutions for Sleep Issues

Sleep—or lack of sleep—is the number-one thing new parents talk about. They have questions about what is normal and what isn't, and many are sure that they are the first to have experienced such problems. Do not worry—you are not alone. The combination of babies and sleep is a hot topic and will always be a hot topic. There are some common sleep-related problems and issues that new and experienced parents alike share.

Babies wake up during the night. You might think that would be an obvious statement, but it really does not sink in until you have been up with your baby at night. Sometimes it does not sink in until after you have been up several nights in a row. It is normal for your baby to wake up in the night. The first step in dealing with this issue is to identify why your baby is waking up and decide if it is normal waking. There are several kinds of night waking. Your response to the situation will depend on the type of night waking your baby experiences. Once you have identified the type of night waking, you will have a variety of options when it comes to handling your wakeful baby. Do not panic about that aspect; instead, see it as an opportunity to try different tactics if needed.

Some babies get up at night because they have wet or dirty diapers. They simply want to be put in clean, comfortable clothes, and then they will happily go back to sleep. If your baby's dirty diaper has soiled the bed, you will also need to change the sheets. It's a sad fact, but sometimes the accident is bad enough that your baby will need a bath before she can return to bed.

The best way to deal with this type of night waking is prevention! Change your baby right before you put her down for the

ELSEWHERE ON THE WEB

▶ Did you know that there is a sleep lab devoted to the study of mothers and babies? Dr. James McKenna runs the lab at the University of Notre Dame. The purpose is to study how mothers and babies sleep and how to get them to sleep safely and to sleep better. You can find information about the lab, interviews, and articles at www.nd.edu/~jmckenn1/lab.

night. Make sure the diaper fits snugly all around the waist and legs. If frequent nighttime leaks become an issue, consider trying a new brand of diaper or using disposables, if you use cloth at other times, at least for the night when wetting can be heavy. I would also advise that you change your baby's diaper every time she wakes up at night.

Your baby might wake up if she is hungry. Nighttime feedings are all about nutrition, not nurturing. Remember that your baby has a tiny stomach. This makes it more difficult for her to do her first job, which is to double her birth weight by around four or five months of age. She therefore needs to eat frequently in the early months. As she grows older, this need lessens, and she will sleep for longer periods of time.

Some parents think that if they feed their baby a large, filling meal just before bed, the baby will sleep longer. This tactic may actually backfire—if you overfeed your baby and then put her down to sleep, she may develop a stomachache. If she is in pain, she won't sleep well at all. It may also cause her to spit up more frequently, which can also cause her to wake up more frequently.

A trick that worked well for my family was to nurse the baby before she went to bed. Then when I was ready for bed, even if it was only an hour later, I would pick her up and nurse her again while she was still sleeping. The key here is to gently move your baby without waking her up. Allow her to eat again while staying asleep, and then both of you go to bed. This might buy you some extra minutes of sleep before her next feeding.

Your baby will let you know she is getting hungry by moving around and making noise, even in her sleep, before she actually becomes hungry enough to scream and cry. If you are close by, you can respond to these early feeding cues and keep your baby calm and (hopefully) able to return to sleep immediately after feeding. Sleeping near your baby allows you to get to the business of feeding without wasting any time and before she is completely awake and fussy. This means that it will be much easier to get your baby back to bed and to sleep if she hasn't been up and screaming for food.

Getting your baby back to bed isn't always easy. Some babies wake up, get their needs met, and go immediately back to sleep. Other parents aren't always so lucky when it comes to getting their baby back to bed.

If your baby wakes up at night, try to introduce as little stimulation as possible into the environment. Do not turn on the overhead light if you can help it. Do not do a lot of talking. If you talk to your baby, do so quietly, gently, and with reserve. Remember, this is about the basics—getting baby fed, clean, and dry. There is plenty of time for play during daylight hours.

Your baby needs to know that there is a difference between night and day. Her 3 A.M. feeding is not also sing-along time or time to read a book. Hopefully it's time to eat, get changed, and go back to bed. The best way to teach your baby the difference between night and day is to preserve this routine of keeping things quiet and simple at night. It doesn't take long for a baby to learn that dark and quiet mean it's time to sleep.

To encourage the baby to learn the difference between night and day, parents do different things. Some go as far as making sure that at night, the baby sleeps in a special place—one that is reserved for nighttime only and is therefore not used for daytime naps. I think that the most important piece to this puzzle is perspective. Remember, your baby has needs that have to be met twenty-four hours a day, even when you are exhausted. If you keep this in mind, you are much less likely to resent or even to notice the night wakings after a while.

Eventually your baby will grow and not need to be up so frequently at night. All parents dream of the day when their babies will sleep through the night. Let me break it to you gently—the medical definition of sleeping through the night is four to five hours, and that's probably much different than your definition. No amount of force-feeding or sleep-training programs will really help your baby sleep through the whole night until she is ready to do so.

Surviving Sleep Deprivation

There is no way to ever truly know the meaning of sleep deprivation until you become a parent. This kind of sleeplessness is nothing akin to the exhaustion that comes from staying up all night in college, studying for finals. It is like nothing you have ever experienced. And yet parent after parent survives this gruesome aspect of parenting and lives to tell about it.

Naps can be lifesavers. You will hear this piece of advice repeated in the form of "Sleep when your baby sleeps." The problem is that no one ever really thinks that this pertains to them. We all think the same thing as we lay our little ones down for a daytime nap—let me just throw a load of laundry in first, then I'll lie down too.

But what invariably happens is something like this. Before you can throw in the load of laundry, you have to fold what's in the dryer so that you can move the wet clothes you washed during yesterday's nap into the dryer and then wash today's clothes. When you're folding, you notice a plate on the counter.

You plan to just put it in the dishwasher before going to your couch to lie down. That's when you see the dishes are clean and need to be put away. And so the cycle goes. Just as your head hits the pillow you hear a familiar cry; your baby is awake and needs you. You just missed your nap again.

This scenario plays out in homes all across the world every day. And all it does is serve to make you more tired, crankier, and less healthy than if you had simply lain down for a few minutes. Why can't we as moms just learn that there is nothing wrong with a little nap? The dishes, the laundry, everything will truly wait.

The best thing you can do to combat sleepiness is to sleep and take good care of your body. Taking energy drinks, caffeine, or even pills to try to stay awake or fall asleep is a bad combination. Pills and supplements tend to be quick fixes or patches that do not work very well.

If you are eating a well-balanced diet, your body will heal faster after giving birth. It will also help you even out any issues you are having with energy and nutrition. Try to fit several small meals throughout the day to keep your energy levels even, allowing you a more comfortable day. Preventing sugar crashes and energy lows through diet will make your life easier.

Avoid eating overly large meals or meals that are filled with sugar. Eating foods in the right amount and avoiding junk food will help your energy levels as well. Fresh fruits and vegetables are better for you than grabbing for a candy bar as a snack.

I found that if I kept healthy foods around in a convenient form, I was more likely to eat them. It was very easy to grab a handful of almonds while I was nursing or to snack on some carrots with ranch dressing. It also made me feel better when I was awake, even if I was tired.

I also found that exercising helped me sleep better. It even made me feel like I needed less sleep. During the first few weeks after your baby is born you're not supposed to be doing a ton of exercising, but I was able to fit some small walks into my daily life. Sometimes I went alone in the mornings before my husband left for work. Other times I waited and went to the mall to walk before it opened to avoid the shoppers and the outdoor elements. This provided me with a burst of energy from exercise that helped buoy me through the day.

Don't be afraid to get some help. If you ever get to the point where you absolutely have to have a nap and your baby isn't game for one, see if a friend or neighbor will come play with the baby while you nap. Consider having a postpartum doula come to help with your baby and the house occasionally so that you can rest one afternoon a week. There were days I had my husband come home for an extended lunch so I could lie down.

There are times when tired is not normal. If you are feeling totally wiped out and exhausted, you may also want to have your blood checked. It is not uncommon to be anemic in pregnancy or to become anemic after giving birth. Your thyroid is another reason you might be very tired, and that is another thing your doctor can easily check. There may be a cause for your state that is not related to sleepless nights, so do not hesitate to ask for help.

ASK YOUR GUIDE

Can I have caffeine while breastfeeding to help me be awake?

▶ Caffeine will travel through your breast milk, so any caffeine you have should be as early as possible in the day to prevent your baby from being awake and irritable. At the same time, caffeine is probably not the best solution to sleep deprivation for a host of other health reasons for you, including inability to nap during the day. I would recommend avoiding caffeine if at all possible.

Get Linked

Questions about sleep are high on every parent's list. Will you ever get enough sleep again? Are your baby's sleep habits good or bad? What can you do to encourage more nighttime sleep? Check out these helpful links for some answers.

NEWBORN SLEEPING

Babies sleep a lot. This is true, but what they forget to tell you is that it happens in five-minute increments around the clock except when it's dark outside. Here are the basics of sound sleep with baby.

↗ http://about.com/pregnancy/newbornsleep

PLACES FOR BABY TO SLEEP

Where you choose for your baby to sleep depends on many factors. Here is a brief outline of all the possibilities.

↗ http://about.com/pregnancy/cribsbeds

SAFE CO-SLEEPING WITH BABY

The rules for safe co-sleeping are fairly straightforward. Here's a review to help you keep your baby happy and healthy in your family bed.

↗ http://about.com/pregnancy/safecosleeping

Chapter 6

Your Relationship with Your Pediatrician

Choosing a Pediatrician

Your pediatrician will help you through the first year of your baby's life in many ways. Of course this person will also help you through the following seventeen years, but there is something special about the first year. Much like dating, it's when you and your pediatrician really form a bond.

Doctors with a variety of different specialties all treat children. The doctor you lean toward will be based on multiple factors, including but not limited to these:

- Your medical history
- The medical history of your child
- Personal and professional referrals
- Your medical insurance

A **pediatrician** is someone who has attended a four-year medical school. Then he or she has chosen to do a four-year residency in pediatrics, or the treatment of young people, from the newborn to the early adult. Most pediatricians stop seeing patients at about college age.

A **neonatologist** is a doctor who went to four years of medical school and chose to do a four-year residency in neonatology, or the treatment of very new and often premature infants. If your baby was born prematurely or very ill, you may remain under the care of a neonatologist for a while, depending on how the practice is set up.

Some people choose to use a **family practitioner** for their pediatrics needs. This is a doctor who attended a four-year medical school and did a three-year residency in family medicine, meaning they can care for the whole family. Some families really like this option because the whole family sees one doctor or group of doctors. Some family practitioners do limit their practice, however, and do not see infants. Be sure to ask this question when interviewing prospective doctors.

Pick a couple of practices to call based on your insurance and other referrals from parents. Make a list of their names, locations, and numbers. First check out any Web sites, if the practice has a site, and then start calling for appointments.

Pediatricians are used to being asked to do a meet-and-greet prior to the birth of your baby. Some choose to hold open houses once a month, where they can meet new parents as a large group. If this doesn't suit your style, ask for just a few minutes at a less busy time of day. You may or may not be asked to pay for this visit, and keep in mind that most insurance companies will not cover this.

If the pediatrician is not amenable to this visit at all, you may want to know why. Perhaps this doctor has a huge practice already and doesn't need or want new patients. Perhaps he feels that he doesn't have the time to visit with every potential new patient. Only you can decide if this impacts how you feel about the practice.

Questions to ask when interviewing candidates for your pediatrician include these:

- Where did you go to medical school? Where did you do your residency?
- How long have you been in practice?
- At which hospitals do you have privileges?
- How often do you take your own calls? Who else is on call with you?
- Do you have a specific time of day set aside for phone calls?
- Will you answer calls and questions, or do you have someone else like a nurse or nurse practitioner?
- How soon will you see the baby after birth? What if the baby is born at home?
- What is your well-child visit schedule?
- Will I always see you in the practice, or will I see whomever is here?
- What are the office hours? Any nights or weekends?
- Where do you send sick kids after-hours?
- Do you have a twenty-four-hour answering service?
- Do you have an onsite lab? X-ray?
- Do you accept routine questions via e-mail? What do you charge for this service?
- What insurance plans do you accept?
- Do you accept payment plans? Credit cards?
- How long is the average wait for a non-emergency appointment?
- How long are your appointments scheduled for?
- Are there separate sick and well-child waiting areas?

○ What is the missed appointment policy?

These questions will be weighted differently for different families. You might have certain questions that are just deal breakers for you. That is all right—simply move on to another interview. Not every pediatrician will be a good match for every family.

Things to consider when choosing a pediatrician include these:

- Type of medical specialty
- Philosophy of the practice
- Issues that are important to you like antibiotic use, breast-feeding, and immunizations
- Insurance acceptance
- Location of the practice
- Number of practitioners involved in your care
- Additional services like lactation support
- Office hours
- Attitude of the office staff

Parenting philosophy can be a big deal when choosing a pediatrician. If every time you go to the pediatrician, she asks you to do things with which you are not comfortable, or if you feel she is implying that you are a bad parent for not following a certain practice or set of practices, then you are not going to have a positive relationship with your pediatrician.

If you have never had a baby, this may be a hard thing to figure out already. Trust your instincts and follow your heart in some ways. Think about what you choose for yourself. Are you a hypochondriac? Do you go to the doctor as little as possible and take a natural approach to things? While this might not be the perfect

WHAT'S HOT

▶ When you visit your pediatrician before your child's birth to interview her, bring your birth plan. Ask her how she feels about the infant portion of your birth plan. If she is willing to support your birth plan and you choose her as your baby's pediatrician, ask her to sign the copy of the birth plan that you will give to your hospital, birth center, or home birth practitioner.

answer, it is a relatively good one for most people to begin to assess their medical beliefs for their new baby.

The Importance of Communication

Let's face it: You will never have all the time in the world to sit and chat with your pediatrician. No matter how much either of you wants it to happen, it simply does not work that way. That doesn't mean that you can't go into an appointment and have your needs met. It simply takes a bit of practice on your part. Effective communication is the key here.

Make a list and check it often. Questions will come up between appointments for your baby. These may seem like inconsequential items, but if they are questions you have, keep them. By making a list of questions, you can go in there and spend time talking about your concerns rather than trying to remember them.

I usually keep a pad of paper on my refrigerator. It is attached with a magnet so that it doesn't fall down, and it's located way up so it's far from little hands. Here I can write questions as they come up. Just before an appointment, I pull the list off and combine questions or reorder them. Sometimes I can even remove some questions. I also use this pad of paper to write down funny things the kids say or when they reach a milestone. It keeps me from forgetting. A couple of my clients use their large family calendar to do the same thing, though they advise you have a separate space for questions so they don't get lost in the jumble of family appointments and birthdays.

Give the doctor information he can work with. Instead of just stating "My baby is sick" when the doctor enters the examining room, start out by offering specifics. You don't want to waste valuable time by slowly working up to stating the problem. Think about it

ASK YOUR GUIDE

Will my premature baby need to see the pediatrician more frequently?

▶ The answer to this question is usually yes, at least at first. After a while your pediatrician or neonatologist will give you the all-clear and tell you that you are free to go to a normal well-baby check schedule. This will usually happen after your baby is off all monitors, is developmentally appropriate, is gaining weight well, and has no further issues that need frequent checkups.

▶ We all need that portable helpmate when it comes to questions about our baby's care. I'm not necessarily talking about questions about how much or what type of medication, but the questions like "Should I worry about this symptom?" "Where should my baby sleep?" "How do I help my baby when he cries?" These are the everyday questions parents have. I enjoy the answers I found in *The Baby Book* by Dr. William Sears and Martha Sears. The authors are a pediatrician and nurse husband-and-wife team with eight kids, so they definitely have the knowledge and experience to help you.

in terms of the major problem or chief complaint in doctor speak. Is it a fever? A runny nose? Maybe you have a concern over a developmental issue. State that immediately and clearly: "Quinn has a fever."

Then give some background. Try to anticipate what your doctor will want to know about the complaint. "His fever started yesterday and it was 100.4 degrees under his arm. I gave him acetaminophen and it brought it down for a bit. This morning it was 101 under his arm and he was pulling at his right ear. He was feeling fine all weekend, but there is a child at his day care who has had a cold. I gave him some ibuprofen and that has really seemed to help."

This enables your doctor to start right in where he needs to begin. He can ask questions of you if he needs to clarify some information. He may just start with the physical exam, but you've saved everyone a couple of frustrating minutes, including your little one.

Ask questions if you don't understand. Sometimes we're so intent on listening to what our pediatrician has said that we miss some of the details. I try to write down what my pediatrician says, but sometimes my hands are full of wriggling baby. Sometimes you may be given written information if it's a fairly common illness or developmental issue. My pediatrician gives out some developmental and safety information at every well-baby visit.

You should also ask questions if you don't understand. This might be about follow-up tests or appointments or medications and treatments. If you don't understand, you can't be as effective in helping your baby get well. It is also easier to get the questions answered while you are there, rather than calling in later. If you get home and realize you don't have all the information you need, however, by all means do call back.

Informed consent means you understand. Since you will be asked to sign informed-consent paperwork about any tests or treatments, you have to know what the test or procedure means. I like to think of it as using my BRAIN:

- **Benefits:** What are the benefits of pursuing the test or treatment?
- **Risks:** What are the risks involved with pursuing the test or treatment?
- **Alternatives:** Are there any alternatives to the test or treatment?
- **Intuition:** What is your gut feeling about the test or treatment?
- **Nothing:** What happens if you choose to do nothing (if you refuse the test or treatment)?

All of this information should be given to you in a language you understand. Don't stand for a bunch of medical terminology you can't comprehend. Informed consent is not about signing a piece of paper; it's about gaining the knowledge you need to make the right decision.

Well-Baby Care

The true goal of a well-baby visit is to ensure that your baby is doing well and developing appropriately. While we call it well-baby care, I often think it's more like parental encouragement. These visits are routinely made through your child's life, though they are more frequent during the first year.

Your baby's well-baby visit will be a time for your baby's measurements to be taken. It is a handy way to follow his growth. It is also a chance to ask questions. You might ask about physical and mental development. Some parents want to get advice on child rearing at these visits. What you do at the visits depends on your needs and your pediatrician's schedule.

What will my insurance cover with regard to well-baby care?

▶ Do a health-care insurance checkup prior to getting pregnant or as soon as you find out you're expecting. One of the big questions will be whether or not well-baby care is covered. If your plan does not cover well-baby care you might consider changing plans at open enrollment. If that isn't possible, ask your pediatrician if she has a well-baby care plan set up. You may also be eligible for other programs that encourage well-baby care in various settings.

A well visit might include:

- Weighing
- Height/length measurement
- Physical exam of baby's body
- Appropriate safety information for your baby's age range
- Discussion of vaccination information and questions
- Medical intervention as needed

These visits to your pediatrician's office are planned for specific ages. How frequently they are done depends on multiple factors including your pediatrician's preference, your feeding choices, your baby's health status at birth, and the age of your baby. These are most frequently done at the following times:

- A few days after birth
- Two to three weeks after birth
- One month
- Two months
- Three months
- Four months
- Six months
- Nine months
- One year

When to Find a New Pediatrician

Let's face it, not every marriage between a pediatrician and parent is perfect. If you are having troubles with your baby's doctor, you need to take steps to rectify the situation. Hopefully the problems that come up will be few and far between, but they do happen, even with great prior planning and interviews.

The important thing to remember is that you are a consumer. This is something we don't often relate to medical care, but it is valid nonetheless. When you think of yourself as a consumer—someone purchasing services from someone else—it gives a whole new dynamic to the relationship of patient and pediatrician.

There are signs that you and your pediatrician are having problems. These might be subtle signs or they may be huge neon signs that this relationship is not working out; whatever they are, learn to pay attention to them. Failing to do so could compromise your child's health care.

Ask yourself these important questions:

- Do you avoid calling your pediatrician for any reason?
- Does your pediatrician really listen to you and your child, and value your input?
- Do you and your pediatrician frequently disagree on treatments?
- Do you and your pediatrician have different parenting philosophies?
- Do you have difficulties understanding your doctor's orders?
- Do you clash with office staff?
- Are office hours frequently inconvenient for you and your family?
- Do you feel uncomfortable going to the pediatrician?
- Does your pediatrician meet your needs?

Your answers to these questions should give you a good idea of whether or not you need to explore the situation further. If you have any doubts, don't tuck them away. They'll only come back to haunt you later.

WHAT'S HOT

▶ One of the best pieces of advice I can give you about your pediatrician's office is to befriend the staff. Be sure that you know everyone's name from the nurse to the receptionist, the lactation consultant to the lab tech. Go out of your way to be polite and respectful. If you're nice to the staff, they will in turn look out for you.

There are some things to try before you leave. Like any good relationship you need to give the other person a chance to help work on what is wrong. I'd highly recommend that you do so before changing your pediatrician.

See if you can set up a time to talk to him when neither of you are harried by patients or sick children. Write down your concerns beforehand so that you don't ramble and waste time—his or yours. Be polite, clear, and to the point. Tell him what you like about his practice and why you chose him, and then tell him your concerns.

That conversation might look something like this:

"I want to start by saying that I appreciate you taking the time to talk to me when it's a bit more quiet. One of the reasons we chose your practice was because you are such a kind and caring physician. I was a bit perplexed when you were not receptive to me holding my son during his immunizations. We had discussed this issue at our prenatal meeting and I thought we were in agreement on it. Is there a reason you have changed your mind?"

Then you need to sit and wait. Be patient. Don't be accusatory. Actually listen to what your doctor has to say; you might learn something. Feel free to speak your mind politely and recognize that it's okay to disagree. At the same time, however, you and your pediatrician each need to decide if your relationship is reparable.

If you leave, you have the right to your records. Most places allow patients one free copy of medical records and more copies for a reasonable fee. You can choose to take your records with you or have them sent directly to another physician. Know that you will be asked to sign a waiver for your records. This is normal and not anything punitive.

We carefully selected our first child's pediatrician before we became parents. I spent much of my baby's first year knowing something was off, but couldn't figure out what was going on. I realized I felt that I wasn't being listened to and that my pediatrician didn't agree with me on basics. Finally I made the decision to switch pediatricians. It was very difficult; this guy knew my daughter's medical history, and a new doctor wouldn't have that history.

In the end we made the decision to switch after a particularly unpleasant visit for both the pediatrician and myself, just before my next baby was born. I did some interviews and selected a new pediatrician. The new pediatrician sent a request for my daughter's medical records and that was that. I did send a letter to my old doctor, thanking him and his staff for the care we had received and explaining why I was leaving. I got a note back saying that they had really been trying to make changes and appreciated the feedback. It was all very easygoing and not as stressful as I had built it up to be in my mind.

Handling Medical Emergencies with Grace

As parents we have to understand that one day we will be in the middle of a medical emergency. We may find that our child had an accident while playing baseball or took a spill down the stairs. With kids in your life, chances are you'll be in a situation to call the pediatrician on an emergency basis.

Emergencies happen. Luckily, by definition, they don't happen frequently. There are some keys to being prepared for a medical emergency with your child:

- Prepare for emergencies by knowing who to contact when and what you can do.
- Take classes in first aid and infant/child CPR.
- Know what constitutes an emergency.
- Respond quickly and appropriately.

Post important phone numbers someplace where you can easily see them in the case of an emergency. You will lose precious minutes looking up a phone number. It is also good for people who frequently are in your house to know how to find these important numbers. Some of these numbers should include your pediatrician, poison control, local fire, and ambulance.

Try not to panic. It may be difficult, but you have got to hold it together. This will help you be able to communicate more effectively, which will mean faster care for your baby.

If you are unable to keep it together, find someone who can. This might be your spouse or a friend. It might be a family member or even a neighbor, but someone who can be rational. They may need to drive you and your baby or help you decide to call for other help, including an ambulance if needed.

You should call an ambulance if the situation is life-threatening, if the situation could quickly become life-threatening, or if you need special equipment. This should be fairly apparent in most cases.

Be prepared. Be like a boy scout or a girl scout and have a plan. Have your emergency numbers posted. Know who to call for what type of emergency. Do you have poison control's number posted where you can find it? Do you have your doctor's number or hospital number handy?

Do you have a first-aid kit? Talk to your pediatrician about what medications you should have around. I also recommend a variety of bandages, gauze, tape, and the like to help in the meantime. If you have a first-aid kit, check it at least once a year for expired medications. I do this twice a year when we change time and fire and smoke detector batteries. Things you might include in a first-aid kit:

- Bandages of various sizes and shapes
- Antiseptic wipes
- Gauze
- Paper tape
- Disposable thermometers
- Instant ice packs
- Pain reliever
- Fever reliever
- Anti-itch medication
- Moist wound-healing ointment

Urgent care centers are good options for some injuries. These centers can sometimes handle "bigger" emergencies than your doctor's office, such as injuries that require x-ray equipment. In my area they handle anything from routine lab work to just shy of a car wreck or major traumatic event.

The nice thing about the urgent care centers is that they are open later than your doctor's office and you don't need an appointment. You can usually find them close to your home, work, or school. They take most major insurances. Some centers offer other specialties, like orthopedics or, perhaps more important, pediatrics.

Emergency rooms should only be used for emergencies. I know this sounds like something I shouldn't have to spell out in black and white, but many families erroneously use the emergency room all the time. When you do this, there are simple ramifications for you and your baby.

First of all, you are unlikely to find a pediatrician on staff at most major hospitals. The exception would be a children's hospital or a specialty pediatric clinic within an emergency room. Without

WHAT'S HOT

▶ During your pregnancy or at any point after you have kids, consider taking a child/infant first-aid course. This can help you feel more prepared in the event of a medical emergency by learning what to do in common emergency situations. You will learn information on preventing and treating choking, CPR and other first-aid skills. I'd also recommend a refresher course every two or three years. Contact your local American Red Cross or hospitals to see if they offer this relatively inexpensive and quick course.

a pediatrician you lose the child-specific care and bedside manner. This may make your child's visit, while technically appropriate, less pleasurable.

It may also mean a very long wait if you are there for a non-emergency reason like an ear infection or a sore throat. This can be miserable on your baby and you. It is standard procedure not to let patients eat until they have been cleared by the doctor, and if you are not an urgent case, you are last on the list at the emergency room—no matter who got there first.

Emergency rooms are perfect for serious accidents and true after-hours emergencies. This is where you will get the best care for these types of emergencies. To help you figure out whether the emergency room is right for you, be sure to contact your pediatrician. She can guide you to the best medical facility to handle your specific problem. Your pediatrician may also be able to make your visit go more smoothly by calling ahead with your child's medical history, orders, or whatever your child may need.

Most calls that need to go to 911 are very obvious. Remember, in any emergency when you don't know who to call, start with your pediatrician. They are your partners in the health care for your baby both during and after office hours.

Get Linked

During the first year of your baby's life, you are going to spend a lot of time dealing with your pediatrician. From well-baby checks to ones where your baby may not be so well, to questions in the middle of the night and ones that come up in the middle of the park, you and your doctor will be working together. Check out these links for more helpful pediatrician information.

CHOOSING A PEDIATRICIAN

There is nothing more important for your child's health than for you to have a great relationship with your pediatrician. Choosing a pediatrician is a very important part of that process. Here is the real scoop on finding the right doctor for you and your baby.

http://about.com/pregnancy/choosepediatrician

WHEN TO CALL THE PEDIATRICIAN

Next to having a pediatrician you like, trust, and get along with is the need to know when to call and what to say. This list will prepare you to handle the biggest or smallest concern via telephone.

http://about.com/pregnancy/whentocallped

WELL-CHILD VISITS

There is a schedule for visits in the first year of your baby's life that are designated as well visits. This well-baby care provides you an opportunity to interact with your pediatrician and learn how your baby is progressing and developing.

http://about.com/pregnancy/wellvisits

IS YOUR DOCTOR SUPPORTIVE OF BREASTFEEDING?

Breastfeeding is something that requires patience and support. A good pediatrician will enhance and support your breastfeeding experience, but a pediatrician who isn't supportive? Well, I'm sure you can figure out what a bad combination that would make.

http://about.com/pregnancy/breastfeedsupport

Chapter 7

Keeping Baby Healthy

Preventing Illness in Your Baby

We all picture babies as tiny bundles with perfect rosy cheeks and a healthy glow. The sad fact is that at some point your baby is bound to become ill. The good news is that you have a lot of control over how healthy your baby stays. From washing your hands often to keeping your baby out of the sun, there are plenty of ways to keep your baby safe from unnecessary dangers.

Wash your hands often. This sounds like a no-brainer, but you would be surprised by how different your life can be with a new baby, even if it is not your first baby. This may lead you to forget to do things that might normally be very common, like washing your hands.

You should wash your hands at least at the following times:

- After using the bathroom
- After changing a diaper

- Before and after preparing meals
- Any time you handle something dirty or potentially infectious
- Before you give baby a massage

If you find washing your hands to be a chore, try to think of how many germs you could prevent your baby from being exposed to by trying it out. Make hand washing a part of your routine. If you have toddlers, teach them to wash their hands and they won't let you forget to do it. It can be made easier by using fun soap like foaming soaps or colored soaps for reluctant children.

Other children can pose a risk to your baby. Obviously I like kids, but let's face it: They bring germs with them. This is true even when they appear perfectly healthy.

While you may not be able to keep all kids away from your baby, particularly older siblings, you can still keep germs to a minimum. Make the kids, or anyone who wants to hold your baby, get screened for fever and illness. Just ask a few question or pull out a noninvasive thermometer. Also encourage hand washing for those who want to hold your little one.

Avoid crowds when your baby is small. This is also a difficult one to define. I had to laugh when I took my seventh baby in to meet the pediatrician the day after she was born. He looked at me and said, "Be sure to keep her away from crowds." We snickered, "You mean like our family?" Then he remembered who he was talking to and chuckled with us.

Seriously, the mall is no place for your baby in the first few days of life. Avoid letting your baby be passed around when you are in a crowd. To do this simply say no to those who ask or offer. If that

▶ Hand sanitizer is great stuff. Don't count on it for complete protection, but do keep some on hand for times when you can't get to a sink with soap. I particularly like my key chain–size bottle that hangs off my diaper bag. It is perfect for diaper changes on the go or when I have toddler hands that need cleaning when I'm out. I also keep several bottles around the house.

doesn't work, I highly recommend using a sling or other baby carrier to "hide" your baby from plain sight. Out of sight, out of mind, as they say.

A sling helps keep well-meaning visitors from touching your baby. If you do have that stray person who won't take no for an answer, try saying that the baby is eating. If all else fails simple physically pull away from them and reiterate your stand.

Breastfed babies are healthier babies. This is a fact. Babies who are breastfed have fewer ear infections, fewer upper respiratory infections, and fewer gastrointestinal problems. This means less pain and heartache for everyone, as well as fewer days off for you and less frequent visits to the pediatrician. The longer you breastfeed, the more benefits your baby gets.

This is particularly true when you are ill. Say you get a cold or virus, as your body is fighting the virus it is making antibodies. These are the very same antibodies that you are passing along to your baby via breast milk, thus protecting your baby right now from whatever you have at the moment.

Avoid poisons like secondhand smoke and lead. Secondhand smoke can cause your baby to be ill more often. It can lead to an increase in respiratory infections, allergies, and even a higher rate of Sudden Infant Death Syndrome (SIDS) in babies who are exposed to this poison. Don't let people smoke near your baby.

Lead poisoning is another serious risk. Children who are exposed to lead can suffer from a wide variety of problems including a lowered IQ, behavioral issues like attention deficit disorder, stunted growth, and more. The most common place for young children to be exposed to lead is through paint, contaminated soil, and dust in a contaminated home.

WHAT'S HOT

▶ If your baby was born prematurely, or even slightly early, or has been seriously ill since birth, you may have special needs as far as when you can take your baby in public. Be sure to talk to your baby's pediatrician about any extra precautions you may need and if you need to wait an extra amount of time before joining the real world with your baby in tow.

Your pediatrician will probably do a routine lead screening of your child around the age of one. They may ask that you do it sooner if you have reason to believe your child has been exposed. You might consider early testing if your child lives or stays in an older home, particularly if there has been renovation or if other children in similar situations have tested positive for lead exposure.

Fire detectors are a must in every home. There are two main types of fire detectors: smoke and flame. I'd recommend that you have both.

You should place a smoke detector on every level of your home and outside each sleeping area. If you have several bedrooms off one hallway, you can use one detector in the hall. You need to stay 20 feet away from bathrooms and kitchens with high humidity. You should also install them in the center of the room for the best placement. If you can't do this put the detector at least 4 inches away from any corner to avoid dead air space where smoke may not go.

Keep your baby out of direct sunlight. This may seem obvious, but it's important to acknowledge that babies can get sunburned too. Most sunscreens are also not baby friendly until your baby is at least six months old.

If you have to go outside, try to stay in the shade whenever possible. If you can't find shade, try shading your baby by putting him in a sling. You might even consider keeping him in just a diaper inside the sling if it is very hot. They also sell a couple of baby sun huts. Though unless you literally lived on a beach, I'm not sure that the expense is worth it for most families. Perhaps you could consider a baby sun hut condo "time share" with other families.

▶ It has been estimated that as many as one-third of all smoke detectors have dead batteries in them. This means that that many families are living with a false sense of security. Remember to check your batteries at least twice a year. I follow a recommended schedule of checking during daylight savings times twice a year. Other parents use winter break and summer break as their reminders to check.

Guns and children don't mix. While you may be thinking a tiny baby doesn't affect how you treat guns, you need to readjust how you think. If you have a gun at home, now is the time to really think about gun safety and your behavior with the gun in regard to gun safety. Good habits formed now prevent many worries down the road.

Do you have to have a gun? If not, consider getting rid of it to prevent all worries. If you must keep the gun, then look into lock boxes, trigger locks, and the like. The more steps you put into putting the gun away and out of reach of your children, the less likely they are to find it and hurt themselves or someone else with it.

Carbon monoxide detectors are also important. Carbon monoxide poisoning is the leading cause of accidental poisonings in the United States, according to the *Journal of the American Medical Association*. Carbon monoxide is a colorless, odorless, and tasteless gas.

Carbon monoxide is not detected by your regular smoke detector. You will need to purchase a separate detector for carbon monoxide. You should have one for each floor in your home. It is best placed at least 5 feet above the floor and it is fine on the ceiling. You should not place it near a fireplace or source of flames.

Monitoring Your Baby's Health

Trying to figure out if your baby is ill can be a tricky thing. While you can look at all of the vital signs and symptoms of illness, I am still a big believer in mother's intuition. By combining a basic knowledge of illness in babies and children with your personal knowledge of your baby, you can usually tell before anyone if your baby is truly ill or not.

TOOLS YOU NEED

▶ I have a really cool product that is a generic home maintenance log. I have seen them sold in bookstores as well. Basically it's a book to keep receipts, phone numbers, and information about home repairs you've had done, receipts and warranties for appliances, etc. This is a very handy collection of information to have as you prepare your home for your baby or as you keep your home safe for baby.

You need to figure out how to tell when your baby isn't well. There are a few things that will always be good indicators of your baby's health, no matter how old they are. I call them the four As:

- Attitude
- Appearance
- Appetite
- Axillary temperature

By monitoring your child for these four things, you can usually pick out when they aren't well. Attitude is about how they are behaving. Is your child normally very calm and easily soothed, but the last few hours wants to be held more than usual or cries more often or easily? This would be a sign that something wasn't right.

Does your baby appear well? Is he flushed? Does he have a rash? Is he pale? You can also take this one step further and ask yourself is he breathing rapidly? How does he sound? Congested? Use your eyes and ears to alert you to subtle signals that your baby may be ill.

Appetite is a huge factor, particularly in little babies and children. Typically when your baby is ill, he will stop eating or only eat very small amounts. This can be very concerning for parents. Try not to worry unless your baby is showing signs of dehydration like no urinary output, sunken **fontanels**, dry mouth, crying with no tears, etc.

And finally, pull out the good old thermometer and take his temperature. You'll notice that I recommend taking the **axillary temperature** (taken from the armpit), as opposed to more invasive options like oral or rectal. If you find that the temperature is above 101.4, you may want to confirm it with a rectal temperature.

Sometimes there isn't any one thing that really stands out. There is simply that feeling that something is going on. Or maybe it's just a couple of really little things that aren't quite right. If you are at all concerned, ask questions and get help. I actually was able to save the life of my eldest daughter because I insisted she was ill, when even her pediatrician didn't believe me. There are times when a parent does know best.

Once you've decided that something's wrong, take action. First you need to gather information about the baby's present illness. How long has he been ill? Why do you believe he is ill? If he has a fever, how high is it? How long has it been going on?

Once you have made a mental or physical list of everything that's happening, you can decide what you are going to do about it. For example, if you look everything over and realize that he has just fed poorly one time today and everything else seems okay, then you are probably best off just watching and waiting for a while.

If, however, your baby has other signs of illness that fit the guidelines for calling your pediatrician, you should do so immediately. I say call immediately because invariably your child will fall obviously ill at 5:01 P.M. as the doctor leaves the office or on the one day of the week when the office isn't open. I always feel better knowing that at least I've talked to the nurse or doctor, even if I don't go in. Then if I'm calling back later that night, they knew it was potentially coming.

By calling your pediatrician early, you may also get information that helps reduce the likelihood that you'll call back or even stops the illness in its tracks. That alone makes the phone call worth it. You may also go over a game plan on how to handle what

How often should I take my baby's temperature?

▶ There is no need to take your baby's temperature on a regular basis. I would recommend that if your baby feels warm to the touch or is acting ill to go ahead and take their temperature. You can then repeat it as often as you think it is needed, until you see a change or as instructed by your pediatrician.

might happen after hours and how to get the best after-hours care, should your baby need it.

The nurses at my pediatrician's office are great about helping me figure out what I need to do next with my kids. They might recommend something I knew about but have forgotten. Sometimes they said, "Bring them straight in!" Either way, I always know I'm going to get the best care when I'm proactive about it. You are your baby's best advocate.

How to Take Your Baby's Temperature

Over the course of your life as a parent, you will develop a very good "baby-meter." This handy way of being able to tell if your child has a fever takes a while to develop and doesn't give you numbers, which are preferred by medical professionals. Until then, the ability to take your baby's temperature is a must.

When you call your baby's pediatrician to discuss your child's temperature, you will want to relate the following information:

- The actual temperature reading
- Type of temperature (axillary, rectal, etc.)
- Time you took the temperature
- Any treatments you have given your baby (medications, etc.)
- Other symptoms your baby is experiencing

Under the arm is a common temperature-taking method. It is also known as an axillary temperature. This type of temperature taking is not as accurate as other methods, but it is easier to do, particularly on squirming kids. It also just seems more humane. This is the temperature you take when overall numbers don't matter.

You can use any almost any thermometer to do the axillary temperature. You will want a clean, dry armpit on your baby, free from clothing. Prepare your thermometer. Then lift your baby's arm up, and place the bulb end of the thermometer deeply into their armpit. Lower the baby's arm and hold it snugly to their side. I usually do this with a firm, huglike stance. Even a tiny baby can flail his arms.

Once the thermometer is done, you will either hear a beep or know that the appropriate amount of time has elapsed. Read the thermometer immediately.

Rectal temperatures are more accurate. Though no fun for anyone involved, you should take a rectal temperature any time you think your baby has a very high fever, to confirm a reading from a different method, or in small infants where accuracy is important.

Rectal thermometers have a blunt tip on the end. Some even come with a guard so that you can't insert it too far into your baby's rectum. This is the biggest danger with a rectal temperature. Due to the risk of glass breaking, I do not recommend you use a glass thermometer for a rectal temperature.

Undress your baby from the waist down. Lay her on top of a towel on your lap, her head away from your dominant hand. She should be facing the floor. Have the tip of your thermometer lubricated with something to help ease the entry.

Use your nondominant arm to brace her head and back, using the hand to help spread her bottom for a better view. Using your dominate hand insert the tip of the rectal thermometer as recommended, about a quarter inch. Gently squeeze her bottom together until you hear the beep of the thermometer.

Do not panic if your baby cries. You would not like this either. This may stimulate her to have a bowel movement or to urinate. The towel is there to catch any mess made by your baby.

When done, remove the thermometer and read it immediately. You can then wipe your baby and place a clean diaper on her. Clean the thermometer using either rubbing alcohol or soap and warm water. I think it goes without saying that once it's a rectal thermometer, it's always a rectal thermometer.

There are other ways to take temperatures. You can buy lots of fancy equipment like arterial thermometers, ear thermometers, and even forehead thermometers. These are fine for screening purposes, though the accuracy of each is debatable. I prefer to use these for screenings and then decide if I need to do a rectal temperature.

Signs of Illness

Let's face it, nearly every baby will have some form of illness during the first year of life. Knowledge is power, and knowing what might be coming down the road might actually help you prevent it, catch it early, and treat it, thus reducing illness and suffering for you and your baby.

Fever is a common first sign of illness in babies. Since humans are mammals or warm-blooded creatures, the temperature of our bodies is one of the best ways to tell if we are fighting disease. While many parents can tell if their baby is warm by feeling her forehead, to really tell if your child has a fever you need to use a thermometer. I recommend digital because it is faster and you don't need to worry about the glass breaking or the mercury escaping.

ELSEWHERE ON THE WEB

▶ Not sure what to do once you've taken your baby's temperature? I can help! Check out the flow chart at http://familydoctor.org/x2575.xml. This chart breaks it down into small steps and tells you exactly what type of treatment your child needs depending on her temperature.

If your baby is under three months of age and is running a temperature of over 101, you should call your doctor immediately, regardless of other symptoms. If your child is running a fever of under 101 it is considered a **low-grade fever**. This is usually treated at home with nonaspirin fever reducers. If the fever is above 101 and does not respond to treatment, call your pediatrician.

Babies often have nose trouble. Runny and stuffy noses are quite common in babies. Your newborn will often sneeze a lot in the first few weeks of life. This doesn't signal an allergy, simply that she is not used to the environment. This usually goes away before you really notice it.

A stuffy nose can make your baby fairly miserable. This is particularly true because it's hard for your baby to eat when her nose is stuffed up. Typically a bit of saline water in the nose will be all that is needed to clear the nasal passages. You can buy brands like NaSal and Ocean or ask your pediatrician how to make your own. Do not use medication unless directed by your doctor.

A runny nose can be allergies or simple drainage. While a clear runny nose is rarely a problem, it is also an old wives' tale that every green runny nose equals an infection. Ask your doctor for specifics on bringing your child in or calling about nasal drainage.

Labored breathing is a warning sign. If you ever notice that your baby's breathing seems labored or that he is having trouble breathing, contact your pediatrician immediately. You should call 911 if your child has blue lips or his ribs go in sharply with each breath.

Some babies will be diagnosed with asthma, allergies, or other breathing difficulties. If your baby has been given such a diagnosis, you will be given special instructions. You may also be taught how to give treatments at home or in the case of an emergency. Reducing the amount of allergens and refusing to take your baby into areas where there is cigarette smoke can be helpful at reducing the amount of symptoms and the number of attacks.

Earaches hurt a lot. Your baby can't usually tell you verbally that his ear hurts, but he will show you. He may cry or be more irritable. He may actually pull at or scratch at his ear. The pain comes from fluid building up in the eustachian tubes in the middle ear.

If your baby has an ear infection, cold, or swollen adenoids, it may be hard for the ear to drain through the eustachian tube as it normally would. This can cause ear pain and infections, which may become chronic or lead to hearing loss.

Earaches and infections are more common if your baby:

- Is around cigarette smoke.
- Attends day care.
- Uses a pacifier.
- Uses a bottle, particularly in bed.
- Has a personal or family history of ear infections.
- Has frequent colds or nasal allergies and congestion.
- Was born early.
- Was of a low birth weight.
- Uses artificial breast milk.

Even if your baby doesn't exhibit any of these factors, you should still be on the lookout for earaches. An earache that goes untreated for too long can turn into a much bigger problem.

Sometimes babies just cry, but it can also be an indication that something's wrong. If your child has a high-pitched, incessant cry for a long period of time that is not settled or soothed by normal measures like feeding, changing, or carrying, etc. then you need to call your doctor. It may be a sign that your baby is in pain.

Remember that crying is one way for your baby to communicate with you. Typically people will try to explain that crying is the only way for a baby to "talk" to you. However, crying is usually a very late signal that your baby needs something. Learning to anticipate what your baby needs and watch for earlier signs can eliminate much of the crying you experience as a parent. This involves getting to know your baby and learning to read the signals she sends you, like rooting when she is hungry.

Look out for diaper rash. A rash on your baby's bottom or diaper area can be caused by a couple of things. Perhaps your baby has a sensitive skin issue and the diapers you are using irritate his skin. Skin irritation could also be caused by the brand of diaper wipes, lotions, or creams being used, or friction. It may also be caused from sitting in a wet or dirty diaper too long.

Be sure to use the most gentle products on your child. Do not use harsh chemicals or soaps. Consider changing the kind of diapers you're using if the rash continues. See if switching for a couple of days makes a difference. We actually switched to cloth diapers and saw a drastic difference by the next diaper change.

Your baby could also have an infection of the diaper area. This could be a yeast infection, **thrush**. Your doctor may prescribe some medicated diaper ointment to have around to help treat these types of infection.

To minimize diaper rash:

○ Change your baby's diapers more frequently.
○ Use cloth wipes and water only.

- ○ Use a preventive diaper cream, like A & D Ointment
- ○ Clean your baby's diaper area very well.

You should consider using a diaper ointment at every diaper change if your baby has a history of diaper rash. You can use the zinc oxide ointments when you need the bigger guns in diaper-rash ointments.

Thrush is a common yeast infection in babies. You may first notice that your baby has large white patches in his mouth. You might think this is breast milk and it may be. You can try to scrape a bit of it off. If it doesn't come off, it is more than likely thrush.

Breastfeeding mothers can get thrush on their nipples too. If you have red, shiny, painful nipples, you may have thrush. This may be treated with an oral or topical medication. Sometimes your doctor will treat you while the baby's pediatrician treats him. Other times the pediatrician will treat both you and your baby since you can pass it back and forth to each other.

Thrush is not particularly dangerous, though it is easily transferred back and forth. Be sure to boil any breast-pump parts, bottles, or anything that will come into contact with the baby's mouth or your nipple.

Don't worry too much about loose stools. The first thing you need to do is to figure out if what you are calling a loose stool is normal. Breastfed babies tend to have stools that are runnier than others. You might hear a normal breastfed stool described as mustardy in color and consistency with small seedlike flecks. This is a normal stool for the breastfed baby.

ASK YOUR GUIDE

Where can I get information about breastfeeding and thrush?

▶ I'd recommend La Leche League for advice: www.lalecheleague.org/FAQ/thrush.html. You need to know what the signs and symptoms are and how best to treat the pain. Since thrush is not the only reason for sore nipples, you will want to be evaluated by someone who knows and understands breastfeeding and thrush.

Your baby will develop a normal stooling pattern. Once this has been established, you will be better able to notice changes in this pattern. More frequent stools may be a sign of diarrhea.

While diarrhea may be alarming, it is generally not a huge problem. Multiple things, including the following, can cause diarrhea:

- Viral or bacterial infection
- Antibiotics
- Milk allergy
- Parasites

Treatment for diarrhea is simply to ensure that your baby stays hydrated. Let him nurse as much as he wants or even add some feedings in addition to normal nursings. Dehydration will be the one problem to be concerned with when it comes to loose stools. Watching your child closely and waiting for the diarrhea to resolve is usually all you will need.

Jaundice is common in newborns. Jaundice is the yellowing of the skin of your baby. It is caused by the failure of broken-down red blood cells to leave the body. The yellowish tinge indicates that your baby's blood has a high level of **bilirubin** in it. This is tested for by blood work.

Typically jaundice will appear in the first week of life. Usually the only treatment needed is exposure to indirect sunlight. You can accomplish this by allowing your baby to lie in just a diaper near a window with open curtains. Just make sure there isn't a draft coming through the window.

Breastfeeding early and often also helps prevent jaundice. This is because the first milk **colostrum** has a laxative effect on your baby. This enables her to get rid of the meconium more quickly, thus reducing the likelihood of your baby having jaundice.

Your baby's doctor will monitor her levels of bilirubin. This may mean extra trips to the pediatrician's office. You might try asking if they will send home health to do these blood draws. It is often covered by insurance and allows you and baby to stay home more comfortably.

In some cases, the bilirubin levels are too high to go untreated. In this case, **phototherapy** is often used. These are usually lights contained within a blanket that swaddles around your baby. This therapy is usually done at home and only lasts a day or two until the levels of bilirubin drop.

Some babies suffer from skin irritations. A baby's skin is so soft and perfect, we hate to think of it as being marred by anything. But there are some common conditions that affect newborn skin.

Eczema is a common skin irritation that may or may not itch. It is most common on the arms, legs, and face, but it can occur almost anywhere. The best treatment is frequent moisturizing, lukewarm baths, and avoidance of irritants like dust mites and other allergens. Most babies will outgrow this type of skin problem.

Your baby may also have small bumps on her face. They can be white or red. This is **milia** or baby acne. Luckily, this doesn't require treatment; the bumps will go away with time. Do not put medication on them or try to drain the area. This may make it worse or cause pain and/or infection.

Medications to Have on Hand

Hopefully you will never need to use your emergency medicine stash, though as a parent I can tell you there is nothing like not having a common medication you need at 3 A.M. You will also find that these are not sold in stores that are easily located in the middle of the night.

Keep some common medications handy. I'm not personally big on giving my kids medication at the drop of a hat, but there is a time and a place for everything. I have actually developed a small stash of medications I consider to be essentials in parenthood.

- **Acetaminophen (Tylenol, etc.):** This is great to have around as it does not contain aspirin and can be used as a fever reducer. It is given about every 4-6 hours. This is good for pain relief of shots and low-grade fevers.
- **Ibuprofen (Advil, etc.):** This product also does not contain aspirin and can be used for pain relief and fever reduction. It lasts about 8 hours. I prefer this one for earaches.
- **Saline Drops:** For that late-night stuffy nose. These help baby breathe faster right away.
- **Simethicone:** These are gas drops. I don't use them often but occasionally you'll have a gassy baby who is miserable. If massage doesn't help, try some of these instead.

Medication safety is important. If you have multiple family members taking medications, you may want to consider color-coding the bottles or finding another way to clearly label which medication belongs to whom.

Any over-the-counter medication needs to be checked periodically for expiration dates. Remember to throw away old medications or medications that have been left over from a prescription. Do so immediately to help prevent medication problems. You should also be sure to store medication according to the bottle's instructions.

▶ While you may need to have medications in your home, it is imperative that you keep them away from your baby and other children. You can use a medication or cabinet lock to help seal the cabinet or box from curious little ones. This will help prevent accidental overdoses or poisonings.

Your pharmacist or doctor will be a great source of information on the types of medications, what they do, and how they act. You should also be given written information with each prescription. Don't forget to read it every time, even if it's a common prescription. It will help put the medication risks in your mind so that you are more aware of what to look for and when to call for help.

Get Linked

Keeping your baby healthy and developmentally on track is the goal of your first year as parents. I include a lot of information on how to do just that on my site. Be sure to check out these and other frequently asked new parent questions.

WHEN TO CALL THE LACTATION CONSULTANT (LC)

Need some advice on breastfeeding? Calling your local lactation consultant can be helpful. Here are some things to look for that indicate you need to call the lactation consultant.

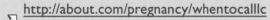 http://about.com/pregnancy/whentocallic

NEWBORN JAUNDICE

Jaundice is something that happens to a lot of babies. When it is your baby you worry more about it. Here are the basics of this condition, including when to worry and when not to worry.

http://about.com/pregnancy/jaundice

Chapter 8

Bath Time

Your Baby's First Bath

Your new baby's first bath is a very special event. Even if you're afraid, you should seriously consider giving your baby his first bath yourself. If you give birth at the hospital and they want to do the first bath in the nursery without you, just tell them you'd like to give the baby a bath in your room. Putting off the bath for a bit helps the baby stabilize his temperature and allows your family to participate in this fun, memorable bath. This is also great if you have older kids.

If you have a family member (your mother-in-law, for example) offering to give your baby his first bath, this person may simply want to help out. Even so, I would strongly advise against it. If you let someone else give your baby his first bath, you might regret it later on. Someone else might want to do it differently than you do, and it's your baby! Just thank the person profusely, tell her you have been looking forward to this moment, and then ask if she can take a few photos or film the occasion for you.

Speaking of photos, remember to take lots and lots of photos of bath time. Definitely snap some shots of the very first bath and then continue to take pictures of your baby bathing as he grows and changes. There can never be too many bath photos of a baby. Have someone else do the picture taking sometimes, too. You definitely want some shots of you bathing your baby.

Bathing Basics

If this is your first baby, you may be a bit nervous about bathing him. He's such a tiny thing, and when he's all wet, you may fear that he's going to slip out of your hands. Don't worry; it's really not as difficult or scary as it may seem. Washing your baby is a personal ritual and one that you'll establish in due time.

Gather your supplies before you start. You will want to have everything you need to use during the bath with you before you begin. It can be dangerous to leave a baby, even a small baby, for just a second to get a forgotten item. Here is what you will need when washing your baby:

- ○ Washcloth or two
- ○ Baby towel or two
- ○ Any soaps or lotions
- ○ Clean diaper
- ○ Clean outfit
- ○ Wipes
- ○ Waterproof apron (if you worry about being wet)

When your baby is still very young, you probably won't need to give her a full bath very often, meaning that you don't necessarily have to have a tub or sink filled with water. In fact, I think it's a better alternative to give small babies something like a sponge bath or

WHAT'S HOT

▶ I am partial to hooded baby towels. When it comes to fighting a baby for a bath and worrying about dropping a slippery baby, there is nothing that beats the confidence a hooded towel provides—because it stays on. Not only that but these fluffy towels seem to really dry a baby better than your average towels. I'd recommend getting a couple to try out.

spot cleaning on most days. This way, the baby isn't dripping wet, and you can leave her diaper on for the majority of the bath. You will need some warm water nearby for wetting and rinsing your washcloths, but your baby doesn't have to be sitting in water.

I personally use two washcloths; the first one being for the baby's face. I use warm water to wet the cloth and then I use one corner to wipe one eye from the nose to the outer eye. Then I change the side of the cloth and repeat on the opposite side.

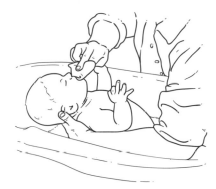

▲ Bathing Baby

Next I use just a touch of soap or shampoo, and I use the same washcloth to do the baby's head. Pay particular attention to the area behind the ears and around the neck. This is an area where babies tend to smell not so fresh. Don't be afraid to lightly scrub a little bit if you find that some areas are dirtier than others. Just don't rub too hard or too long, as this might irritate your baby's skin. Rinse your cloth out well and wipe the baby clean.

Uncover a small area to wash and repeat until the front of baby is done. After the head I usually do the trunk, then the arms, and then the legs. Then I flip the baby over, diaper still on, and wash the back of the baby the same way. Once everything else is done, I take off the baby's diaper and use wipes to clean the diaper area.

ASK YOUR GUIDE

How often should I bathe my baby?

▶ The truth is that babies don't get very dirty very often. Some parents like to give a bath every day as a part of a routine, while others find that every couple of days works best for them. I play it by ear, some babies are sensitive to soaps, lotions, or even warm water drying their skin, so I might do a full bath a couple of times a week and do spot cleans daily as needed.

After that I switch to the clean washcloth and wipe front to back, which is particularly important to do for baby girls in order to avoid infection.

When you are done with the bath, quickly wrap up your baby in a clean, dry towel. This will prevent your baby from catching a chill. Use the towel to rub her until she is dry. If your baby has sensitive skin, consider patting her dry instead of rubbing her.

Last, do not let the water out of the tub while your baby is still in the tub or nearby. The sound of the drain releasing and the water going down the drain can frighten a baby. As your baby gets older, the thought or sight of the water going into the drain can scare her away from a comfortable bathing experience.

You might consider using other items to wash rather than a washcloth. Some people feel like a regular washcloth is too slippery. They prefer to use a bath mitt. This might be a better option if you are a bit leery of washcloths. The bath mitt comes in a mitt or glove style. It can make you feel like you have a better grip on the baby if that is making you nervous.

Other parents use cloth diapers or cotton balls. It is never recommended that you use cotton swabs in your baby's ears. I usually just wrap the washcloth around my finger to help me get to the external part of the ear.

You can do hair washing separately. Some parents prefer to wash their baby's hair separately from the bath. This would probably depend on how squirmy your baby is and how much hair he has. Once a baby is older, it is more common to need to wash his hair, sometimes after every meal.

I like to swaddle my baby in a towel like a burrito before washing his hair. This type of wrapping prevents flailing arms. You can tuck him under your arm, with his legs toward your back, and wash his hair in the sink. This makes it hard to get soap or water in your baby's face, meaning that you run less risk of causing a fear of hair washing down the road.

One phenomenon that you might encounter while washing your baby's hair is **cradle cap**. This refers to flaky or scaly patches on your baby's scalp. It is not a sign that you are not caring for your baby properly; some babies just get it. Typically these patches require no treatment and will clear up on their own within a few months, although some parents want to treat it and try to remove it. Before you try to treat cradle cap yourself, discuss it with your pediatrician.

Tubs and Other Bath Products

You have a lot of options when it comes to bathtubs and products like soaps and shampoos. I'd encourage you to try several different items before deciding on just one arrangement. In fact, I often find myself switching back and forth depending on how dirty the baby is and how long it's been since his last bath.

There are a few different choices in tubs and tub substitutes. One option is to use a bulky plastic baby bathtub. These usually fit over the sink and allow your baby to rest in a reclining position on an attached foam mat while you bathe him. The dirty bath water drains out the bottom. You can find variations with holders for toys and soap and even small sprayers attached, but they are all basically the same.

I personally find these bathtubs to be okay when bathing a baby, but the cleanup is a pain. Even if the water drains out the bottom, you have to dry the whole thing before you move it. I invariably get something wet that doesn't need to be wet, no matter what brand I use. Also, it's big and takes up space. I don't have a lot of extra space to store this piece of baby equipment, particularly when it's

When can I introduce bath toys to my baby?

▶ At first you don't need bath toys for your baby. As your baby grows, you may want to consider them. I find small plastic toys without sharp edges create the perfect distraction for an older baby who dislikes bathing. These toys will usually buy you enough time to get at least the basics of a bath completed.

wet. The bottom line is unless there is a real reason you need to use a baby bathtub of this nature, it is probably not worth it. The added stress and strain would make me go longer periods of time between baths than I wanted.

A foam pad that either goes on the counter or inside a regular bathtub is another option. These are very inexpensive and readily available. You can purchase these at nearly any store that carries baby bath products.

To use this bath sponge, all you do is you lay the baby on it and gently clean him, turning him over slightly as you wash. I still use a towel when using this method to prevent my baby from getting cold. The sponge is a soft place for baby to lie and collects water that you wash with so it doesn't go all over the counter or other surface.

This one can be a bit messy but is obviously smaller and easier to store than others. Some mothers tell me they just leave it in the bottom of their bathtub and push it aside when others bathe. If you let the sponge sit around wet, it can get mildew. It also feels cold and weird to step on when you hop in for your bath. I do find it nice for moms or dads who are worried about dropping their baby, as they know baby will land on the soft sponge.

A third option is a wire frame with a piece of cloth over it. This allows baby to sit at a reclining angle and water goes all the way through this special material. It is not as hard to store as a bulky tub, but not quite as easy as the sponge. Nevertheless, I actually like this one more than other options for bathing with equipment.

I find it easiest to bathe my babies in my bath. I simply sit in the tub and rest them against my legs. I can calm them and hold them tightly. I am constantly testing the water for the right temperature. I can even nurse if the baby gets super fussy.

When I'm done, I hand the baby off to dad who is waiting with a baby bath towel. Then I can finish my bath alone. Dad finishes up by diapering the baby and finishing the bedtime routine.

As your baby gets older, you can actually allow him to sit up in the tub with you or sit just outside the tub. I also have fond memories of bathing the kids in the kitchen sink. You will need to decide how to bathe your baby based on what works for you and what your baby likes.

Babies don't need a lot of soap. In fact, your baby may not need any soap. I usually start by washing my babies in pure water. Then as they get older I will try tiny bits of soap to help really dirty areas, like under the neck or the diaper area.

When choosing a soap for your child, keep your family history in mind. Do you or your partner have any skin sensitivities? Do you have any allergies, particularly in the area of soaps? This can help prevent breakouts in your baby and make her skin less sensitive if you plan ahead.

You can also choose soaps that are naturally based. The fewer ingredients and the fewer chemicals and colorings, the better it is for using it on your baby. This is particularly true if your baby has eczema.

If you find that your baby's skin seems irritated in any way, stop using that particular soap. Irritations can be a rough spot, flaking skin, redness, or any other marring of the delicate skin. Go to plain-water baths and then re-evaluate the soap situation.

Baby lotions are a gamble. Some are great for moisturizing baby's sensitive skin, while others are just creamy chemicals that coat but don't protect. Be careful what you select, particularly for a very young baby.

TOOLS YOU NEED

▶ SolarVeil Pouches or summer slings are great products for bathing your baby. You simply put on the sling, put the baby inside, and jump in the shower. The material allows you to wash the baby right in the sling; meanwhile you've got a great grip on her. It also works as a lightweight summer sling.

WHAT'S HOT

▶ Burt's Bees Shampoo Bar is one of our favorite products. It is not liquid so it doesn't spill everywhere. You can't use too much. The bar is easy to hold, smells good, doesn't irritate most babies' skin, and it lasts forever. The cost may seem high for a single bar of soap, but it's going to last you the baby's entire first year. Plus, I love how it smells.

Think about what your goal is for the product you are considering using. Is the goal of the lotion to make your baby smell good? A plain-water bath may remove any smells on your baby, particularly if you hit the hot spots like the diaper area and under the chin and neck. Don't be afraid to lift up the folds and clean really well.

Are you thinking of lotion to cover a rough patch? If so, what is causing your baby's skin to be rough? Is it eczema? A rash? Or normal newborn skin adjusting to air? In that case a thick cream with few chemicals might help relieve itching associated with very dry skin.

A good rule to keep in mind when picking baby lotions is to look at the lotion. If it's pink or purple, it's probably got a lot of unnecessary chemicals. The same goes for overly smelly lotions. These may only serve to make the problem worse, not better. When in doubt, ask your pediatrician for a recommendation. Some good standbys include Aquaphor® and others that help seal in moisture to your baby's skin. This can also reduce the redness, itching, and irritation without harsh chemicals or medications.

Ten Cord-Care Tips

Nothing strikes fear in the heart of a new parent like an umbilical cord stump. From the moment the cord is severed from the placenta until it dries up and falls off, you are likely to think about it at every diaper change.

The cord is clamped to help close off the blood vessels after birth. By using a metal, plastic, or string clamp, you protect your baby from bleeding through the umbilical cord. The clamp will stay on for several days and be removed by the doctor or midwife. Should you notice any blood, call your pediatrician.

Here are ten basic cord-care tips to get you through those first few weeks:

1. Don't panic about the cord. It is not worth worrying about it. By watching for a few small details, you can basically just ignore it for the few weeks it is on your baby.

2. Know the signs of infection. Rarely a cord stump will become infected. When it does, it is usually red and swollen. Sometimes it is hot to the touch. It may even ooze yellow or green and smell foul. If you notice any of these, call your pediatrician for advice.

3. Know how to clean the cord. Gone are the days of swabbing the umbilical cord with alcohol at every diaper change. In fact, now it is usually recommended that you don't use anything on the cord. Your doctor might recommend something if you have problems, but ask for details at your first well-baby visit or at birth.

4. Don't stress about whether your baby will have an innie or an outie. There is not really any way of knowing. Usually you will know within a few weeks of the umbilical cord stump falling off. Don't be tempted to tape quarters to your baby's belly button or try other ancient methods to control this.

5. Keep a watchful eye on the cord stump. All you need to do is to monitor the cord stump at diaper changes. That's all you need to do. It doesn't require hourly checks or anything.

6. Be gentle with the cord area when diapering and dressing. If you accidentally snag it or pull on it, you can cause pain for your baby, or even cause it to bleed. Simply folding the diaper over can prevent this. I also use side-snap T-shirts until the cord is off to avoid it.

7. It used to be said that you shouldn't bathe your baby until the cord fell off. Now we know that while you shouldn't let the cord stay wet, it doesn't hurt to get it slightly wet.

ELSEWHERE ON THE WEB

▶ Caring for the intact penis is something for which there is a lot of literature. The basic idea is that you want to leave the intact penis alone. You do not need to retract the foreskin during bathing now or ever. Left alone it will retract on its own as your son grows. For more information on care of the intact penis, visit www.cirp. org/pages/parents/peron1.

Just dry it off. You can use a clean cotton ball to dry it off. You can also use a very light, no-heat setting on a hair dryer to help air out the stump.

8. At the very end, just before it falls off, the cord seems to hang by a thread. One diaper change your baby's cord is there—the next it's gone. Most of the time you can find the stump by shaking out the clothes. Simply throw it away.

9. Normally it will take two to three weeks for an umbilical cord stump to fall off. If it is much sooner than this, like within a few days of birth, there is a risk that your baby can start to bleed. This is very unlikely though, even if the cord does fall off so soon.

10. What happens if you don't clean it? Numerous studies have been done on the safety of not cleaning the umbilical cord stump. Your baby is not in any danger from not doing it, despite what other members of your family may say. Any questions? Just refer the nonbelievers to the pediatrician.

Bath Safety

It's normal to be a little nervous about bathing your baby. Like every new skill, it will take time to develop. Even when you do become comfortable with it, it's important that you keep bath safety in mind. From having a good grip on your slippery baby to making sure the water is the right temperature, you need to make sure the bath is a safe environment.

Wet babies can be slippery. The good news is that certain bathing methods will help you keep a good grip on your little one. For example, some parents like to keep their babies wrapped in a towel while they're being bathed, and others like to bathe with their babies and hold them on their laps. You could also wear special hand mittens made to wash the baby's body; these can create extra friction and give you a better grip. Once you become more accustomed to bathing, you might feel you can stop wearing the mittens.

Whatever you do, don't let fear prevent you from bathing your baby. Try the baby-bathtub method if you're overly concerned about slippery babies. You could also have someone else, such as your spouse or parent, help you bathe your baby the first few times. After a while you'll gain the confidence you need to continue solo.

Check the water temperature before you use it. Hot water has the ability to scald your baby; babies have been given third-degree burns with only bath water. Even slightly hot water will dry out her skin and make her uncomfortable. Always test the bathwater temperature before touching it to your baby. You can test the water with the underside of your forearm, as that skin is closest to your baby's skin in sensitivity.

Here's another great tip: To avoid accidentally burning your baby with water that is too hot, go to the source: your water heater. You can use one of the anti-scald devices on the market, or you can turn your water heater down to 120 degrees Fahrenheit. Either choice goes a long way toward child safety, particularly as your child grows older.

Worried that your baby will bump her head in the tub? When your baby is small, this isn't much of a concern since you'll be holding her. But as kids get older, they often like to stand in the tub, which can put that big, metal faucet right at head level. My kids always seem to find the faucet and bang their heads. Here's an easy fix: Simply cover the faucet with something soft like a wash-cloth or a foam guard. You can also buy bath products like foam mats and rubber slip guards to help soften the tub environment.

Here's another rule: Never let your child stand alone in the tub, and never take your eyes off your child while she's in the tub. Don't answer the phone or even turn around to grab something. Kids are quick and unsteady. It will be several years before your baby is old enough to handle bathing on her own.

Get Linked

Learning to wash and care for your baby need not be a daunting task. There are lots of visual classes and other forms of help on my About. com site. Here you can enjoy the pace you set for yourself in a baby-care class and find even more detail on caring for your baby.

NEWBORN-CARE CLASS ONLINE

This newborn-care class is designed to teach you nearly every aspect of baby care, including bathing. Each class will focus on a different aspect of caring for your baby to help you increase your knowledge and confidence.

http://about.com/pregnancy/newborncareclass

HOW TO BATHE A BABY

Here is a great step-by-step review of bathing your baby.

http://about.com/pregnancy/howtobathe

UMBILICAL CORD CARE

This photo essay shows you what a real umbilical cord stump looks like and how to best care for it.

http://about.com/pregnancy/cordcare

BABY BATH PRODUCTS AND LOTIONS

Here is a listing of some of the baby bath products that I like and dislike. This listing tells you why.

http://about.com/pregnancy/bathproducts

Chapter 9

The World of Baby Clothes

It's All about Comfort

Stop! Put down that pink frilly outfit with a billion tiny buttons down the back. Ask yourself, "Would I want to sleep on my back in this outfit?" While it may be tempting to select something because of how it looks initially, you will find that this is one of the worst ways to choose an outfit for your baby.

When you go to buy clothes for a baby, ask yourself the following questions:

- Is it washable?
- Is it comfortable?
- Does it have easy access for diaper changes?
- Does it pull over your baby's head? Or does it have snaps?
- Is it the right style or size for this baby?

ELSEWHERE ON THE WEB

▶ Baby shoes are not necessary until your baby learns to walk, which usually happens around one year of age. Some people can't resist because baby shoes are so cute; but I would not recommend it. Your baby's feet should not be so restricted when they're still so small and sensitive. Socks, booties, and similarly soft items are fine. If you like the look of shoes on babies, try Robeez as a shoe alternative: www .robeez.com.

Finding the right size can be a task. Before your baby is born, you may be tempted to shop at clothing sales or snatch a cute outfit you're dying to have off the shelf. The problem is that you don't know what size your baby will need.

Most babies are born weighing about seven and a half pounds, but there is a huge difference between a six-pound baby and an eight-pound baby. If you spend your entire clothing budget on clothes that would fit a six-pound baby, your baby probably won't be wearing these clothes for very long.

That said, clothes that are too big for your baby could also make your baby uncomfortable. Extra material will bunch and gather in uncomfortable ways, and you may not even realize it's happening.

Just as you can't predict your baby's birth weight, you also can't predict how quickly your baby will gain weight after birth. The average baby is going to double her birth weight by the age of six months. Around the time of his first birthday, a baby's birth weight is usually tripled. This leaves a lot of room for change. Some babies gain very slowly and steadily, while others grow quickly and then sit at the same weight for a very long period of time.

My advice is to make sure you have a variety of sizes before your baby arrives so you'll be prepared for anything. Chances are you'll get a bunch of different sizes of items as gifts, and you can always buy more clothes once your baby is born.

How the outfit opens and closes is important. You will want to ensure that the closure of your baby's clothes is simple. If you have trouble with small baby-sized buttons—and who doesn't?—then consider alternatives. Baby clothes frequently come with snaps and zippers.

I find most of the clothes we have use baby snaps. Sometimes it feels like a maze getting one side to match up with the other, but they are much easier for me than buttons. You will find some clothes with zippers. Zippers can work well, though I do not recommend them if you have a hard time getting your baby to sit still. This is because it becomes very easy to accidentally catch baby flesh in the zipper.

Typically baby clothes will have openings at the neck. If the neck is too tight, it can be dangerous and present a choking hazard. Some have cloths flaps to add to the width but still provide coverage, while others use snaps on one side to widen the hole for the baby's head to go through easily. Either works fine for most clothes.

Also keep in mind that you will be doing frequent diaper changes, so the baby clothes you buy should have easy diaper access. The last thing you want to be doing is struggling with a complex closure or completely undressing your baby to change her when you're in a hurry or out in public.

Texture can make or break an outfit. Don't you hate when a sweater is itchy and irritating to your skin? So does your baby. But while you are able to just take off the sweater, your baby can only cry to announce her discomfort. And if your baby starts crying, you'll probably assume she's hungry or tired before you figure out that her outfit is bothering her. Remember: Your baby doesn't really care if Aunt Rosie gave her this adorable outfit; if it's uncomfortable, it won't work.

But texture isn't only about material. While you definitely want to stay away from itchy or coarse fabrics, you also want to avoid chunky weaves, knots, and any other features that might irritate your baby's sensitive skin.

One other texture problem occurs with the tags on some clothing. Tags with washing instructions are not usually a nuisance (and instead are quite useful) for most adults, but tags can really irritate the back of a baby's neck. If you notice a skin irritation there, a tag is probably the culprit. Go ahead and cut tags right off,

TOOLS YOU NEED

▶ Bulky winter coats and snowsuits for babies can be a real pain, especially when you're trying to strap your little one into her car seat. To remedy this problem, I recommend car seat covers to keep your baby warm. Rather than fight with a winter coat, you simply use this elastic-edged "coat" and put it over your baby's car seat. This product makes taking a baby out in the cold a lot easier.

but make sure you cut them down far enough so as not to make the problem worse.

Designs are cute but potentially dangerous. Make sure that any designs on your baby's clothes stay on your baby's clothes. Logos and decals should not loosen or come off. Something like glitter is a definite no-no, as it can easily fall off and get in your baby's eyes, nose, or mouth.

In addition to her health, also keep your baby's comfort in mind when you look at clothes with designs. While you may really like frilly necklines and other types of lace for a little girl, you have to remember how they will feel. They will be scratchy.

Having Fun with Fashion

Clothes that you choose for your baby should be a mixture of sensible and fun. This shouldn't be too hard if you follow a few simple rules for dressing your baby: Keep it sized appropriately and safe. Other than that, feel free to express yourself!

Different parents prefer different looks. There are some really adorable baby clothes out there, but not all of them will be the style you're looking for. For example, you can dress your baby as a little adult if you want to. We've all seen little boys wearing small suits and a tie. It looks cute, though I'm not sure it meets the criteria I have for comfort. Also in this category are T-shirts that have sayings aimed at adults. Think: "My grandma loves me." "Little sister." "100% breast milk." If you like these items, that's fine. If not, don't feel like you have to choose them to be trendy.

The most common choice is just to dress your baby like a baby. Lots of clothes have pictures of animals, flowers, and other dreamy or childlike things. You will probably even find clothes that take this motif too far and enter the "sickeningly cute" realm. Just choose

▶ Premature babies need even more warmth than full-term babies because they have trouble maintaining their body heat. If your baby was premature, you will want to be sure to add an additional layer of clothing and always use a hat until your pediatrician has said it is okay to take the baby out without the extra layer. This is usually only a matter of a few days or weeks.

whatever you like for your child and don't worry about what you see other babies wearing.

Don't sweat the color game. Most colors are fair play for either sex these days. Gone are the days of choosing only pink for a girl and only blue for a boy. When you start shopping for kids' clothes, you will see what I mean.

Primary colors are very popular in infants' clothing lines. You will find these for both genders. Girls are definitely wearing blues and greens, just as boys wear reds and yellows. To me, the primary colors are the most neutral palette.

Pastels are popular in the very young sizes. They are also very traditional. White usually goes into this category. I like white Onesies in the beginning, mainly because they are easy to bleach and let me monitor my baby's color. I think that the use of pale yellow should be banned in newborns because of its tendency to cast a shade of yellow, which might lead you to worry about jaundice.

You will find out which colors work best on your baby. Some might play off his hair or eyes better than others. You may notice that other colors wash him out. Find what works for you and him and go for it.

Dressing for Seasonal Success

No matter what climate you're in, every baby needs some clothes. You can choose to stock up before the birth or wait to meet your baby and find out his specific needs, but I would recommend that you at least have some basics to get started with. The following checklist contains some of the starter items you might want to have.

- ○ 6 T-shirts
- ○ 2–3 gowns
- ○ 4–6 stretch outfits (with or without feet)

ELSEWHERE ON THE WEB

▶ If you are so inclined, there is also the option of making your own baby clothes. You can sew, knit, or crochet, and you can make anything from simple dresses and shirts to diapers and even some baby carriers. The Sew Baby Web site has lots of patterns, ideas, and accessories for sale. If you are interested in making your own baby clothes, check it out at www.sewbaby.com.

- ○ 8 pairs of socks
- ○ A blanket for swaddling
- ○ A pair of mittens to cover hands to prevent scratching
- ○ 1 sweater
- ○ 2 hats

These basics may have additions based on the season or your local weather. Babies really do not need much, though the more clothes you have the less frequently you will have to do laundry. Then the problem becomes space related: Where do you put all of these clothes?

A new baby has trouble regulating her temperature. This means that you need to help her do that. Don't worry; it's not as tricky as it sounds. You simply need to choose clothing that is appropriate for the weather and situation.

Here's a general rule to follow: Your baby needs one more layer than you do. If you are wearing a very light top and you are comfortable, then your baby needs to wear a light blanket or spring jacket over her outfit. If you are wearing a long-sleeved top, pull out a T-shirt to layer under your baby's long-sleeved top.

Summer is the one time that you might want to be less stringent with the one-layer rule. If you are sweating to death and wish you could remove your skin, chances are that your baby is hot too. Assuming your baby is not in the sun, having your baby go around in merely a diaper is perfectly acceptable.

I cannot tell you how many times I've gone out in the middle of the summer to visit a client and her new baby and the child is wrapped in two blankets and wearing a thick sleeper underneath. This is going a bit overboard. Your baby's skin should be warm to the touch. Not hot or cold, just warm.

▶ Newborns will keep their umbilical-cord stump for up to several weeks. This can make dressing your baby a challenge. I typically use the wraparound T-shirts that don't fasten under the diaper area. This leaves the middle slightly exposed if the shirt pulls up. Then just add a stretchy outfit over the T-shirt to cover the whole baby. This prevents the cord from falling off too early from clothing issues.

Summer babies don't need many clothes. I swear there is nothing as cute as a naked baby crawling around in the summer. That said, it is not always appropriate for your baby to be naked.

I usually have my kids dressed in one-piece T-shirts that snap under their diaper area, usually called Onesies, though that is a brand name. These T-shirts are lightweight and yet keep everything covered. They can be very simple such as a one-color or white T-shirt or they can be very fancy with embroidery or designs on the front.

The nice thing is that these versatile T-shirts allow you to add pants or a sweater for a completely different look. I use them in the cooler months to layer clothing as well. They also make great sleepwear.

There is a version for girls that are called bubble dresses. It is basically a one-piece T-shirt with an extra piece of fabric that makes it look like a dress, though the diaper area is still covered.

You can also get shirt-and-shorts sets for summer wear, along with little dresses. You may want to consider adding some of the following items, specifically for warm weather:

- Sun hat to block sun from baby's face
- Swimsuit
- Sunscreen for babies older than six months

Winter babies need different clothes. This is because babies are more frequently found inside the house while it is cold outside. How warm you keep your house may determine how you dress your baby.

Obviously you need some different clothes for a winter baby. Additions might include:

TOOLS YOU NEED

▶ Baby hats are a must for everyone, no matter what time of year your baby is born. While winter babies will see more use of most hats, hats are also good for new babies, even in the summer. Your baby's head is a good percentage of his body and the fastest way for him to lose his body heat. Keeping his head covered is the easiest way to maintain his body temperature, particularly in the first few weeks of life.

- A thick hat for outdoors
- A coat
- A sweater
- Thicker blankets for naps and bedtime (not quilts)

Washing and Maintaining Baby Clothes

If you start to accumulate baby clothes during your pregnancy, don't just stuff them in a drawer. You need to wash all of your baby's clothes before your baby wears them. This will remove any remaining chemicals or dyes that are on the surface of the clothing, as well as soften the fabrics.

Once your baby arrives, you'll find that keeping his clothes clean can sometimes be a challenge. Not only are babies messy in general, but parents are messy too. I'd like to blame all the messes on the kids, but the truth is I've spilled my dinner on them, usually while trying to multitask.

With all the potential messes out there, laundry can seem overwhelming on some days. Finding ways to make laundry less of a chore is always on my priority list.

Develop a basic laundry schedule. This can be just for baby, though I find it also helps to do all household laundry on a schedule. What your schedule looks like will depend on how many clothes you have for your baby, how many clothes your baby goes through, and how many other people there are in your family. You may also be limited to the availability of a washer and/or dryer.

Since I have a large family, I usually choose a day of the week and do a specific set of clothes. I currently do my clothes on Sunday, baby clothes on Monday, girl clothes on Tuesday, and boy clothes on Thursday. I let my older children and my husband do their own laundry, but only on my off days or days I specifically approve.

Are secondhand clothes safe for my baby?

▶ Absolutely! Secondhand clothing, whether it be from an older child of yours, a neighbor, a yard sale, or a clothing store is a great idea for baby clothes. Babies spit up and stain clothes. They outgrow clothes at phenomenal rates. Whether you're on a tight budget or not, secondhand clothes can be a huge help. Just be sure to wash the clothes thoroughly and check for loose buttons and snaps before allowing your baby to wear them.

This works well for us and allows us to wash clothes differently, if needed.

You might also only have a handful of laundry to do for each family member. If this is true you might be able to do all of your laundry on one intensive day. This works well if you are sticking around the house for a period of time. If you don't have the time to stick around, consider putting a load in the washer on your way out the door. When you return, put the clothes in the dryer right away. Then you can fold the clothes at some point later.

It is important to keep in mind that the schedule will always have exceptions. There will be times when you absolutely need a specific outfit and it is dirty, so you just do the laundry early. You can also adjust your schedule as life changes.

Stains are a part of life. You will become the master at removing stains made by your baby. The biggest stains that come from babies are from food and diapers.

As soon as you see a stain, take action! If you are changing a diaper and there is a small area on her sleeper's leg that has some stool on it, set it aside and finish changing your baby. Then once your baby is safe, rinse the soiled area with cold water and treat it with whatever stain pretreatment you have on hand. I like the gels because I can see where they are on the outfit. Which pretreatment you use is a matter of choice.

Once I've pretreated a stain, I let the outfit sit for a while. The stain treatments can stay on until you wash the outfit, so there isn't really any hurry. I also find that the longer I leave the treatment on, the better the chances that the stain will go completely away.

Once I wash the outfit, I pull it out of the washer to inspect it for the stain. If the stain is still present, I will try to treat it again. I do not use the dryer, I simply add the treatment back onto the stain

▸ When washing your clothes, you can wash them together with everyone else's clothes if your baby seems to tolerate that. The only real exception is cloth diapers. These need to be washed alone. I like to do these on heavy duty with hot water. I also use a second rinse. You can then either dry them in the dryer or on the line.

and set the whole outfit aside. Some moms say they use a different treatment at this point.

If the stain is still there, I try sun-drying the outfit. This can also work wonders. Just lay the outfit out in a sunny area and leave it. The problem is you have to remember to bring the outfit in. This works better on white outfits in my experience.

There are some stains that don't come out, like artificial breast milk and brightly colored foods. If you find that you keep ending up with stained clothes that you can't get clean again, you might resort to the "strip your baby to feed him" method—at least until your baby gains more muscle control or is old enough to eat neater foods. Bibs can also be helpful if you prefer not to strip and feed the baby.

Your baby will wear several outfits a day. This is particularly true in the beginning. You can plan on at least three changes of clothing a day. You will have the main outfit, a spare, and a set of pajamas.

If your baby is particularly prone to accidents, you can either handle the laundry appropriately and frequently or you can do something to try to prevent them. If the stains are coming from feedings, consider stripping your baby down to a diaper to eat when possible. This is a very handy strategy during the days of early solids, around six months or older.

Sometimes it is a diaper accident that you can't seem to prevent. When my babies started having more frequent accidents, it was time to check the size of the diaper or even the brand. If this still does not prevent most problems, consider double diapering. With cloth diapers, you can even use something called a **diaper doubler.**

Keep Dressing Baby Simple and Safe

You've already read about choosing clothes that will be comfortable for your baby, but it's also important to select clothes that are safe for your baby. The basics of choosing safe clothing are simple. Remember that you should have no ribbons, cords, or strings in the outfit. Even baby gowns should have elastic in the bottom to be truly safe. These ribbons can become loose and actually choke the baby.

There is an easy way to dress a baby. Other than finding clothes that are simple to use for you and your baby, you need to learn a few tricks to clothing your child. These are simple to learn and will become automatic very quickly.

Many moms and dads find that sitting the baby on your lap works well. Alternatively you can stand at the diaper-changing table or someplace where you can stand up straight and not hunch uncomfortably over the baby. Keep the following advice in mind when dressing your baby:

- Don't let the neck of a shirt rub your baby's face as you pull it over her head. Stretch it so that there is some distance there.
- Don't pull on your baby's arms or legs to get them through sleeves and pant legs. Instead, gather the material in your hands and pull it over her arms and legs.
- Separate the garment from your baby's skin before you close any snaps or zippers.

In the early days, when your baby is so small and has no real strength to hold himself up, you may feel more worried about hurting your baby while handling him. This is a normal fear, but injuries of this sort are not very common. Just read your baby's signs and signals, and you'll be just fine.

Be careful: Babies wiggle! And if they dislike having their clothes changed, they wiggle a lot. This can make changing your baby's clothes not only challenging but also dangerous.

Be prepared for your little one to resist being dressed. Try calming your baby by talking to her. Tell her what you are doing in a calm and soothing voice, even if she gets upset. Be sure to hold her firmly, no matter how she wiggles.

If your baby is constantly wiggling or rolling around while you are changing her, stop. Move the whole operation to the floor. Kneel down and continue once you've moved everything safely to the floor. This will prevent you from worrying about dropping your baby and it will keep the baby safe in case she is able to squirm away.

You may have to use the floor tactic for a while if you have a squirmer. This is usually short lived. And in general, you only need to do this for older babies, say, past the six-month time period. New babies are rarely so wiggly that you can't get them dressed.

Get Linked

Hopefully now you have a pretty clear idea of how to choose safe and comfortable clothes for your baby based on a variety of factors. Here are some other articles on my About.com Web site that will help you keep your little one happy and healthy, in addition to well-dressed.

BEFORE YOU BUY BABY CLOTHES

Buying baby clothes can be very simple if you follow a few basic rules about dressing your baby. Here are the rules, written in an easy-to-follow format to help you make buying baby clothes a breeze.

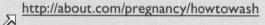

http://about.com/pregnancy/bybbabyclothes

HOW TO WASH BABY CLOTHES

Not sure who to listen to when it comes to washing your baby's clothes? Factors that you need to take into consideration, types of detergent, and more are discussed here.

http://about.com/pregnancy/howtowash

LAYETTE LIST

With all of the options out there, you need to be able to decide which clothes and other layette items you and your baby really need. Here is a complete list that covers all seasons.

http://about.com/pregnancy/layettelist

About.

Chapter 10

Baby Proofing Your Home

Different Approaches to Baby Safety

It is so hard to believe that this small baby you've brought into your lives will ever move around on his own. You look down and see a small helpless bundle, but I am here to tell you that the small warm bundle you've got today is tomorrow's wild child. Plan today to keep your baby safe, for the times when you blink and they've gotten into something.

Too many parents take the wait-and-see approach. This means that you figure you have got plenty of time before you'll need to do anything about the baby's safety needs. Perhaps you have picked an arbitrary date in the future. Many moms I have talked to have picked a developmental milestone like crawling or walking as their personal deadline to baby proof.

It is great to have future plans. I am also a believer that baby proofing is an ongoing process. There isn't one big sweep and you are set for life. You will need to bend and grow as your child does.

▶ I admit it. I am a terrible judge of what is too small to give a baby to play with. Apparently I am not alone. This is why they sell a small tube for a couple of dollars that allows you to see if you can pass a toy or object through the opening. If you can't, the toy is safe for a baby. If the toy fits in the tube, it means that the toy is actually a choking hazard and should not be given to your child.

This also applies to subsequent children who will have different needs when it comes to child proofing.

You might also believe that you don't need baby proofing because you will always be there to watch your baby. Even if you were with your baby twenty-four hours a day for the entire first years of his life, you will eventually have to sleep. Sometimes all it takes is a blink of an eye to give your child the time to do something to cause himself harm. This is usually from curiosity rather than mischief-making, but the results can be disastrous either way.

It may simply be that you become comfortable. You let your guard down, or your baby suddenly sees something in a new and different manner. You've sat in the kitchen cooking dinner every night with your baby playing on the floor under you and today is the day he's decided that the light socket looks like it might be fun to play with. You've not changed, nor has the light socket. What has changed is how your bright and inquisitive child sees the world.

The problem with forward thinking means that your baby is not protected today. And let's also not forget that some baby proofing is really just a matter of things even a newborn needs, like not using fluffy crib bedding, and safe co-sleeping rules. I can't say enough for planning ahead, even if you only do a bit at a time.

Planning ahead is the only way to baby proof. This means that you know that there are things to think about and problems to correct. You are never really done baby proofing. This is a huge problem with many of the parents I know, they have a fix-it and forget-it mentality. The problem here is that it will not grow with your baby.

Take baby proofing a bit at a time for an easier go at it. You will want to start with some basics that matter right now. When I'm helping people get started, I usually recommend that they start with a couple of products to get the big dangers that are easily seen. So they might put some socket plugs in the wall. For tiny babies, and the best place to start is with the basic products and go room by room.

Ten Baby-Safety Products You Need

The gizmos and gadgets that you will use to keep your baby safe from harm are both ingenious and wonderful. For me, they also provide peace of mind because I don't have to be the end-all, be-all, know-it-all of child safety. I don't need to invent something to prevent a fork from going in a light socket or keep my baby from strangling on the cord to the blinds.

While there are literally hundreds of products available, you will probably not need most of them. The products I have listed here are the most basic level of safety products. They do not take into account if you live in city or the country, if you have tall windows or low stoves. This is where you will have to personalize your needs. But these products will cover the basic baby proofing of your home and really make you open your mind to the possibility of dangers.

Outlet plug covers are as basic as it gets. They are probably the number-one baby-safety product used. You can get a pack of ten basic outlet plug covers for about a dollar. These are used to prevent your baby from sticking anything in the outlet.

Outlet plug covers come in several styles. The most basic plug is clear or white plastic cover having pluglike prongs that fit into the socket. You can also buy plug covers that have swivel tops, allowing you access to the outlet, but only if you have the dexterity to swing the cover up or over, depending on the brand you get.

The more complex covers require installation, but we're talking a screwdriver—not rocket science. They provide you with more

TOOLS YOU NEED

▶ *The Safe Baby: A Do-It-Yourself Guide for Home Safety* by Debra Holtzman is a great guide for at-home baby proofing. Not only will she show you how to work on the physical aspects of your home, but she teaches you how to help your child as he continues to grow to keep himself safe, including basics like washing his hands.

coverage as well. Many parents like these for obvious reasons, including the fact that a small child can't simply pull them out.

A bathtub spout cover prevents bumps. These are usually inflatable covers that simply slide over the faucet in your bathtub. They prevent your little one from hitting his head or face on the hard spigot.

The faucet is hard and can cause a number of injuries. The most common would be cuts or bruises. I have a neighbor who, for years, showed off a scar from his encounter with a bathtub faucet. The other thing is that after running a warm bath, the faucet may be hot. The cover will prevent your little one from touching the hot metal. The good news for parents is that they are easy to place and remove.

Gates for stairs are a must. You should always use a gate or some other way to block the top and bottom of your stairs. The blocking of the top of the stairs is obvious—you do not want your baby falling down the steps. The bottom is protected to prevent your baby from going up and then tumbling down.

The problem with stairway gates is that you have to use them at all times. The older versions made them really hard to pass through, meaning they were often neglected or only improperly used. Newer models will be marked with versions that are easy to pass through. Be sure to see if the store has a live demonstration, then imagine carrying a child or a bucket of laundry through the gate one-handed. If it passes this test, you're good to go.

In the same breath I would be remiss to ignore stair railings. There are many products sold to protect this area. Some are made of mesh while others are clear plastics. This simply covers the area between the slats of the railing to prevent your child from falling through. Don't think your child's head is too big. I came out one day to find my three-year-old child happily dangling over the landing between the railings.

Baby gates are great to have. These gates are used between rooms. It might be used to keep your baby in the room or prevent your baby from accessing this area.

Some are easily removed to make them temporary. This is great for rooms that aren't open a lot. I use one like this on the door to my scrapbook area. It is right off the play area, so I open the door and lock myself in. The kids think it's great that Mommy is locked in her room. I can still hear and see everything from my vantage point without the hassle of little hands covered in glue and feathers.

For rooms where you will need a stronger or a more permanent gate, there are ones that actually attach to the wall with hardware. Gates are really more user-friendly these days with a variety of attachment options. Which type of gate you choose will depend on what type of protection you need.

Kitchen locks are must-have items. They sell locks for all of your drawers and cabinets. While there is a wide variety, you really need to test some of these out. That is because you will constantly be using them every time you are in the kitchen or bathroom.

I also find that they can be difficult to install, so make sure you know what you are doing. Since they are complicated to install, I try to ensure I have good quality locks so they don't break after a couple of months of continuous use.

These are used for all the floor-level cabinets and drawers that are at counter level. Various parents will disagree about whether they are needed on cabinets that hang from the ceiling. My personal opinion is that you need to put locks on any upper cabinet that contains items such as poison, medications, or cleaning supplies. I would also encourage you to think strongly about installing locks on all upper cabinets. You never know which child will be a climber. and you don't want to find out when your grandmother's china is in pieces on the floor after your toddler has played Frisbee with it.

Refrigerators need locks, too. No, this is not to help you lose baby weight; it actually is meant to protect your child from getting inside.

Children are small enough that they can actually get inside the refrigerator and be closed in. This can cause them to suffocate inside the refrigerator. These locks are made of Velcro and are easily removed for fridge access.

Did you know they also make electronics blocks? It started with simple blocks for VCRs. I really didn't understand the need until I saw a child put a slice of pizza in a VCR. Luckily it wasn't my kid or my VCR, but I watched it happen before my very eyes.

So now you can buy blocks to keep small fingers out of VCRs and DVD players. You can keep tiny fingerprints from the screen of your computer or television, and you can even program your computer or television to block certain channels, games, or shows. These blocks can start out simple and progress as your child's ability to program increases.

Don't forget to lock the potty. Don't laugh, but you need to have locks on your toilet. There is nothing like finding an older sibling giving the baby a swirly or watching small toys being flushed at such an amazing rate that your plumber can't even keep up. We once had to call the plumber for a clogged toilet, only to be told that it was $1.87. Not the plumber's bill, but the change clogging the toilet.

▶ I was never really a rubber corner–type of parent. I figured if you weren't smart enough not to buy sharp corners with your little ones… well, you know. But then I moved into a house with a brick hearth with an edge that was already covered. After watching my kids' heads bounce off of one a couple of times, I was grateful and completely sold on their use.

The obvious safety hazard for the toilet is drowning. Infants and small children can easily drown in a toilet, but they can also get stuck from the other end as well. Save everyone a headache and buy a quick-release toilet lock.

Stove blocks are handy to have around. I like my stove block. It's a clear piece of plastic that fits over the bottom edge of the stove. It keeps little hands from reaching up onto the stove and burning themselves. I recently found out it also blocks mommy from dripping hot liquids on little ones.

The stove block took me a minute or two to install. It is made to fit a variety of kitchen stoves, so I had to figure out how to make it work with my handles and knobs. It was only a couple of dollars, but it's my most recent purchase. The biggest complaint I have is that it is only good for the front of the stove. If your stove's side edge is not bordered by cabinets, you need another one or you must find a different solution to get total coverage.

Door handles come in many styles. And every door handle deserves a good lock. Again these are used to keep children out of places they shouldn't be, although the toughest part is finding door locks that are easy enough for an adult to use. My favorite kind fits over a door knob; you just grab it and squeeze while turning, like a cap on a medicine bottle, and then the door opens. But little kids would just spin the lock around without opening the door. My four-year-old twins who are into everything still haven't figured these out yet.

Something else that fits this category are products designed to prevent doors from slamming on little ones. Kids are fast to discover the joy of slamming doors. I like the foam wedges that fit around the top of the door edge to prevent slamming. They don't hurt the wood and are easy to remove. I can't tell you how many fingers this has saved in my house.

ELSEWHERE ON THE WEB

▶ Baby and child proofing doesn't end in the home. Truly speaking, car seats and booster seats are an extension of baby proofing—that is, they keep your baby safe. Each state has laws on how to keep your child safe in the car and how long to keep them in what kind of car seat. Save your sanity and read this list of the state laws: http://about.com/baby products/carseatlaws.

Is there anything to help my child be taller and help in the kitchen?

▶ The Kitchen Learning Tower by Little Partners is your best bet. This is an enclosed area that is a platform, so your child has a bit more area to feel safe and secure on. The height is adjustable. This works well for an older child who loves to help. My only complaint is what to do with it in a small kitchen!

Rooms to Baby Proof

Every room that you go through will have some basic steps to make it safer for your family. Following some simple steps can improve upon that safety for your whole family.

Here is the basic list:

- ○ Are outlets covered?
- ○ Is furniture away from windows?
- ○ Are cords shortened on appliances, electronics, and window blinds?
- ○ Is furniture secured to prevent it from tipping over?

The kitchen is a hotbed of danger. Pun intended. You need to be sure that you keep your little ones away from the stove and refrigerator. You also need to be certain that you have drawers and cabinets locked.

I like to leave one cabinet with items just for my little ones to play with. This is usually a couple of plastic bowls and wooden spoons. Little ones are particularly enthralled with measuring spoons, such as the tin ones that clink. This makes them feel like they have their own area to play in while I cook.

If you have a stool or some other device to have your child help you cook, be sure it has a nonskid surface on the stool. I don't really like doing this because it allows my child too much access. So if I need help, I'll bring a bowl and spoon for him to stir to his level so he can help. It also makes it easier on the child because he isn't worried about keeping their balance.

The living room has a lot of living going on. This means a lot of potential dangers. You will want to ensure that all of the rugs, if you have any, are nonskid. If they aren't, you can add nonskid pads underneath them.

Check to be sure that all electrical cords are really out of reach of little ones. It also works out well to have cords banded so that you don't trip over them when carrying a small baby. If you must have cords through the middle of a room, be sure to tape them down or secure them in some manner. The best bet is to always place cords behind furniture whenever possible.

Also have things like VCR/DVD locks in place, and tidy up any messes like piles of magazines. These can easily topple over onto an inquisitive toddler or a baby learning to cruise, not to mention they are slippery to stand on.

Bathrooms are an area I leave to products. Between the drawer and cabinet locks, the lid-lock on the toilet and the variety of tub products I use, nearly every surface in my bathroom has something to help me out. The bathroom is potentially such a dangerous place. Be very careful in this room. I keep mine locked when not in use.

Outside areas need baby proofing too. Two of the biggest safety areas outside your house are the garage or shed, and the swimming pool. Now, many of us don't have a pool, but if you do, you really need to pay close attention to some of the safety issues surrounding water. Some of the ideas might actually save you money on your home insurance.

The garage and shed are often neglected areas of our home. I know mine tends to be a lot less organized and tidy. Let's just say I won't be hosting dinner parties out there any time soon. It is where you shove leftover or semi-broken furniture, and you also might use it as a place to store paint or chemicals, like cleaning supplies.

Spend some time and money organizing and baby proofing your garage. Buy some hanging racks to hang your lawn equipment

WHAT'S HOT

▶ If you have a swimming pool or spend a lot of time around a pool or other body of water, you will want to do everything you can to keep your baby safe. This will probably include early and often swim classes for you and your little one. You should also have a variety of things like safety belts, special swim suits, and other protective swimwear.

and to store your chemicals safely. Buy a cabinet that can lock to allow you to hide these items away from prying hands—and the cabinet alone is not enough.

Make it your family policy never to let anyone ten years old or younger go into the garage alone. Children should never be left in the car asleep. They shouldn't go out to get a ball or toy from the garage or car. Something as simple as a trip to the deep freeze can end tragically for even an older child. They will whine and cry about it, but it's still the best policy for all involved.

The nursery is usually the easiest to baby proof. I mean, you can't have your baby in a nursery that isn't safe, right? The problem with this mentality is that parents often let the fun of building a nursery over-ride the safety instructions. For example, the lovely, adorable quilt that you spent so much money on to match the sheets is not safe for the baby's bed. You should also forego the bumpers.

So while you're working at keeping your baby safe in his room, be sure not to let your baby become a victim of fashion. The largest part is safety in toys and bedding. Remember no soft toys or bedding, and only use approved sleepwear in the appropriate size for your baby. Large, loose-fitting clothing can be a strangulation risk.

Baby-Proofing Services

There are actually people who baby proof for a living. These good folks actually come to your house and look around. They tell you how and what to baby proof—for a fee.

The services they provide vary. Some services are discussions and information only. They come to your house. They inspect every room. Then, they sit down with you and give you a detailed

WHAT'S HOT

▶ Take that adorable quilt and turn it around. Use your brand-new, not-safe-for-baby quilt as the newest decoration in the nursery. Tack it up on the wall as an adornment and continue to use the theme as a jumping-off point for decorating the whole place. It will add color, texture, and a theme.

list of everything that you need to do to baby proof the house. But they do not provide any products or installation services.

Other companies do things differently. They will come and do a walk-through inspection. Then they give you an estimate for the products and installation on all of the recommendations. Some parents choose to just purchase the products and do the installation themselves.

While some of the baby-safety products are a bit trickier to install, the majority are very simple. If you choose to have anything installed, I'd opt for the more tedious tasks like the drawer and cabinet locks. I'm also a big believer in hiring someone to install anything that requires a drill, like big gates. This can also apply to products that hold large pieces of furniture in place when children climb on them.

You should find a reputable source to do your baby proofing. See if you can find references for people who do this work. Some of my clients simply figured out what needed to be done and did it with a local handyperson simply because there weren't any baby-proofing services.

Others might be fly-by-night services that haven't been around long. You do have to worry about putting your baby's safety into someone else's hands, even if the guy only wields a screwdriver and hammer. So I'd stick with companies with a history and no complaints filed on them at the Better Business Bureau (BBB).

To find a service, you can try the phone book. Many times I've found great sources of help from local mothers' clubs or even the twins clubs in your area. Some hospitals offer a referral service for any baby-related service.

When you find someone, ask to speak to satisfied customers.

ELSEWHERE ON THE WEB

▶ The Nanny Cam is the newest weapon in your arsenal on child safety and baby proofing. Having the ability to watch your child when you're not home is something that most parents at least think about. With the many options available, do you really know what you are looking for or if Nanny Cams are right for you? Check out http://about.com/childcare/nannycam.

Do I need to baby proof differently if I have twins?

▶ Absolutely! Twice the fun is twice the trouble. Your multiples will always be able to think twice as fast. They have someone to give them a mental or physical boost. Two minds moving that quickly are bound to figure out many things sooner. One mom points out that when one of her children hit a wall the other was already problem-solving the solution—which spelled trouble.

You can ask questions like:

- Were the people who worked for the service on time and professional?
- Did they seem knowledgeable about baby proofing and children?
- Did they have all the tools necessary and clean their work area before leaving?
- Do they offer any other services like CPR?
- Will they contact you for birthday visits to upgrade baby proofing at specific developmental ages?

Test It Out: Borrow a Baby or Toddler

While it is possible to hire grown men and women to help you baby proof for your tiny newborn, there are other options. One way to look ahead into your future when it comes to making your home safe is to borrow a baby.

I got this idea when I had finished baby proofing my home for my first baby. Our daughter was only about three months old, and so far, she hadn't done anything to get in trouble. But then some friends came over with their fourteen-month-old who tore through our home. When they left, we had a whole new list of things to accomplish.

The developmental stages are the keys. Remember how much your new baby will grow within the first year alone. I am not just talking about gaining weight and outgrowing clothing. I am talking about learning to interact with you and everyone around you. Part of the process of learning to interact is to manipulate the environment.

This all goes back to the idea that you need to do first things first. Being that one step ahead of your baby is the best policy.

After you're getting settled into a new routine at home with a new baby, think about the upcoming milestones. What will your baby be doing next?

If it is rolling over, what do you need to do to prevent accidents? Well, you can remind yourself about not putting the baby down on a high surface like a couch, counter, or changing table. If you have been neglecting that strap to buckle your baby into the changing table when you switch diapers, now is a good time to teach yourself to do it. This helps prevent you from learning the hard way when your baby shows you he has mastered a new skill by rolling onto the floor.

These developmental stages are fairly predictable. Rolling over leads to sitting, which leads to scooting or crawling, which leads to cruising and then to walking… While a couple of steps might come in a different order depending on the children, they will usually happen within a few months of each other. Appendix B has many of the developmental milestones to look for in your baby.

A toddler's-eye view is best for baby proofing. I prefer real, live toddlers for this activity. Invite a few over for the afternoon. You can usually entice the parents by offering a few hours off from parenting duties.

You don't need to do anything except watch the child, but watch is the operative word here. She will run everywhere. Make note of where she goes and what she does. Toddlers can give you a great idea of where the danger spots are in your home. Does she find change in the couch cushions? Did she find a frayed wire on the lamp in the hall? Maybe she grabbed at a corded telephone you had forgotten about. These are the types of things you are looking for her to find for you.

Keep the list handy. After you're done watching the child-proofing expert, have a plan. What needs to happen now? What

▶ Breakables do not have to be banned when you have children, although keeping glass items on a level that your child can access might be a bit like the proverbial bull in a china shop. I highly recommend placing these items high up on shelves or on top of very tall furniture. Some parents choose to put certain items away for a while. The choice is yours.

can wait? Remember to keep the developmental milestones in mind when choosing which projects come next.

If you aren't in a situation where you can find real toddlers to come over, try getting down on the ground yourself. Have a play date and crawl around the floor. Look around for dangerous items close to the floor that aren't often seen from your perspective above.

You might also try lying flat on your back on the floor and staring up. Do you see any dangling strings? Does the recliner footrest look inviting to little fingers? Can they become trapped under a rocking chair?

Baby proofing is a large job, but it does not have to be done immediately. Do a bit at a time and plan ahead for developmental milestones, although giving yourself a head start during pregnancy can be a lifesaver. Just knowing some of the basics will go a long way in keeping your baby safe.

Get Linked

Baby safety often seems to fall at the bottom of our to-do lists. Thinking ahead in the area can actually save a life. Check out some more tips and products on my About.com site to keep your baby safe.

BABY SAFETY

You can find general guidelines for keeping baby safe here.

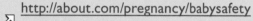 http://about.com/pregnancy/babysafety

TOP 10 BABY SAFETY PRODUCTS

I've gathered a list of 10 products I have personally used to help protect my family.

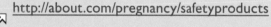 http://about.com/pregnancy/safetyproducts

TIPS FOR BABY PROOFING

These tips will help you get some of the basics of baby proofing done very quickly and easily. This really helps set your mind on the right path to go along with the products to help you.

 http://about.com/pregnancy/babyprooftips

About.

Chapter 11

From Slings to Car Seats: Stuff for Your Baby

All about Car Seats

A car seat is the basic piece of baby gear that nearly every parent must have when expecting a baby. In fact, there are many hospitals and birth centers that will make you bring in the car seat for inspection before allowing you to go home. When we had our seventh baby and brought her in for her first well-baby checkup, our pediatrician got really anxious because we left the car seat in the car. I had to send my husband out to get the car seat, just to prove we had one! Bottom line? Get a car seat.

Car seats are designed to be safe. The basics about car seats are that each one made in the United States has to meet the minimum safety standards. This is not true of car seats purchased in other countries. However, there are car seats that test better than others in safety tests. Consumer Reports and other similar places often have lists of the best car seats in their studies.

There are a lot of types of car seats available. There are those that fit the smallest to the tallest babies or toddlers. There are car seats that swivel. They even have really wild and outrageous prints on some car seats.

When you first have your baby, you're going to need an infant car seat. This is a car seat designed for babies. Usually the weight limit on this kind of car seat is around twenty pounds. It is designed to be a rear-facing car seat for the safest ride for your baby.

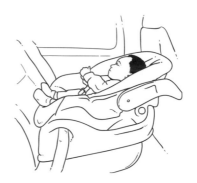

▲ Rear-facing car seat for an infant

These types of car seats usually have a base that gets buckled into the car. The actual car seat can be easily snapped into the base and then just as easily removed. This allows you to use the car seat as a baby carrier as well. You can usually buy multiple bases for multiple cars. The base system also helps you ensure a safe ride by not having you put the tight base in over and over—which gives you a chance to be lazy about it.

After your baby reaches a weight of twenty pounds, she will go into a larger car seat. Your baby's age and weight will determine when the car seat gets turned around to face the front of the car; in general, this happens at about one year of age. As the seat—and your child—gets bigger, it doesn't make as much sense to take the seat in and out of the car or to use it as a carrier. We usually leave ours in the car, with only periodic removals to do safety checks and clean out the car's interior.

▲ Forward-facing car seat for an older baby or toddler

Convertible car seats technically hold your baby from newborn all the way until they are about 40 to 45 pounds. These car seats can be rear or forward facing. They are not useful as baby carriers. Some mothers and fathers find that their tiny babies are swallowed up by this huge car seat, while other parents aren't bothered by it.

A booster seat is never appropriate for your baby. Typically, a booster seat is for an older child around four or five years of age. These are always forward facing and have various ways of working with the existing car seat belts. Different states have different laws concerning how long your child has to be in a car seat or a booster. In some places, it is as old as 8 years of age.

What are you looking for in a car seat? Make a list and take it with you when you are out shopping for car seats. Talk to other parents about car seats. What car seat features do they love, and what could they live without? Sometimes something in an ad sounds good, but when you get that feature, you find it's really awful for whatever reason. My husband fell for this one, a few kids back, when he saw a car seat that had bent handles for carrying. He thought it looked easier to carry, but it turned out to be a big pain.

Use the following checklist to establish that the car seat you're considering has all the features you require:

- ○ Does it fit in my car?
- ○ Will it fit in any other cars we use?
- ○ What are the weight ranges on this car seat?
- ○ Can this car seat be used forward facing?
- ○ Can this car seat be used rear facing?
- ○ Does it have a five-point harness?
- ○ Approximately how long will my baby be in this car seat? Will I need an additional car seat?
- ○ Does it have a base system to allow it to be easily removed and installed in a car?
- ○ Can I buy an extra base for this car seat?
- ○ Does this car seat come with any optional items?
- ○ If my child has special needs, will the car seat accommodate them?
- ○ Is this car seat in my budget?

There are a couple of issues with used car seats. First of all, let me make the distinction between different kinds of used car seats. One type is the car seat you used for your first child or the car seat your sister used. These car seats have a known history and are probably relatively new. Then there are the car seats from a yard sale or even eBay. These have an unknown history.

A used car seat with a known history is obviously the safer choice. If the car seat is a couple of years old, double-check with the maker to ensure that there are no outstanding recalls for that make or model of car seat. Clean it up and wash the padding, and you're good to go.

A used car seat with unknown history is problematic. If a car seat has been through an auto accident, no matter how small, it should be considered unusable. This is because of small or undetectable problems that make that car seat potentially very dangerous for your baby. Unfortunately, even if the current owner says it hasn't been in a wreck, you can't prove it. Is the uncertainty worth the risk? Probably not, even if you are saving a few bucks.

One of the biggest problems with a car seat is that parents use them improperly. This can be from using the wrong car seat at the wrong time, like using a booster seat for a child who is too small or using an infant seat for a baby who has outgrown it.

Putting your baby in too loosely is dangerous, too. Your baby's harness should be as tight as a tight hug. You should not be able to slip fingers easily between the straps and baby's body. Remember, this is supposed to hold your baby in place in the event of an accident.

Having a car seat that faces the wrong way is also a problem. Infants should be in rear-facing car seats until they are about a year old. Turning him around sooner may place your baby at a greater risk of injury should a crash occur.

Being sure that the car seat or car-seat base is strapped in correctly and tightly is also important. If you're having trouble getting it installed or tight enough, ask for help. Many times you can find Certified Child Passenger Safety Technicians at automobile dealers, fire stations, and police stations. Call around locally to find someone to help you install the car seat for that added protection.

TOOLS YOU NEED

▸ Car-seat entertainment is fun and hip. I'm talking about the toy bars and seat-back covers that can keep your baby entertained for hours. I particularly enjoyed, as did my little ones, the cute things you hang on the handle bar that smile down at your baby and occasionally chime when he bats at them. I think everyone needs a couple of these car-seat toys to keep baby entertained for the car trips, even just around town.

What is the LATCH system?

▶ There is a rumor going around that the LATCH system of installing a car seat is the safest way to get a car seat in the car. While it's true that LATCH is safe, it should not imply that you can't get a baby car seat safely into a car without it. What LATCH cars and car seats offer is an easier way to get a safe car seat installation. Don't think you necessarily have to ditch your car to have a safe place for your baby to ride.

Once the car seat is installed, I prefer not to take it out unless absolutely necessary. This is where a base really comes in handy; although I want to warn you that if you have a car seat that never comes out of the car, you still need to check that the base or car seat remains secure. I cannot tell you how many times I have found that the seat belt has been undone accidentally or the straps have become loose. Older children are great helpers at reminding you to look and helping you watch out for loose straps.

Some car seat add-ons are dangerous. Usually items that go into the car seat are more dangerous and are not necessarily approved for use. This could be the inserts that the baby lies on, a headrest, pillows, and blankets. Be sure that anything you use that affects how your baby fits into the car seat is approved for safety use before you use it.

Get your car seat inspected. This can be done anywhere there are Certified Child Passenger Safety Technicians. Many times this is at a local fire station, police station, or even at certain baby-centered stores. Ask when you purchase your car seat about these inspections. They can give you all the safety information you need. You should get your car seats inspected whenever you remove car seats, get new car seats, or are worried.

Highchairs

A highchair is a baby staple. It is a way to incorporate your baby into your daily life through mealtime. I am always really excited when one of our children becomes old enough to join us at the table on his or her own terms.

Highchairs come in a variety of options. Today's highchairs offer so many things to choose from it can be difficult. So you may need to think about what you are looking for in a highchair before you go shopping.

Consider the potential functions of a highchair:

- A place for baby to sit while eating
- A place where baby can lie down while being in the kitchen
- A play station for baby
- A portable table for baby

Which functions you are looking for will ultimately guide your decision in highchair purchases. Some highchairs are used as stand-alone chairs. This means that they do not require a table. They stand on their own and have a tray for food. Other highchairs attach directly to the table or attach to a chair that pulls up to the table; these are also called booster chairs. Some highchairs are convertible and pull directly up to the table after you remove the tray table.

If you intend to use the seat for a very young baby, you will want an adjustable seat that reclines. How far back it reclines will depend on the make and model. Some highchairs are designed to accept very small infants. These are used more as table baby carriers that later convert into feeding centers.

Keeping a highchair clean can be a chore. For this reason, you will want to consider the highchair carefully. Does it have small crevices that easily trap food? Can you run the tray or trays through the dishwasher? (I love this feature!) It is also true that the sooner you wipe it up, the easier it is to clean. I usually use a washcloth on my baby's face and then turn it on the highchair. Then simply toss it in the washer. The same holds true if you use baby wipes. Be careful not to use chemically laden wipes accidentally on the baby.

ELSEWHERE ON THE WEB

▶ There are a ton of new baby products coming out every month. It is important to stay on top of baby-product safety trends as well as product recalls. You can register your baby products with the companies that made them. There is usually a postcard included with the purchase packet. You can also stay alert to trends and recalls at http://babyproducts .about.com.

The extras that seem to come more frequently with highchairs these days appear to be more difficult to clean. These are usually fancy toys with the ability to hold onto baby goo better than anything. If the highchair you choose has an electronic toy pad for a tray insert, be prepared to clean it a lot even if you don't use it when food is near.

You also had better be very sure you are capable of listening to the electronic din over and over before you purchase it. If you did not buy it and cannot return it, consider not letting your little one know about the super-secret electronic table top.

Some parents choose vinyl or other plastics for the highchair pad, so that they can wipe it down easily. I personally am fine with highchair pads made of cloth, as long as they are washable. Be sure to read reviews to see that the highchair pad will hold up to washing. I wash the pad every couple of weeks or whenever baby has made a huge mess. I just take it off at night and run it through the washing machine on gentle and hang it out to dry overnight. It is usually ready by the next morning's breakfast meal.

Safety matters in highchairs too. The resounding theme of any baby product is safety for your child. A highchair is no different. Before you buy any highchair, you will want to ensure that you have a safe option.

Your highchair should at least offer straps that go between the baby's legs to prevent her from slipping out and around the waist. I personally prefer the five-point harness, because it prevents your baby from coming out the top. While you might not believe it possible from a tiny baby, as soon as your baby gets some leg strength, a good solid push with her legs on the tray table and she can flip out the back of the highchair with no problem.

Any tray tables that are removable should lock into place. Having a one-handed removable tray is not a problem, but the tray should lock and be locked every time your baby is in the highchair.

Things to consider when getting a highchair include:

○ Does it have a removable tray?
○ Will the tray go into the dishwasher?
○ Does it have a five-point harness?
○ From what material is the seat padding made? Vinyl? Cloth?
○ Is the pad removable for washing? Is it washable?
○ Does the highchair have additions like toys or other trays?
○ Does the chair offer multiple position settings to accommodate the baby's age?
○ Does the table have an adjustable height to allow it to fit easily at your table?

Swings and Baby Bouncers

Baby swings are all the rage in new mothers' circles. These handy baby carriers have been around for a very long time, although the swings of today make yesteryear's swings look positively archaic.

Nowadays you can get swings that fit into small spaces, use batteries, hand-wind, fold up, and more. The choices seem to be unlimited. You can find every kind of swing from a very simple swing that only swings to more intensive models that swing in various directions, have removable sleeping baskets that interchange with chairs, and offer music interludes.

Baby swings are dangerous if used incorrectly. Be sure to put together the swing according to the directions included in the box. You should also try to get a swing that offers a five-point harness for added safety. Each swing will have weight limits that need

ASK YOUR GUIDE

Can my baby sleep in a swing?

▶ While a swing can be a nice, temporary home for your baby for a few minutes, keeping your baby in the swing for hours on end deprives him and you of valuable touching time. It also develops very poor sleeping habits. While an occasional nap in a swing isn't going to be the end of the world, a daily (or nightly) ride in the swing can be the beginning of a very hard habit to break.

▶ *Consumer Reports Best Baby Products* is a great tool for a new parent. I would carry it with me whenever I went shopping and write all of my notes right inside the book. Keep in mind, though, that this is something that you'll need to replace every other year as new safety standards are put forth and new ratings are given. Use this book in conjunction with reports from other parents, and you should be good to go.

to be heeded. So be sure to keep the instructions around. This is particularly true if you intend to use the swing for multiple children. You'd be surprised how you really don't remember how to put it together or where that tiny little plastic part goes—even a year or two down the road.

Some swings set up on the floor and are about four feet high. They are usually not meant to be portable. There are other swings that are very close to the ground, with maybe only a couple of inches of clearance. They stand about two feet off the ground. These are meant to be a bit more portable. However, they should not be used on higher surfaces because of the risk of falls for your child.

Which type of swing do you want? Do you need a swing that swings forward and backward or side to side or vibrates? While some models do all of these, your basic models do not. I personally have found that not all babies like every type of swing. Therefore, I usually recommend to parents that they leave a baby swing off their baby shower gift wish list and wait until they've had the baby. Let the baby try out a swing at a friend's house to see what her preference is before plunking down the money on a swing.

Most swings now have open areas over the baby's head. I actually have children old enough to remember when swings didn't have that open area—you tended to bump their little heads trying to get them out of the swing. So I do recommend that you look for this feature.

Another handy feature to have is silent winding. Old swings operated with a hand crank that was so loud it invariably woke the baby up whenever it was wound. Most swings today are actually battery operated, which means winding is not needed. If you choose a battery-operated swing, I have a couple of words of advice for you: rechargeable batteries.

Baby bouncers are swing alternatives. These are usually floor toys that are not very portable as far as moving from location to location, though they travel well within a house. I used one of these in the bathroom so that baby was safe and occupied while I took a bath.

These come with a variety of options and in a range of prices. You can have the basic models that bounce when the baby moves and have a simple toy bar over the cloth seat. The more expensive and fancy types offer battery-powered bouncing and vibrating. They may also include music toy bars or lights and sounds.

Most of the children I know, including my own, have truly enjoyed the simpler version. Not only did it require fewer batteries, but I thought it was a nice, basic science lesson in cause and effect. It is also easier to put together and less annoying to listen to.

Take a Load Off: Slings and Carriers

Carrying your baby around is something that is lovely to do. You will find that it makes life much easier just to attach your baby and go. I always wind up getting more done—including exercise, housework, and just plain fun things—when I have my baby in a carrier.

Using a cloth-type carrier helps the baby feel more secure and comforted as well. She can feel the warmth of your body. She is able to hear the rhythm of your heartbeat and movement as you walk. This helps keep the baby more calm and relaxed.

Slings are one type of carrier. These are usually a piece of fabric that is either tied or held together in certain positions on an adult's body to firmly and safely attach the baby. These can be used with babies from newborn all the way to toddlers. They can also be used by almost anyone.

Are there any slings or carriers that work with twins?

▶ There are two options here. One is to have two people each carry one baby, though this is not always possible. I used to actually take two Maya Wraps and sling one over my left shoulder and one over my right to carry both of my twins at the same time. This worked great from about three months through their second birthday. When they were younger, I would lay them side by side in a single Maya Wrap. It worked like a charm! They also make slings that work specifically for two babies.

Your baby can face in or out in a sling. You can carry your baby on your front, your side, or your back. This type of sling provides you with the most positioning choices available. It also takes you the longest in the way of how old your baby is and how long you can use the sling. These carriers also enable you to breastfeed discreetly.

Many of the slings have rings to hold them together. If the sling you choose has rings, you will use the fabric and the ring combination to adjust the carrier to fit you and the baby. This can be altered at will depending on the growth of your baby or the position you're using.

Some slings are simply one long piece of cloth that you tie around you in various configurations. These work really well for people who have differently shaped bodies—for example, a really long torso or wide shoulders. Slings also come with really great instructions on using them in a variety of positions. These are also the easiest types of slings to make by hand or at your home.

▲ Carrying baby in a sling

Some slings offer padding around the edges of the fabric. Whether or not you choose to have padding is a personal decision. There are also some slings that offer padding for the parental shoulder. The padding works well, but I've also found that it isn't needed if you have a properly adjusted sling.

Pouches are another easy way to carry baby. These pouches can be worn by anyone and can go on the front or back. They are able to hold a baby in multiple positions using the same carrier.

Pouches are different from slings in that they are usually one piece of fabric that is not adjustable in the same way your typical sling may be adjustable. However, you can use them with the baby sitting up, lying down, and riding forward, or inward facing. This makes them fairly flexible carriers.

Pouches also make it easy to breastfeed while carrying your baby. You can use the pouch to nurse discreetly without having anyone know, though it does take a bit to figure out how to do it all. Many moms really like this aspect of the pouch.

The pouch is great for all ages of babies because of the multiple positions available. The age limitations are more weight limitations. Each pouch will have a weight limit based on the fabric used. Many pouches have a weight limit between 35 to 45 pounds, meaning that they will accommodate even a large toddler comfortably.

Front carriers are also popular. I have to admit these are not my favorite types of baby carrier. I think it has something to do with feeling nine months pregnant whenever I put one on. Still, there are many different styles available and many moms and dads rave about these carriers.

Front packs can carry a baby either forward facing or inner facing. Some front carriers only carry a baby one way or the other.

WHAT'S HOT

▶ Dads really enjoy baby carriers these days. I know when we had our first baby you didn't see many men out there with slings, backpacks, or carriers on. But now it seems that they have many more options as far as types of baby carriers, colors, and fabrics. This opens it up to allow more and more people to feel comfortable carrying a baby hands free. You might even consider getting two carriers—one for you and one for him!

When investigating which front carrier to choose, be sure you know whether or not you have these options.

Front carriers are great for slightly older babies. Newborn babies have a hard time holding their heads up. Some of the products come with props or special things to try to help baby hold his head up. Some babies find these annoying and wind up screaming rather than enjoying the experience.

Older babies really enjoy being able to be close to you. They also enjoy the ability to look around. This can provide them with a great source of entertainment.

The front carrier places the baby in front, putting the weight up front. The restraining device usually attaches in the back. So you will snap the carrier on and then snap your baby into the carrier. Older models made it difficult to remove a sleeping baby without waking them. I'd highly recommend making sure whichever model you get has an easy access for removing a sleeping baby. Also make sure that the carrier fits your body frame for your comfort.

Front carriers usually cannot be used as backpacks. These are two separate items, and it can be dangerous if you try to turn a front carrier around to try to use it as a backpack. Follow all written instructions to ensure a safe and comfortable experience for your baby.

Backpacks are fun too. I'll admit that I often see more dads with backpacks than I see moms, but those numbers are evening out. Backpacks are great forward-facing, rear-only carriers.

Many models of backpacks can be used as a stand for the baby. This enables you to remove the back and still have the child being held upright. I also find it very handy for getting the things on.

These packs are great for everyday use as well as for sports like walking and hiking. You can usually use a backpack once your baby

ELSEWHERE ON THE WEB

▶ Wearing your baby is very comforting for both of you. The choices available for how to wear your baby are many. Different products are each worn slightly differently, making it a likelihood that there is the perfect sling or carrier for you and your baby. But that means that you probably need some instructions on how to wear it and what amazing tricks each carrier or sling can do. That's why I love the videos and clips at this site: www.mamatoto.org.

is between six months and a year old, depending on his ability to hold his head up and be upright.

Since the baby is staring at the back of your head, let me warn you about long hair. It will either be pulled by the carrier or the baby. Be sure to pull your long hair up before using a backpack.

Another type of carrier is one that looks like a car seat and has a handle. Don't be fooled, though; these cannot be used as a car seat. While many car seats do convert to baby carriers, some of them are still very bulky and awkward to carry around. A carrier that is just a carrier is a handy tool on its own. I think they work perfectly as an extra place for baby at a relative's house.

Your Baby's Sleeping Needs

You might think that you know everything there is to know about babies and sleep. You simply put the baby in a crib and she sleeps—hopefully all night long. There are actually many places that you can sleep safely with your baby, though even the American Academy of Pediatrics agrees that your baby should be near you while sleeping.

Your baby should never sleep:

- In a waterbed
- On a couch
- With someone who has been drinking, smoking, or taking medications

Bassinettes are nice for the early days. These beds are small and mostly portable. You need to be careful not to use them after about three months of age or when the baby starts sitting up—whichever comes first. This prevents your little one from rolling out.

Bassinettes are fairly easy to move around the house at will, though you shouldn't try it when the baby is in the bassinette. This is a nice place for overnight sleep or daily naps. This works well if you have a very small space and still desire to have baby near your bed.

Co-sleepers are perfect for new parents. A co-sleeper is an attachment to your bed. It is like adding a three-sided crib to wherever you currently sleep. This allows you the best access to your baby short of sleeping with your baby, with a small distance. It allows you to hear your baby immediately and comfort yourself with the sounds of your baby. It always provided me with peace of mind to hear my babies sleeping. These come in wooden and plastic models.

▲ A co-sleeper

Need a portable and convertible bed? There are a bunch of smaller criblike items cropping up. These beds are a combination portable crib, changing table, bassinette, and play yard. Not every portable crib comes this way, but you can get many of these options. Some families use this as a second bed for their baby—think naps on the first floor versus sleeping upstairs during the day.

These can be fairly inexpensive particularly for all the potential savings from not purchasing multiple items. The actual crib part is good until your child figures out how to crawl out as a toddler, but the other areas usually have weight limits and the removable bassinettes are usually good for only a couple of months. These also fold down fairly small, making them ideal for travel.

Cribs are the most common places for babies to sleep. A crib is also potentially very dangerous, with many babies dying every year because of safety issues directly associated with the crib or things placed in the crib.

When buying a crib, you want to make sure that the crib meets the minimum safety standards. The slats should be no more than 2 ⅜ inches apart to prevent your baby from becoming trapped between the slats. It should be put together with all of the parts it came with. If you have extra pieces lying around, you've done something wrong.

While it is possible for your baby to be safe in an older or used crib, you want to be sure you know what the crib is painted with (no lead-based paint, please) and that it meets the current crib-safety standards.

There are many crib choices available. Some cribs are built to be very small and can be used in small spaces; usually they are the same width but just about a foot and a half shorter. Other cribs are full size and actually convert to be a bed frame and headboard for an older child. Some cribs convert to toddler beds or day beds. At the other end of the spectrum are round- or oval-shaped cribs, which are not commonly found and usually need to be specially ordered.

Other Baby Products and Tools

There are a ton of products that are made to make your life with baby easier or more stylish. Some of these items become bestsellers and things you couldn't live without. Other items become cult favorites or even things of legend. Here are some of the other items you'll hear frequently discussed when it comes to babies.

Baby gyms and floor mats are fun. These are simple toys that are used to encourage your baby to play. The matting is usually slightly padded and basically acts as a floor cover. Typically, you'll find either a mat designed for babies to lie on their stomachs for tummy time or ones that encourage them to look up and play with toys strung overhead.

These come in many varieties—some with lots of bells and whistles and others that are plain versions. Decide what you like and go from there. These are easy to cart about and can be handed down from your firstborn child. Do not be tempted to make your own, as they may be dangerous.

Baby-propping pillows are popular shower gifts. These cute, fabric-covered pillows help your baby hold her head up or encourage her to have tummy time. There are a couple of different brands, but the real winner is the Original Boppy. I love my Boppy and have had one for each child, mainly because it was too difficult to wrest the Boppy away from the older child. While I love the Boppy to play with the baby or help him sit comfortably, I have one piece of advice: don't use it as a nursing pillow.

Moses baskets are nice for little ones. The last few kids I've had have really fallen in love with the Moses basket. These woven baskets often come with a complete set of padded bed, sheet set, small blanket, and matching bumpers. They make a really handy and portable place for your baby to sleep anywhere.

I used the Moses basket with my last baby as a bed for the first floor. This enabled me, in those early postpartum days, to simply

▶ A baby-shower gift registry is a great thing to build. This lets people know your ideas on what you need for your new baby. Heck, even if you're not planning on having a baby shower, I like using these as a way to track what I need to get for a new little one. Most registries allow you to say what color or style you're thinking of when decorating. I also like that they simply tell people what you need so that gifts aren't duplicated. It's also being used as a handy way to help you make gift returns should you need to do so.

tuck her in downstairs while I napped on the couch. This made catching a few minutes of sleep here and there work better for both of us.

Breast pumps are handy to have around. Which breast pump you need depends on how often you pump and what your breastfeeding goals are for your baby. I think everyone ought to at least have a breast pump for emergency purposes. I like the Avent Isis for a hand-held pump. It's quick and easy and won't damage your nipples like some of the other cheap pumps.

If you will be pumping long term or often during the day, consider hiring the big guns. I preferred to rent the hospital-grade Medela Symphony, though many women do well with the purchased Pump in Style Advanced or Pump in Style. There are other brands and many women I work with love them equally as well. Brand loyalty here is not as important as the grade of the pump. In general, the higher the grade the better the pump. You need the big bad pumps when you're trying to establish your milk supply or trying to overcome difficulties. After that, nearly any pump designed for everyday, long-term use will work well.

Changing tables are not as popular. These days, people do not seem to be spending money on plain changing tables that are set up solely for the purpose of changing. You will see more changing table/dresser combos. This is where a removable pad is used on top of a dresser and later is just removed. You may also find people using the portable crib as a changing station. This leaves you with a bit more room to work with, particularly if you're tight on space.

Rocking chairs never go out of style. Being able to sit and rock your baby is an amazing feeling. This is why the rocking chair

ASK YOUR GUIDE

Will insurance cover my breast pump?

▶ Some insurance companies will cover the cost of renting your breast pump. This is because they realize that your baby will require less medical coverage if she has the benefits of breast milk. Your employer may also have a deal because of the time they save by having you in the office and not at your pediatrician. Ask your insurance company if they require a prescription for a breast pump. If you are having difficulty with the medical insurance paying for the pump, check with your flexible spending account company.

has been a nursery staple for so long. It provides you with a comfortable place to sit and hold or feed your baby.

Not all rocking chairs rock anymore. There is a new fashion among rocking chairs—gliders. Gliders go back and forth on a track, rather than rocking on rockers. The movement is easier to maintain and feels smoother to most people. The gliders often come with matching stools.

Get Linked

Getting all that "stuff" associated with baby can be fun and costly. You really don't need as many things as ad companies would have you believe. Here are some basic products and the high points for how to pick the right one for your family.

BEFORE YOU BUY A CAR SEAT

This is one of the most important purchases that you will make. Not only does your baby need to be comfortable, but he also needs to be safe. Check out the many varieties and find what fits your lifestyle and your budget.

http://about.com/pregnancy/bybcarseat

BEFORE YOU BUY A STROLLER

Interested in getting out and about? Well, look no further, because here you'll find information on all types of strollers, from the simple umbrella stroller to the stroller that holds more than one baby and even some jogging strollers. So form, function, or fitness—we've got your style.

http://about.com/pregnancy/bybstroller

BEFORE YOU BUY A CRIB

If you decide that a crib is the right choice for your family, you need to look at your options carefully. One of the biggest issues in choosing a crib is safety and function. Here are the basics of crib design and how to pick the best crib for your baby.

http://about.com/pregnancy/bybcrib

BABY-PRODUCT REVIEWS

If you are interested in my reviews (the good, the bad and the ugly) of other baby products, both specifically and as individual products, check out the link below for the latest reviews and comments from other parents.

http://about.com/pregnancy/babyproducts

Chapter 12

Baby Play and Entertainment

How Babies Play

Play is the important work babies do, though it is often something we take for granted. As adults, we often don't play enough. How and why we play with babies is not as important as simply playing.

Your baby learns in three major ways: by watching, by listening, and by doing. Each of these ways are ways for your baby to experience the world. You can encourage learning by using these three types of input for your baby all by playing lots of different ways.

Play is important for all sorts of reasons. Your baby will learn many of the skills he needs for the rest of his life. They help your baby develop physically. Your child will learn to use muscles and gain strength as he moves around. Something as simple as dancing with your baby will help him feel close to you, allow him the interaction he craves, and give him exposure to music.

Mentally and emotionally, your baby learns to interact with others through play. He learns to be social with people. He becomes accustomed to the flow of conversation. He learns cooperation. He figures out problems that present themselves. In addition to all of this, babies really want to be with their parents, making them the best playmates for kids.

Being with you should happen often, but taking the extra time to play is also important. You should play alone with your baby sometimes and sometimes with other kids, like a group setting at day care, with siblings, or in a play group. You should also allow your child to play alone or alone with other children at times, without your direct supervision.

If I put a ball into the middle of the floor, how does the baby get around it? The baby can push it with his arms or legs. The baby can roll it back to you. Or your baby may choose to go around it. This type of play helps stimulate and develop his brain. And all you were doing was putting a ball down!

There are also things to remember about playing, rules if you will:

- Play often
- Be silly
- Ask them questions, where appropriate
- Know when it is time to stop to avoid overstimulation
- Be ready to do similar games over and over
- Play with toys and without

There are several types of play that babies do. Each type of play offers its own rewards, and children should be encouraged to do many of them.

WHAT'S HOT

▶ Tummy time is very important, especially since the advent of the "babies should sleep on their backs" campaign. Tummy time is when you allow your baby time on her stomach. This will allow her to strengthen her upper body and neck. Your baby should have awake time on her stomach every day.

Socialization is important to all kids. This starts at a very young age. There is a natural give and take in the flow of communication. Mommy says something to you and then waits for you to respond. Your baby will learn to share communication skills as well as the rules of social interaction, such as manners, kindness, and playing nice.

Many types of play involve physical activity. Fine-motor skills are exercised with certain types of play. Fingering small toys or pieces of food help your baby with her fine-motor skills. You will be able to watch the baby pass toys and other objects from hand to hand. Offer a bright, shiny toy to your baby, but offer it on different sides of the body and in the middle, making her figure out how to use her body.

Moving around develops large or gross motor skills and this helps build strength and balance. This means that you can do whatever gets your baby moving, even before she moves on her own.

You can also teach your child rules. Simple games for toddlers like "Red Light, Green Light" teach your child how to play the game. There is a set of rules. If you don't follow them, you can't play well because the whole game structure falls apart.

Pretend play is fun for all. It's a chance to act out roles that you may not get to do. With toddlers, it is certainly fun to switch sides. Let your toddler be the mommy for a while. You can show your baby what her behavior is like on certain occasions or ideal behavior you're hoping for. This also allows her to try out new behaviors, actions, and words in a safe environment.

Being Silly

Most of us don't really think about being silly as a requirement of parenting. But I am here to tell you that the ability to laugh at yourself, your kids, and life is a good one when you have little ones. It will help keep you cool and keep them entertained if nothing else—and it always makes me feel better!

TOOLS YOU NEED

▶ There are multiple books available on games to play with your baby and toddler. I would suggest finding a couple in the library and bring them home to try out. Some are just great reminders of songs and games we thought we'd forgotten, while others are new takes on old games or things we had never learned. Most books have a theme like summer games or baby games. The theme doesn't matter, just the variety. When you find one you like, you can buy it.

▶ Using sign language with your baby is a great way to help you communicate with your baby before he can talk. We have done it with a couple of our kids, and we all love it. You simply start with a couple of signs like please, thank you, eat, or more; and go from there. After watching you for a while, your baby will eventually begin to make the signs back to you. There is nothing as thrilling as being able to communicate with your baby and often before he has learned to talk! Try *Sign with Your Baby* by Joseph Garcia.

Silly is as silly does. Silly may be a state of mind, but it's also a great way to play with your baby and toddler. Kids can really connect when you're acting a bit "immature." They can laugh and learn at the same time.

One of the things we do with our kids is to take a very familiar book and tell it incorrectly. This will send your toddler into giggles. For very young children, simply try reading with a silly voice or voices.

Sing songs if you need to be silly. Nothing like a good old round of kids' songs to bring out the silly, even in the stuffiest of adults. I also find that when I feel my blood beginning to boil (at anyone or anything), singing a silly song helps me put it into perspective. Okay I can forgive that you dried a box of crayons in the dryer accidentally, as long as I can sing "Old MacDonald Had a Farm" for a few verses. Don't laugh; it really works. Give it a try!

The car is a great place to carry a set of CDs of kids' music. I like to have a couple on hand like Raffi, Laurie Berkner, They Might Be Giants (Two of my favorites are *No!* and *Here Come the ABCs*). We also have a hilarious CD we made ourselves of the kids singing songs. That always makes a long drive or a wait in traffic much more tolerable for everyone. Even though my husband dislikes the repetition, the kids love it!

Ten Must-Have Baby Toys

Baby toys are so much fun. They are one of the ways that your baby learns about the world. Don't misunderstand me, though; you don't have to have the latest, most expensive toys on the market. Start thinking outside the toy box and give your baby some unconventional toys. Read on for ten of my suggestions.

Your hands are a great toy. Not only are they free, but they provide your baby with the tactile stimulation and human contact she craves. You can use your hands to make puppets or shadow creatures on the wall. Your hands can hide your face in a fierce game of peek-a-boo. You can also use your hands to add movement and characters to sing-a-longs—think "Itsy Bitsy Spider."

Your baby will learn to use her hands in response. She will watch your fingers and enjoy the interaction. Your fingers are always around, which makes them very handy.

The human voice is also a great toy for a baby. Babies and kids love to hear people talk and sing. They also adore funny voices. Be silly and create voices for the characters in a story you read to your baby. You'll be surprised how much she likes it.

You will also notice that your baby will begin to play with her own voice as she begins to recognize it. I love listening to this happen. One day you might think she is asleep and then you hear her "talking" to herself. This is the first step in talking.

A mirror is a great basic baby toy. Babies love faces, even their own. A soft-sided mirror is the perfect toy for a small baby. They come in many models, such as one to hang over the side of a crib or a car seat version. I liked the Lamaze version that I can place on the floor at a perfect angle for a baby on her belly.

The mirror that you choose should not be made of glass. Only use a mirror that is designed for use by babies. This will prevent the baby from becoming hurt by broken glass or being hit by a heavy mirror.

Everyone loves to build with blocks. Beginning just before your baby's first birthday, some nice wooden blocks can become a favorite toy. You will find them in many shapes, sizes, and colors.

I would recommend that you start with a small, basic set. I prefer the natural-colored wood.

You can show your child how to build towers. You can use your imagination to build cars, houses, animals, etc. When he gets older, he will also start building; but don't panic when he builds something and seems to get a huge kick out of tearing it back down. That is part of the natural progression of the game and not a sign of destructive tendencies.

Nesting toys have been a favorite for a long time. These toys can also be simple or complex. I love the look of the nesting dolls, but they are not very appropriate for little ones; save these for older kids. For babies and toddlers, I would focus on the simple toys like the Discovery Toys nesting cups. These brightly colored cups count one through twelve. They come in a set of four colors, allowing you to sort by color as well. You can also teach the basics of addition—a water-filled "1" cup plus a water-filled "2" cup equals the "3" cup. But mostly they stack up tall, fall nicely, and nest.

There are also nesting squares and other variations. Some are made of wood, others plastic, and now you can even find some that are cloth. The one concern I have with cloth is that they can be so soft that they don't stack well, which can frustrate your child.

Toys that require imagination are fun. They are also incredibly popular. You might not even realize what constitutes imagination play. It ranges from pretend food or kitchen sets to costumes for dress-up.

When your child uses her imagination, she is stretching and growing her mind. At first, she simply wants to imitate others in her life. Often this revolves around daily activities, like cooking,

▶ Toys these days actually have suggested age ranges on the sides. Sometimes these should be considered absolute, like warnings of small parts that are choking hazards for little kids. Others, like cards and other games, might not distinguish between your seven- and eight-year-old; that would be a parenting decision. If you aren't sure, err on the side of caution and use the upper age limit.

cleaning, driving a car, and getting dressed. There is nothing as enjoyable as being served pretend food and gobbling it up much to the delight of your child.

A tea party is a great game for all toddlers—boys and girls. Even my older sons get sucked into being served the little girls' favorite snack: hot chocolate or lemonade with brownies. I teach them table manners and how not to break the tea set, and they get to practice life skills. The same goes for pretending to eat a banana or wearing clothes that belong to daddy.

Don't think these toys have to cost a lot of money. Many of these types of toys can come from your own kitchen or home. Do you have an old, nonbreakable bowl? Perhaps a pair of shoes and some shirts that aren't good for work anymore? I keep a huge basket full of dress-up clothes nearby for spontaneous play.

Have fun with musical instruments. I have been seeing a lot of these given as gifts lately, and it really made me think about them. While I cringe at the thought of giving my child a noisy drum, I totally see the value of music and rhythm in their lives.

So I picked up a packet of baby- and toddler-sized musical instruments, and there wasn't a drum in sight. There were maracas, a triangle, a tambourine, and various other shakers and noise-makers. They are easy to incorporate with music that you are playing. This helps your baby learn to enjoy being a part of the music.

One of my daughters suggested that we pull out the musical instruments when I was reading one night. She assigned each child a sound and said when they would make it based on the story. I was a bit concerned about a three-year-old director, but even our not-yet-walking child got in on the fun with some help. It was quite fun and something I wouldn't have thought of before this.

Are hand-me-down toys a good idea?

▶ Hand-me-down toys can be a great way to save money and resources. Handing toys down within your family or extended family is best simply because you would know more of the toy's history, but some toys are fine from yard sales and secondhand shops. I look for very sturdy toys that will stand a good scrubbing to remove unseen dirt and germs. I also avoid personal-use toys like teethers. But things like books and blocks are perfect.

Trucks and dolls are good toys for both sexes. Don't get wrapped up in gender-specific toys. Girls benefit from zipping around the kitchen floor with a miniature car, and boys certainly enjoy parenting a doll, male or female.

Assigning roles to your child through toys is not the best way to go. If your daughter is in love with trucks, be sure to let her enjoy them. Don't force her to give them up in favor of a toy that doesn't thrill her. Your son may like to play with the doll house. It is absolutely appropriate. The more you discourage the use of these toys, the less likely your child will be to play in general.

Your baby can never have enough books. These are the foundation of learning so many things, and the children's book market has exploded. They still have all of our old favorites, but now they also have so many more books as well.

Have a variety of books available for your child. You can have books made from different materials like wood, cloth, plastic, and paper. (Paper books aren't great for tiny babies because they tend to put them in their mouths.) You can also have books that offer a variety of textures. Some of these books were meant to teach about texture, but others are just different textures.

You can have books that are simple and offer no stories. These may be a word on a page. They may revolve around a theme, like colors, numbers, or animals. Others are simple stories that engage even young readers. Find what kind of stories your baby likes and read them over and over. While we tend to dislike reading the same books over and over, kids love it.

Remember that books are not just for bedtime. To develop a love of reading in your children, they must be read to often. Let them see how you read throughout the day and encourage them to do the same. I like to show my kids signs all over town while driving, in the grocery store, and even menus. It really puts reading in perspective.

If you think you have too many books, remember that you can actually rotate books. Take a few beloved favorites and keep them out at all times. Pull out any special books, like those for holidays, a few weeks before each of the holidays in question. Then take the books you have left and split them into two piles.

Take one pile and put it away. The remaining pile will be used for a month. This group of books will be your active reading selection for that period of time. When a month is up, switch the books with the pile you put up before. This helps keep the books fresh and yet helps you hit all of the great books you own. Otherwise books have a tendency to get buried in your bookshelf.

Toys that go are a must. I'm talking about wagons, push toys, and pull toys, particularly things your child can ride on or in. However, they should not be motorized.

As your child is learning to walk, being able to practice walking while pushing a small, mobile toy is a great answer. You can also still enjoy taking a walk and pulling her in a wagon. You might be thinking that a stroller works just as well. The problem with a stroller is that she isn't learning to sit alone or getting the chance to be a big kid as she does riding in the wagon.

The TV Dilemma

The debate over television rages on when it comes to kids. You have got various factions talking about why television is or is not good for your baby. You have educational programming and popular children's characters adorning everything from clothing to carrots. But what is the real deal when it comes to the benefits and risks of television?

Babies do not need television. Pediatricians from the American Academy of Pediatrics (AAP) say that a child under the age of two does not need television at all. They also believe that these young children don't need any **screen time**, such as computers and the like.

Once your baby is over two, the AAP recommends that she get no more than two hours of screen time a day. Considering that most American children spend four hours in front of the television a day, you can see why this number needs to come down. Their claims are that the kids see too much violence, sex, and other adult issues. They also rail against commercials aimed at children.

That's all well and good, and I think most parents agree that much of what is on regular television is not appropriate for little ones. But what about educational programming? From classics like *Sesame Street* to new, trendy shows, there really are some great programs out there that help kids learn. There are lots of companies putting out excellent educational videos and DVDs too. So don't throw the baby out with the bathwater. Do your research and choose the programs and videos you deem valuable.

Most parents will use the television anyway. Sometimes it's difficult because you have older children watching a show. Your younger child watches it without you even thinking about it. I didn't think about this until I realized that our youngest played in the room where the television was on. How many times have you nursed the baby in front of the television?

I think the key here is to be realistic. There is a huge difference between having the television on in the same room with a small infant and plopping him down and turning on the television, even educational programming, for hours on end.

The harder part for me is that screens are popping up all over. Watch out for televisions and DVD players located in the watch seat of the car. I personally love mine, but the rules of use are that we only watch television when we are going more than two hours from home. The only time I broke this rule was when I had newborn twins and couldn't get the toddlers to quiet down in the evenings when my husband was in class. We'd sit in our driveway and watch a thirty-minute show while the babies actually napped.

Some guidelines for television and screen viewing with older toddlers include:

- Watch television with your children
- Preview what they watch before they watch it
- Point out commercials or unrealistic content
- Plan your viewing before you sit down—don't channel surf

When you follow these general guidelines your children will pick up your good habits and learn to emulate them as they grow older. This early preparation will definitely pay off down the line.

Playgroups and Classes

Playgroups and new mothers' groups are great ways to meet others who share a similar interest—their kids! You can find these groups in all sorts of places and with a variety of goals in each.

Finding what you're looking for shouldn't be difficult if you define it. Do you have a new set of twins at home? Consider the local twins club. Do you have a new baby and a toddler? A standard play group with siblings might be great for you. As a new mother, are you looking for a bit more education or sharing of ideas? This can often be found at your local birth network.

TOOLS YOU NEED

▶ There are many educational videos available for purchase these days. They are everywhere. Chances are that you will have some given to you or buy them yourself. Before you think about letting your child watch it, be sure to watch it all the way through. If you decide not to use one, it will probably be fine to save for later use. Many even have audio only and play great music. Pop it in your CD player and see if that works!

Some groups are purely social in nature. They meet for fun and to allow the babies to play together. Usually these groups have a specific age range for the kids. They may meet at each other's homes. When joining, ask if you will be required to share the meeting location responsibility. Get the scoop first!

A new mothers' group is often designed for mothers with babies under one year. They usually have an educational component to them, although this topic is usually relevant to the life of a new mother. You might find topics like sleep issues in new babies or baby proofing. All of the meetings will include a kid-friendly atmosphere, making it easier for you to attend the meetings with your baby.

Occasionally these groups will have a specific educational topic. For example, La Leche League International has four topics they teach on a rotational basis, but how they teach is completely different each time. Their courses revolve around infant feeding from breast milk to solids and weaning; babies and personal sharing are welcome.

Finding the right group might take time. When I went to my first twins club meeting, I was still pregnant. I sat there and listened to some of the mothers talking about raising newborn twins and I panicked. Here I was, already a parent of four children and they made me nervous. What were the people who had never had kids thinking? I almost didn't go back to the group, but that would have been a huge mistake. The others who had been there, or who were currently living through it, wound up being a great source of support for me when my twins were born.

Finding someone out there who is living through something similar is a great way to start; just don't expect that everything will be the same identical situation. That would make for a boring group. You need some identifying factors and form there; the variety helps you move along.

When trying to decide if a group is right for you, ask yourself some questions:

- Does the group meet in a convenient location?
- Are the times of the meetings easy for me to get to?
- Are there policies I need to know about? Hosting? Other kids?
- Do I share a core belief with the group or is this a general group?
- Do I know anyone in the group?
- What is the group format?
- Are there additional opportunities to be together, to learn, or to socialize?

If you can't find a group that meets enough of your needs, try to create one yourself. All you need is another mother and baby and a location. These things have a way of growing on their own. I started one without even trying. It all started one morning when I invited another mother over for coffee. Our babies lay on the floor playing nicely and we had a blast just talking, even though we had very little in common.

Before long, it was a routine date for us. Once a week we met up and let the babies play while we chatted. From there, we found another mom who we invited to join us. Soon, we had seven routine members, and one mom had left to start a group in her own neighborhood because we lived too far away from her. We considered it a success! You will hear stories like this all the time.

ASK YOUR GUIDE

I found a group, but it doesn't feel right. What should I do?

▶ The first thing I would do is to try to figure out why you don't feel right there. Is it that you're simply adapting to a new environment? It's possible the other mothers or fathers have simply been together longer and their friendships seem a bit harder to break into as a newcomer. As long as there isn't anything really wrong, such as religious, ethnic, or other discrimination, you might try sticking it out to see if time heals all. If there are other groups available, by all means go to one of those groups as well.

Knowing that your baby needs to play and how to pick games is a part of the parenting process. One thing I'd remind you of as a parent is to enjoy playtime. Don't come to think of it as something you have to do; make it something you enjoy. This time with you and your baby should be one of pleasure.

Bring others into the mix as your baby grows. Invite other family members and friends to play to explore different areas of growth and development. You can also find groups to play within. But enjoy the education playtime and choose the appropriate toys.

ELSEWHERE ON THE WEB

▶ Matching Moms is a group that helps you find other moms and play groups in your area. It is a free group with more than 700 play groups listed. There are also sections on how to start your own group so that you can find others like you. Visit www.matchingmoms.org.

Get Linked

Babies, games, and toys go together. These links to my About.com site offer some ways to make smart decisions on toys to buy, games to play, books to read, how much television to watch, and how to incorporate playing into your daily life.

BABY-SHOWER GIFTS

Toys are very common gifts for baby showers. Here are some of the best baby-shower gifts for you or your friends.

 http://about.com/pregnancy/showergifts

TELEVISION FOR BABIES

A great discussion about using television with babies. What do you need to know as a parent? How do you make the best decision you can?

 http://about.com/pregnancy/babiesandtv

LARGE PLAY TOYS FOR BABY

Play centers, exersaucers, and other large toys are where infants spend much of their playtime. Here is a section of reviewed items available for babies.

http://about.com/pregnancy/largetoys

Chapter 13

Out and About with Your Baby

Important Travel Tips

Traveling around with a baby in tow can be a lot of work. But most modern-day parents don't let a little thing like a trip with a baby scare us away from traveling. With some proper planning and a bit of luck, a trip with a baby can be fairly straightforward, whether you're traveling around the block or around the world. Just keep in mind some basic wisdom.

Plan for frequent stops along the way. A baby takes time. That is a true statement if you're sitting at home or traveling. You will need to build time into your itinerary to care for your baby. This can be time that is required for feeding, changing, napping, or playing. Though you can always figure out that less time is needed than you originally planned for, but it's often harder to create time within a schedule.

You might plan, during a car trip, to stop the car about every two hours. This would be to take care of your needs and the baby's needs. However, during the trip, you find that you don't need to stop at every one of those breaks, and thus, you get to your destination a bit early. It provides a buffer in case your trip is longer than expected or if your baby (or you) needs an extra stop.

First aid still applies while traveling with a small baby. Though you won't be expecting your child to injure himself during a trip, you will want to plan ahead for medical issues. I usually travel with a small kit of some useful medications that are often hard to find. These usually include:

- Ibuprofen (fever/pain)
- Acetaminophen (fever/pain)
- Teething gel
- Simethicone (gas drops)

These will cover the basic baby medicine emergencies. I actually took a trip with my four-month-old baby and wound up walking from the hotel to a "nearby" gas station looking for infant fever reducers. It was a long, hot walk, with a very cranky and unhappy baby. After walking four miles and trying several gas stations, we finally found a drugstore that carried the products we needed. I never made that mistake again.

Bring a change of clothes. This change of clothes is usually expected, but I would actually recommend that you bring two or three changes for the baby for every day you will be away from home. Maybe you will need fewer outfits if you have access to a washing machine, but you typically don't want to be doing laundry away from home.

▶ The clothing you pick for your child when traveling is very important. While you want to plan for the weather at your destination, you also need to be cognizant of the weather on the way. Remember airports are often a bit chilly, even if you're flying to warm weather. Cars can also be a bit drafty. Consider packing long sleeves and pants for your little one, or at least a lightweight blanket.

There should also be an outfit or two for you. This is particularly necessary when on the road or flying. I usually travel with a light-weight sweater to cover up baby spills, although a friend recently taught me the trick of flying with a button-down shirt covering my nice clothes. Then, when I arrive, I can remove the shirt for a quick change into clean clothes, which helped me feel less worried about my appearance when being out with the baby.

Baby food that travels well is a must. Once your little one starts eating solid foods, traveling is not quite as easy for a bit. You can pack those jars of baby food, but they often are in glass containers. These containers have a tendency to roll around in the bottom of the diaper bag or suitcase. I also have a really bad history of breaking them open. I don't think I need to tell you what a mess this is for everyone.

Sometimes you can get away with finding a couple of great foods that are fairly baby friendly, like a plain baked potato. You may also want to try to hit food stops where you can get some fresh produce, like bananas. These are easy to mash and can be cut without much fuss for anyone. I also like to pack applesauce of the unsweetened variety, although you can find it at almost any grocery store no matter where you are going. When in doubt, pack a ton of snack foods your baby enjoys, such as baby-friendly cereals, including some packets of cereals that just require you to add liquid.

Cloth diapers are travel friendly. I do not believe in discouraging those who use cloth diapers not to travel with them. I have occasionally taken trips of a very short length with cloth diapers. I traveled with a large-sized waterproof bag that served as a diaper bag for dirty diapers. It was great and didn't smell at all.

TOOLS YOU NEED

▶ I have often found it easier to make my own baby food while on the road. My husband bought me a baby food hand grinder with our first baby and it is still working. I just purchased another one, but only because it now comes with a handy travel case. This has helped me turn many meals that wouldn't be appropriate for my baby into baby-friendly servings. I just rinse it off in the hotel room when I'm done.

There are a few problems with traveling with cloth diapers, but they have solutions. The first is what to do with the dirty diapers: I kept them in a waterproof bag. Another is what happens if you run out of cloth diapers. The answer is simple: you buy disposables or let your baby go diaper free. The last issue is getting the diapers home. If you're driving in a car, just throw them in the trunk. If you're flying, they can take up a lot of room. One mom had her diapers shipped home. Whatever works for your family is perfect!

Baby-sitting is often available on the road. Whether or not you use it is another thing. I have noticed in my travels that many large hotel chains offer a sitter service. This usually means they call a local service that then finds a sitter for you in your room. These sitters are able to travel to you. Some parents have no problem with this, while others are very leery for many reasons.

Another option is using family to watch the baby while you're out of town. So you're going to grandma's house and she lives far away. You and your husband want to have a nice romantic dinner alone. So you decide to leave the baby with her. The only issue here is one of familiarity.

I have not personally tried sitter services away from home, but I can tell you what we did do once. We used the sitter service at Disney World. You drop off your child over three at the playhouse on the hotel site and they have caretakers dressed as Disney characters, as well as food, games, and crafts. We did this while we enjoyed dinner not too far away. Something about it being Disney and having characters made it easier for us to take. The kids loved it!

Plan ahead for sleep troubles. Traveling always disturbs my sleep. Add to the mix a tiny baby or a toddler in an unfamiliar situation and you've got some trouble.

You can call ahead to arrange for a crib at most major hotels, although I personally have never liked the old broken-down cribs I've found.

You can also pack your own travel bed of the folding variety. These are very handy to have for travel and are fairly easy to fly with or drive with and can be used for many reasons. Co-sleeping can be a bit more difficult on the road. See if you can get a king-size bed for you and baby and remove all of the fluffy bedding.

The unexpected will occur while you are traveling. Planning is great, but you can never plan for every eventuality. Remember to carry some cash, your credit cards, and a cell phone in case of emergency.

When traveling with a baby, allow for extra time everywhere you go. Do as much research ahead of time as possible to help familiarize yourself with the area. If you find yourself in a rush and unable to prepare as much as you would've liked, keep in mind that most hotels offer free maps of the surrounding area, as well as recommendations for eating out, local attractions, and transportations options. Remember the best advice is not to sweat the small stuff. Babies who eat at a slightly later time or who stay up too late one night are generally fine, if a little bit sleepy the next day.

You may find that something happens and you wind up traveling without your baby. This may be a business trip that you may or may not have known about; or perhaps it is a family emergency and you have chosen to leave the baby at home for the time being. These trips are often short and intense, and tend to not be very baby friendly. The other type of trip you may take without your baby, when she's a little older, is the often-discussed weekend away. For either type of trip, planning is the key.

Child care while you're away may be an issue if your husband is not available either because he is with you or otherwise engaged at work. Finding someone you trust to stay with your baby can be difficult, particularly when the baby is young. Determine the hours you need care. Is it twenty-four hours a day or just during working hours? Do you have family you can use?

Provide your child's caretaker with a handy list of his likes and dislikes. Try to organize the list to include what a typical day might look like for your child. This will help your baby feel more secure, particularly if he isn't in his own home. You should also give detailed feeding instructions—do not assume that the person caring for your baby knows anything about taking care of him.

If you are traveling away from your baby while you are breast-feeding, you will want to find a way to express your breast milk. Most women choose to use some sort of a breast pump. Though there are those who also hand-express and do just fine. Decide ahead of time how you will empty your breasts to maintain your milk supply. There is nothing as bad as sitting in a business meeting with engorged breasts.

You also will have to make a decision about what to do with the milk you express. Will you do what's called pumping and dumping—throwing away your breast milk? That's a personal decision. Most of the time I make the decision based on the age of the baby, the length of my trip, and what my stash at home looks like. A one-year-old child who is eating solid foods doesn't need the ounces I'll make on a two-day trip. So then I pump for my comfort and dump the milk. (It's still hard for me to do!)

Recently I took a four-day trip without the baby, who was still completely breastfed. I had enough of a stash in our freezer for her to eat plenty while I was gone. However, I liked having the freezer stash. So I requested a small refrigerator at the hotel, which even had a tiny freezer. I brought freezer gel packs and insulated lunch bags with me. Then I pumped my breast milk into collection bags and laid them flat in the freezer. When it was time to leave, I placed all the bags and freezer packs into the insulated bags and put them in my checked luggage. They were still frozen when I got home. Other mothers actually have found ways to overnight their milk back home.

Breastfeeding is very handy while traveling. The food is prepackaged, travels with you everywhere, and is always served at the right temperature. It also can't roll down the aisle on a plane because you can't drop it!

Breastfeeding was very handy for me when flying with a baby. During take off and landing, it really helped keep my little one's ears from hurting. It also kept the baby and my mind occupied.

If you choose to bring bottles on board, remember to bring milk, water, or juice to put in them and all the accessories. You will also want to bring a spare bottle in case you lose one. Don't laugh; it can happen. I've done it.

What's in Your Diaper Bag?

A diaper bag is a necessary evil of parenting. It's great for carrying all the things your baby needs, but you'll probably find that it gets very cumbersome very quickly. It's also a personal thing. While many people will try to buy one for you or your husband, it just doesn't work that well. You have to have so many personal things inside and out of your diaper bag that you need to be in charge of it. This is never more important than when traveling.

Your diaper bag will be the command center of your trip as far as your baby concerned. It is a great place to hide, stuff, and store. It should be ergonomically in tune with your body and style. Are you left handed? Do you hate digging in deep pockets? Or do you love the deep pockets that store all the little bits and pieces of baby stuff that accumulate in a pocket?

TOOLS YOU NEED

▶ When you're traveling with a baby, dirty diapers are bound to happen. You certainly don't want to be trapped in a small space with a dirty diaper either on or off your baby. I'd recommend taking along small plastic bags that can be used to wrap up smelly diapers. This also works for wet clothes. You can buy packs of small bags that hang off a diaper bag, or you can also use the ones you get with your groceries.

Put a lot of thought into what goes into your diaper bag. Overpacking is just as bad as underpacking when you're traveling with a baby. Your diaper bag should easily hold all your stuff but should not weigh three hundred pounds. You should be able to lift it fairly easily; remember you might be carrying it for quite a while.

What you pack will depend on where you are going and for how long. For example, if you are flying from one place to another, what you need only needs to last a bit longer than your flight. You will also know what some of the things you could purchase in an emergency would be. But your diaper bag would be it in terms of having a place for your baby's stuff, unlike a car trip.

A diaper bag checklist for a flight might look like this:

○ Diapers and wipes
○ Food needs
○ Utensils including breast pumps and bottles
○ Clothes
○ Lightweight blanket
○ A few toys

A diaper bag packed for an hour or two might look like this:
○ A few diapers
○ Small packet of wipes
○ Small toy

To avoid overpacking your diaper bag, ask yourself what would happen if you didn't have an item. Would it totally ruin your trip or event? Can you buy it when you get there? Does it require any special attention like ironing or batteries? How heavy is it?

Pack the things you are most likely to need on top. Use the outer pockets to hold your flight items like tickets and boarding passes. I usually recommend ditching your purse altogether in favor of a small wallet that tucks easily into your diaper bag. Some moms choose to get a wallet on a string to keep their purse close by, though sometimes this just gets to be a tangled mess on the plane. A wallet with a detachable string might be a nice compromise.

If you are traveling with a stroller as well, you will probably want to find a way to attach the diaper bag to the stroller. This means you don't have to carry the diaper bag. You might find parents who carry the baby and use their stroller as a shopping cart–type of device for their belongings. This is perfectly acceptable, until you want to have your baby laying down in the stroller and have no place to put the bag. I'd recommend that you find a diaper bag with special connectors—plastic is fine—that attach it to your stroller.

Road Trips

Taking a car trip with your baby is often easier in many ways when you need to travel with your baby. One thing I really like is the extra travel space and the ability to leave whenever I want. This keeps the baby and me from being on someone else's time. You can go across town or across the country in a car, although statistically you are safer in the air.

Car-seat laws in other states are important rules to follow. Sometimes I forget that the laws in my state are not the same as laws in every other state. When traveling, you are still required to follow the rules of the state you're in. Some states have laws that will be more lax, but it is always best just to stick to the highest level.

My diaper bag is so heavy that it makes my stroller tip over. Is there any remedy for this?

▸ You will want to find a small weight that is meant for most strollers. It slips over a front rail to balance out the hanging diaper bag and basket items when you remove your baby from the stroller. These are usually inexpensive, though you may have a more difficult time finding one.

Feeding issues are different in a car. If your baby is hungry while you're flying, you simply feed him. In a car, it is not so easy if you're the driver. If you are not the driver, you can successfully nurse if you sit in the backseat—and still keep the baby in a car seat.

I have also used a breast pump in the car. It works better if you have a hands-free bra while you are pumping. Then you can decant the milk in the pump into a bottle for the baby. This works but adds a whole other step to the feeding process. To keep extra breast milk cool, you can use a small cooler. I have used both freezer gel packs as well as just regular ice. You do need to have a replenishable source of ice, but gas-station ice works fine. One mom I know actually travels with a small car refrigerator.

Plan to play with your baby. You will need to plan for ways to entertain your baby both during your journey and at your destination. Easy games that do not require anything but you are best for the trip. For example, peek-a-boo is an awesome game. Your baby gets to watch your face, hear your voice, and interact with you. This can be done anywhere!

I also really like the board books that are on heavy board with a laminated top. They hold up very well while traveling. They also double as teethers when not in use as a book. Cloth books are also nice, though they may require washing.

Age-appropriate toys are always best, but you also need to factor in what your baby loves. As soon as one of our children could grasp anything, she wanted to play with the Duplo Legos. She would happily teeth on them, wave them around, and click these two pieces together for hours. She would even talk to them as she started babbling. In short, it worked for her, despite the toy technically being for an older child.

Air Travel

If you live far away from relatives and close friends, chances are you're going to need to travel on a plane with your baby at some point. I would recommend that you try to keep from flying with a new baby for as long as you can; instead, suggest that friends and family come to you. Not only is traveling with a very small infant not a pleasant experience, but if you just gave birth, it can be hard on your recovery as well.

There are travel restrictions on very young babies. While these rules may vary from airline to airline, there are some general guidelines. Typically they will not allow an infant younger than two days to fly except on medical emergency transports. Between two and seven days, some airlines will let you fly if your baby's doctor will write a note to allow her to fly.

The other thing to factor in is how well developed your baby's immune system is at this point of time. A baby who is three or four months old will be better able to handle the stress of flying on the immune system and the exposure to germs than a younger baby. If your baby was premature or has had any illnesses, it may be best to postpone your travel or use a different mode for travel for this trip.

Taking your car seat on a plane might be a good idea. The good news about taking your car seat on a plane is that it is safer than holding your baby. It also gives you a place to lay your baby down during a flight if your baby were to fall asleep. This is preferable to handing over your baby to a flight attendant or stray passenger should the need arise for you to go to the bathroom or even stand up occasionally.

TOOLS YOU NEED

▶ I thought driving nine hours with a baby and a fourteen-year-old girl would be not only fine but fun. Thankfully I had an iPod for the teen and one of Dr. Harvey Karp's baby-calming CDs for the baby. I played that CD in the car for hours and it kept her from crying. Check out Dr. Karp's Web site at www.thehappiestbaby.com.

Some parents are hesitant to fork over the extra money to pay for a seat, since most airlines will not charge you for an infant flying in arms under two years of age. These parents have never flown across the country with a baby in arms. Of course I have done it, and I used a sling, which helped a lot. I still think that the car seat might have been a nice touch. If you ask, sometimes they will give you a discount on a seat for an infant or child.

You also have the option of flying with the car seat on standby. This means that you bring it with you. Sometimes you luck out and there is an extra seat available for free. If no such seat opens up, you can do a planeside check-in of the car seat so you don't have to lug it around.

Your stroller can also travel this way. It is very handy to have your stroller when you're traveling. If you weren't planning to take it because you're dreading lugging it around, remember you can also check in a stroller planeside too. You drop it off right next to the plane and it's waiting for you as soon as you deplane. Very handy!

Keeping Control on the Go

Traveling with your baby doesn't have to be a harrowing experience. In fact, it really can be a lot of fun. You just have to set yourself up for success by planning ahead. Remember, your baby thrives on familiarity. Find small ways to keep your baby's day on as normal a schedule as possible. Be close to the baby. Listen to what she needs. Small breakdowns will only lead to big breakdowns if they're not addressed.

Have a plan for dealing with the baby and baby-related issues. A backup plan is a great thing too. This is because we don't know how the day will go or how the baby will react to anything. By addressing potential problems ahead of time, you can prevent problems.

A good example would be what you are going to do if your baby cries and you're driving. How will you handle it? Let's say you want to stop, but those you're traveling with want to keep going. What do you do? My advice is to head this off at the pass. Work it out with everyone you're traveling with that you plan to stop when the baby cries. Driving with a crying baby can be dangerous for you and the baby.

By stopping, you can end the crying jag more quickly. This will help you stay on track for your travel and make everyone happier. By agreeing to this ahead of time, you can also prevent conflict in the car. The same techniques works for flying. But in this case you would want to talk about who helps calm the baby—even down to who will walk in the aisles.

If you are driving, you will also want to plan out where your stops are going to be. Check out a map and see what cities and towns you'll be passing through. Know the general area as far as what they will have available. From gas for the car to a meal on the road, you'll probably need to stop for various things along the way. It might be a good idea to check out where the rest stops are on your route, so you know when you can expect to stop.

Listen to experienced parents who travel frequently with kids. They have a lot of great advice in this arena. Most of it has been learned the hard way—through experience.

Some parents swear by traveling as the baby sleeps. You will often hear of parents leaving for long car trips in the middle of the night. This way the baby sleeps in the car. This works great if you are traveling with two or more adults. Then you can take turns sleeping while the baby sleeps and another adult drives.

WHAT'S HOT

▶ When you are traveling away from home, particularly if you are leaving your own time zone, you should consider keeping a single watch on your local time. This can be attached to your diaper bag just as a reminder of what your baby would be doing at home. That can be useful for figuring out why the baby is sleepy, or hungry.

▶ A handful of great baby toys is always appreciated—by your baby, you, and the others around you. Have one or two that clip onto the car seat, a larger one for the stroller, and a couple of hand-sized toys that can clip onto the diaper bag. This prevents them from being thrown down to the ground.

Singing can often help small children and babies calm down. Even if you're just singing the ABCs, you can help keep a situation under control. Even if you feel like an idiot singing the instructions or plan—you're fine. Babies are a bit confused about the happy tones, but seem to play along.

Baby-friendly hotels and resorts get a really big thumbs-up from parents who have used them. They provide you with lots of extras to help you be a bit happier with baby in tow. You'll find larger bathrooms and baby-changing facilities in all the restrooms—not just the women's restrooms. And many of these places actually have nursing stations where you can stay and nurse. It's these little things that can often make a difference.

Plan ahead and travel safely with your baby. Pack wisely and with intention. Walk the fine line between overpacking and under-packing. Ask others who have been there and plan for support at your destination. You'll have a great trip and will not have to worry about anything other than enjoying your time with your baby.

Get Linked

So you think you're going to take the baby on a trip? Well, it is definitely possible, but you will need to do some planning before walking out the door. Whether you're going to the grocery store or across the country, you'll need a plan of action. Check out these helpful links on my About.com site:

ROAD TRIP WITH BABY

Here are some great tips for traveling by car with your baby. Fun ideas for making road trips seem less like long, boring rides and ways to pass the miles without listening to your baby scream.

 http://about.com/pregnancy/roadtrip

DIAPER BAGS 101

Every parent of an infant or small child needs a diaper bag; it is a baby necessity every time you walk out your front door. Here are the basics that will make sure your diaper bag is always perfectly packed. This includes sections on how to choose the right diaper bag and more.

 http://about.com/pregnancy/diaperbags

AIR TRAVEL WITH BABY

Taking your baby on a plane can be worrisome, but here are some answers to your most common questions, including how to make the trip less stressful on you, your baby, and those around you.

 http://about.com/pregnancy/airtravel

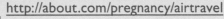

Chapter 14

Child Care

Back to Work Versus Stay at Home

One of the potentially nastiest debates in parenthood is that of the stay-at-home parent versus the working parent. I personally think it's ridiculous to think that we can tell anyone what will work best for their family. I spend my time with clients trying to figure out what they want to do and then work with them to figure out how to make that happen. There are many factors to think about when it comes to this situation.

Stay-at-home parents worry about loss of income. So if mom stays home and does not return to work, how will the loss of income be managed? Some families are lucky enough that the other income will support the family, even if it is at a slightly lower standard of living. By this, we're usually talking about eating at home more often and maybe going back to basic cable rather than the 300 channel mega-pack.

To make the determination as to whether or not you can afford to stay home, you need to do a cost analysis of how much money you spend working. This might seem ridiculous; of course you make money and don't pay to work! But there are hidden costs.

- How much is transportation? Do you add miles to the car? Spend money on gas? Is your car insurance higher because you drive to work? Do you take the bus or subway to work?
- What about your clothing? Do you need special clothes to work? The cost of uniforms or suits adds up.
- Will you add expenses in child care? If you're having your first baby, you may not currently be paying for child care.
- What about other costs associated with working? There may be professional licenses, lunches out, dry cleaning, and more. All of these add up to money from your pocket.

If you were planning on working simply because of the money you'd be making, you may find out that there is more money to be made by not working. Many mothers tell me that where there is a will, there is a way to stay home, though they all acknowledge that it does take effort.

Stay-at-home mothers are quick to point to the benefits of being home. They often list being able to raise their child exactly how they want to do it. They are there for every life event and pediatrician appointment. They don't have to share the decision with anyone outside of the family.

I think it is also important to point out that it is not always the mother who makes the choice to stay home with the children. More and more dads are opting to be at-home parents. My husband did this for several years. While he was the only guy in many mommy-and-me groups for a while, he eventually began to meet

ELSEWHERE ON THE WEB

▶ Trying to add up all of the costs associated with being a working parent can be completely overwhelming. I love the About.com Financial Planning site because it gives such great examples of how easily money adds up when working outside of the home. Even if you decide that working is right for you, I'd encourage you to look at this to see where you could save some money. Check out http://about.com/financial plan/stayhomefinance.

other dads. He formed a lot of long-lasting bonds with other dads, not to mention all the bonding he did with his kids. It was a difficult transition for us, but one that we are both really glad that he and our children experienced.

If you have made the decision to stay home, you need to figure out the best way to leave work. For some mothers, if they tell their bosses prior to going on maternity leave, they find that their benefits are terminated immediately. This means that many mothers I talk to wait to tell their workplace that they are not returning until after their maternity leave is up. Others know that their benefits are secure. Either way, I would also advise that you leave on a positive note. Offer to help at least partially train your replacement. Leave a very detailed notebook on all aspects of your job. This will always put you in a good light and help you later in life.

Working outside the home is another option. Some mothers and fathers choose to work outside the home for a variety of reasons. It may be a money issue, it may be insurance, it could be where they are in their career, or they may simply want to work outside of the home. There are not any right or wrong reasons to go back to work as each family needs to do what works for them.

Many mothers say that they feel that going to work provides them the best of both worlds. They get to be a large influence on their child's life, but they also get the thrill, education, and value of working. For some, the value is the monetary rewards; for others, it is the sense of well-being and accomplishment of a job well done.

If you choose to return to work, you will need to begin thinking about maternity leave well before you may need it. You will want to know your company's policy on leave as well as federal guidelines for the Family Medical Leave Act (FMLA). Do you have to use your vacation? Does your place of work qualify for FMLA?

▶ If you choose to stay home, be sure to figure out insurance coverage before you leave your job. You may have to do some rearranging to make it work. You may even want to look at additional or primary coverage outside of the workplace. You may be able to do this through work or you may need to find an independent insurance agent. This is also a good time to do a life insurance checkup.

When should I go back to work?

▶ I always encourage you to take as much time as you can afford to take off, but to leave a bit of your FMLA time in case of an emergency. That said, I always try to encourage new moms to go back to a shorter schedule. Can you start back at half days for a week? What about going back on a Wednesday or Thursday to ease you back into work? See where you have flexibility and where you don't.

How long can you take off paid? Unpaid? Does it depend on how you give birth?

You will also need to prepare for your return. Did you leave specific instructions on projects and day-to-day tasks for your co-workers? Where will you be using your breast pump? How will you schedule the times to pump?

Some parents choose to work from home. This unique option has become much more of a possibility as you hear of people **telecommuting** to work or even running home businesses. If you have a special skill or talent or just plain good business sense, you might consider running your own business as well.

Of the families I know that work at home, many say it's much harder than working away from home; mainly because of the temptation to work twenty-four hours a day. Here are some tips:

- Set regular business hours and really stick to them.
- Get a cordless phone.
- Get a fast Internet connection.
- Consider hiring short-term child care occasionally.
- Be realistic about what you can do.
- Avoid scams and get-rich-quick schemes.

What to Look for in Child Care

There is not one particular aspect that is likely to make or break a place of child care in your mind. The perfect child-care setting for you is most likely a set of ideals that you and your partner have come up with. Following are some of the major areas most parents think about when it comes to child-care choices.

Location is incredibly important. I would encourage you to choose something that is either close to your home or work. You want to be able to quickly and easily drop your child off at child care. You will also want to easily pick your child up should you need to go to the pediatrician or take him home because he is ill. This is one place where having in-home child care usually wins hands-down.

You really will begin to hate the drive in the opposite direction if you choose someplace out of the way. I had chosen a child-care setting that met every need I had except location, but it also offered me some other benefits. It was a preschool affiliated with an organization I belonged to, most of my children had previously attended there, and we knew the teachers (before we moved from the area), and we had a small discount because we belonged to the group. While I was highly motivated to go there, I spent 90 percent of my mornings asking why I did it. So think long and hard about making the decision to go out of your way.

On the same note as location, you want to make sure that the physical space is to your liking. Is it warm and inviting to a child? Is it childproofed and safe? Is there adequate area to play? Are there appropriate toys in a state of good repair for the children?

The rooms should be safe as well. Do you see evidence of childproofing like electrical outlets covered? Do you see medications, chemicals, or cleaning products out within reach of any child? Do the cabinets have safety locks?

Be sure to check outside too. Look at the playground facilities. Are the toys there age appropriate? Do they get inspected frequently enough? If there is a sandbox, is it clean?

Also check more deeply into things like the soil in play areas. Has it been tested for lead and other poisons? This may be mandated by state agencies or it may not be. It doesn't hurt to ask.

TOOLS YOU NEED

▶ Every state will have its own agency that provides licenses to day-care centers. This should also include some home day cares. These agencies typically have information about the state laws regarding child care as well as helpful ways to spot if your chosen school is in compliance. Start your search with a call for information to your local agency.

Do all the children get outside time? Or is it only certain ages? Can smaller kids be taken outside in a stroller? Some child-care centers have special strollers for just such a walk.

Cost is a factor in child care. Before you even go to look for child care, you need to figure out what your budget will hold in terms of expenditure for child care. Then you can add or cross things off your list as you begin with that one question. Although, if you are finding that the majority of places you are calling are out of your price range, you may have to reconsider your budgeted amount.

In addition to how much the care itself costs, find out how often you have to pay the fees. Are they weekly or monthly? Are they due at the first of the month or every Monday? You will also need to ask about potential fees you may not have thought about. Some day cares charge for a yearly registration fee, educational fees, and supplies fee. Be sure to get this information up-front and before you sign up.

You will want to know if there is a contract to sign. This applies to all child-care settings. What type of notice do you need to give to the center or sitter before leaving their care? What will the charges be for breaking your contract early? What fees are involved? How is notice given and how much time is requested? In my area there are not fees involved, but you must give two weeks' written notice before you leave. This may be waived in certain circumstances, but clear it beforehand with the director.

Staff/child ratio is directly related to how much attention your child gets. The fewer kids to teachers, the more attention your child has from the teacher. In general, though state laws differ, there should be more teachers for smaller children. So you might have six toddlers to one teacher or four infants to one teacher.

This number is usually posted proudly. Many centers strive to do even better than what is recommended by the state. Though there will always be certain times this number is pushed, like lunchtime for the providers. Most child-care centers have the teachers move around to accommodate lunches or breaks. If you notice at various times that there are fewer teachers than required, don't hesitate to say something. It may also be a scheduling issue that the director of the center needs to be made aware of to prevent it from happening regularly.

The activities offered and schedule can be helpful. These glimpses into your baby's day will tell you a lot about the center. There should be a nice mixture of downtime to do things like free play, eating, and nap times to balance out any structured activities. Remember, small babies do not need much in the way of structured play. A few books and songs here or there are fine, but it should be more of an integration into the whole day than a specific 15-minute period.

Some child-care centers offer themes each month. They may change the decorations of the building to go with the theme. For example, a theme might be transportation. The threes and fours will draw pictures and read books about various modes of transportation. The twos might play with cars and build snacks that look like boats; think banana boats or celery boats. And infants might listen to "I've been working on the railroad" and other transportation-themed songs.

A highly scheduled class for small children is usually not realistic. It may be a sign that the person who schedules the day isn't a part of the classroom, or it may be a sign of inflexibility. What happens if it's singing time and your three-month-old needs a nap? The nap should probably trump sing-a-long time, particularly if that is your desire.

WHAT'S HOT

▶ One of the things that works for me is to watch the staff at the place I'm considering change a diaper. I usually try to get whomever is giving me a tour to stop in the nursery while I ask questions. Does the person changing the diaper keep a hand on the baby? Do they wear gloves? Do they wash their hands before and after the diaper change? These are all things that will quickly make me say yes or no to a certain child-care center.

▶ SIDS education at home
is important, but it also
extends to child care. When
you're examining a nursery,
look around and see if there
are cribs with stuffed animals, blankets, pillows, etc.
Are there any kids sleeping
on their bellies? Of course,
you can—and should—also
flat-out ask the teachers
about their SIDS prevention
steps.

Emergency plans are for every center. This is the basic emergency drill. What happens in the case of fire? Tornado? Flooding? Do the teachers know where to go and who to call?

Is there a formal manual? Who is in charge of it and how often are there drills? I didn't even think about this until I asked one day why there was always an empty crib with the words "Evacuation Crib" taped on it. That was the dedicated crib to place all the tiny babies in to evacuate quickly. It made me realize how much of the safety and emergency planning I'd taken for granted. But it is particularly important when dealing with small infants who can't evacuate themselves.

Know what you want to happen in an emergency. Do you want to come get your baby? Who would you release the child to if you were unavailable? These are all questions you need to think about when filling out the paperwork that goes with a school enrollment.

Staff credentialing is important. Usually in larger centers, you will have a lead teacher and an additional teacher, sometimes even more. Does this leader teacher hold any special qualifications? A degree or special training?

What type of training do all the teachers have to go through? How often do they have to renew? You should look for answers like, "Everyone is child/infant CPR certified and required to update early child education classes every year." This shows an ongoing dedication to keeping your child on track.

It is also important to note if your child would potentially ever be alone with a teacher. Some parents worry that this should never happen, while this would penalize small classes. Some smaller centers feel that by having an open visitation policy, a director moving from class to class, parents going in and out, and windows really negates any alone time a teacher may have with any child.

References are also a must. You should be able to talk to other parents who have sent their children to this place. Perhaps they are parents you already know and trust. Otherwise, you can ask the child-care place for names and phone numbers of other parents willing to talk about the setting.

Ask them questions about how the staff treated them and their children. Did the staff follow instructions from the parent on all topics? Did the child want to go to child care?

How they communicate is very important. I like daily notes home, particularly as the parent of an infant. When did she sleep and for how long? What did she eat and when? Did she have dirty diapers? Did she get medicine? Do you need any supplies (like diapers or wipes)?

As the kids get older, there is less need for this detail. You might get a list at the beginning of the week that announces the activities for the week. Though don't be surprised if when you ask your toddler what he did in school you get simple answers like "Nothing." Or "We colored." It's just his nature.

If you need to talk to the teacher about a problem, be sure to approach it open mindedly. Remember you are the parent, not them. Creative solutions are always the best answers when you work together with the teachers.

An example might go like this:

> **Mom:** "I noticed that Sally seems to be hungry when we pick her up. Is she being offered an afternoon snack?"
> **Teacher:** "Yes, but she doesn't like it."
> **Mom:** "Maybe we can offer to bring in something she'd enjoy more. If we were to do that, would you be able to offer it to her?"
> **Teacher:** "Yes, that would be fine."

If your concern is not followed up on, then you can ask the director of the center to become involved. Always keep notes about communications like this to help you remember who said what and when.

Is Day Care the Right Choice?

Day care usually involves a group of other children being together throughout the day. Depending on the setting, your child may be in a small group of children of a similar age or in groups with different ages. There is not one right choice for day care, and there are many great options including in-home day care and larger establishments that may or may not be chains.

In-home day care is an option in most cities. These are licensed by the state or local government. This means that the person running the day care has had at least a minimal amount of training in topics like child development, safety, first aid, and some business topics.

Most parents who choose this type of setting for their child list the following as the benefits of an in-home day care:

- Smaller number of children
- Only one or two providers to get to know
- More homelike atmosphere
- May be closer to home or have a personal relationship with provider

This homelike atmosphere and smaller number of children can be perfect, particularly if your child has some special needs. A small group setting might mean that you have the only baby, although that will depend on the state laws that govern the number of infants or toddlers per adult.

ELSEWHERE ON THE WEB

▶ Day care is a huge topic. There are plenty of questions to ask before you decide that it is the right option for you, but there are also plenty of things that can come up during your stay with a day care. From how to deal with carrying baby stuff back and forth to dealing with biting and more, I really enjoy http://daycare.about.com.

All of the same questions apply when choosing a day care that operates out of someone's home, although there may be additional questions that you would have which may include:

- Will anyone else be at home with the children? Are they approved by the state?
- What happens if the main care provider is ill?
- Will the provider ever run errands or otherwise take your child out of the home?
- Is there an area that is off-limits to the children?
- How are multiple age groups handled?

The very things that people like about home day care tend to be where things go wrong. This is usually because the parent and provider have very different ideas of details. It is easy to forget that a home day care is a business and not your best friend. Therefore you need to remember be respectful of their home as a business. For an example, you would not stay and chat for hours on end, particularly about off-topic subjects.

Most day-care centers are big centers or chains. The benefit to this is that they tend to be very good about spelling everything out for you. You will typically be given a large packet of information that can seem very overwhelming. Be sure to read it before having a tour of the facility.

The parents who choose larger centers have many reasons for choosing the larger or chain day care. These may include:

- Preference for corporate control
- A deal with their place of business
- No concerns over care not being available when the provider is ill

TOOLS YOU NEED

▶ Be sure to ask to see a copy of their state license or certification. It should have a seal or number on it. Also copy this information down and call to verify that there are no outstanding issues with the facility and that they are up-to-date with the state. You can also ask if any complaints have been lodged. The Better Business Bureau may also have some records that you will want to know about.

This last issue was the kicker for me. I loved using in-home day care. I had some really great experiences. But one day when I really needed to have child care, my in-home provider had to take her daughter to the doctor. That left me scrambling. I just didn't have the flexibility that may have helped that situation.

There are also some things that some parents have issues with in large centers.

○ Will my baby and I be treated like numbers or people?
○ Is there any flexibility in the rules that I may need?

Live-In Help

Finding someone to live with you can be useful if you need care every day. The benefits of having someone in your hours are enormous if you leave for work at a horribly early time or if you have on-call hours. Those who choose live-in help are often very happy with their choices, but they will tell you that finding the right person can take a great deal of work.

You might consider an au pair. This is usually a female between the ages of 18 and 26 from a foreign country. The country she comes from will depend on the agency you use and your preference. All au pairs are supposed to be fluent in English, though in truth, this can be the one place where the agency's definition of English and yours differ.

Families who choose an au pair really like the international flavor it brings to their lives. I have some friends who wanted their young children to grow up bilingual in Spanish, so they hired an au pair from a Spanish-speaking country to aid in this development. The au pair spoke Spanish to the children and helped the parents learn as well.

While having live-in help sounds like a dream, there are plenty of restrictions placed on au pairs. They may not work more than 45 hours a week. The lines between work and play have to be carefully drawn. The best way to do this is to have a written schedule and clearly communicate the expectations of work versus playtime.

Most au pair agencies conduct interviews. Then, they try to match your information and expectations with a good match. From there you do phone interviews with the potential au pairs. Once you choose an au pair, she will book her travel to the United States. Normally she will have a week or more of training in child development, safety, and health issues through the agency during that time period.

The downfall is that most agencies make you pay the bulk of the fees for the year up-front. This can be between $5,000 and $10,000. Then you pay the au pair a small allowance during her stay. Au pairs can only stay a year or two maximum due to immigration constraints. This can be difficult if your child really develops an attachment.

A nanny is also an option. These are usually females from your area. You can find one by advertising in the newspaper or in specialty papers. You might even luck out with a personal referral. Again, an agency may be a nice option, simply because for a fee, they provide you with nannies to interview, but have done a lot of the prescreening.

With a nanny you do not have as many restrictions on how long she can work, although this is an expectation that you want to work out ahead of time, particularly to avoid misunderstandings. Many families set out a base salary for an average number of hours per week. Then they set up an overtime fee to pay the nanny for hours over that original number.

ELSEWHERE ON THE WEB

▶ The U.S. Department of State has information on their Web site about the criteria that must be met for au pairs. This applies to all au pairs and every agency. Being sure you're in compliance can be very helpful. This includes information on hours available for work, special-needs children, and educational needs of the au pair. You can read their information online at http://exchanges.state.gov/education/jexchanges/private/aupair.htm.

Some nannies will live in your home, while others won't. This will depend on your needs and desires. If you need help at early or odd hours, like the middle of the night, having a live-in nanny can be very helpful.

The Occasional Baby Sitter

Hey, we all need a day off, right? Or maybe you're ready for a date night out with your husband. Either way, it's always a good idea to have a few names on hand for last-minute or occasional baby sitters. These are sitters who stay for an hour or longer on an irregular basis.

Some families use baby sitters creatively. You might find that there are people who use a baby sitter for all the reasons you might think: going to the movies, a dinner party, or even a doctor's appointment. But there are other reasons why a sitter might prove to be very handy.

For example, have you ever thought about using a baby sitter while you stay home? Many mothers and fathers are choosing to bring in an occasional baby sitter to help them with the baby or other kids while they stay home. This might be that you'd like a bath alone, just you and a book. But some parents use an occasional sitter to allow them to get some important business done or make phone calls.

While I don't suggest using a sitter while you do housework often, it can be handy if you have some really important things like out-of-town guests staying at your house or trying to mop the floor your unentertained toddler likes to walk across while you're still working.

My husband actually had a regular person stop by for several hours every week so he could work on his dissertation. This worked out well because he said he felt like he could devote his attention to the baby when he was there, because he knew he'd have reserved time just for his work later.

Some parents also choose to use a baby sitter just to get the baby used to being around others. I have had a local teen come over after school so I could work out alone. The point is that you can do creative solutions for problems by using part-time, occasional help.

Local sitters are usually your first choice. Finding a baby sitter does not need to be difficult, though sometimes it seems like all the good baby sitters are taken. This is because the baby sitters who stand out are often busy. Some of the things you want to consider about an occasional sitter include:

- The age of your child(ren)
- The age of the sitter
- How far away is the sitter? Do you need to provide transportation?
- References from others
- What they charge
- How often are they available?
- Does your child like the sitter?

Be sure to find out who your neighbors are using. These are often neighborhood teens or those who reside part-time in your area. I usually find that teens make great baby sitters from about seventh grade until they get their driver's license.

You will want to think about the age of the sitters that you use based on the age of your child. You may not want to use a seventh-grader for a newborn baby, but that age is fine for an older toddler.

WHAT'S HOT

▶ If you can find a baby sitter who has younger siblings, you can almost always know that she has some great qualities and skills that other sitters may not possess. I know that my oldest daughter is often sought after as a sitter simply because people know that with six younger siblings, it takes a lot to shake her sitter confidence.

It will also depend on the time of day that you will be gone and how long you intend to be away. Longer times away from home usually call for older sitters.

You can also use a sitter service. These are businesses set up to help you find sitters. The nice thing is that the majority of these places prescreen the sitters for warrants, criminal records, etc. They may also be able to provide you with references locally. The sitter services generally only hire those who are 18 years old or older.

One of the nice things about using a service is that you can simply call and let them know when you need someone. They have multiple sitters to choose from for your needs. This means you are rarely left without a sitter.

The sitters employed through these agencies will often be able to drive themselves to and from your house. This can definitely save you time and energy. The sitters also may be more mature simply because they are older, though this is not always true.

The services usually have you pay the sitter directly for her time and gas. You may pay the total fee to the sitter. Or sometimes the service will invoice you for their portion of the fees, usually a dollar an hour on top of the sitter's fee, which the service also sets. The local sitter services also charge a yearly membership even if you're not using them regularly. It's usually about $30, but can vary from location to location.

I use a sitter service occasionally when I need a sitter who is going to have to stay late or long. This may be an overnight situation. I usually will use a sitter a lot before allowing an overnight, but it has always worked out well. The sitters we usually have are really nice college students who do this on winter break and in the summer. The one time I had a sitter I did not like, I simply told the service not to use her again for me. It was very easy, and worth paying slightly more depending on why I need a sitter.

▶ One thing that I did not know when using a sitter service was that there was a minimum number of hours I had to pay for, even if I didn't use all that time. You may also pay a premium if you use sitters on special days like New Year's Eve, spring break, etc. So be sure to ask about this policy. This may also extend to local special events that draw big crowds like annual sporting events or parties.

Get Linked

Child care and maternity leave are high on the list of worries for pregnant and new families. You need help to figure out what all of your options are and which will realistically work for your family. This doesn't have to be horrible, but you do need guidance in finding the answers. Here are some helpful links on my About.com site:

MATERNITY LEAVE 101

Knowing the ins-and-outs of maternity leave can save you a lot of trouble. From deciding when to start maternity leave to how soon you have to come back and everything in between, this information will help you navigate the murky waters of maternity leave.

http://about.com/pregnancy/maternityleave

CHOOSING CHILD CARE

If you are looking for child care for your baby or older child, there is a set of questions that you will want to ask any potential provider. Here are ideas of what to look for to get the best child care for your baby.

http://about.com/pregnancy/childcare

RETURNING FROM MATERNITY LEAVE

Nothing can be as frazzling as returning to work after an extended absence; add the whole postpartum and new baby issue and you've got a lot on your plate. Here are some ideas to help make the transition a smooth one.

http://about.com/pregnancy/backtowork

WORK OR HOME?

Making the choice to return to work or stay at home is not an easy one. There are many options and ideas to consider when deciding if this is the right choice for your family. Here are some tips and tricks to help you decide.

http://about.com/pregnancy/workorhome

About

Chapter 15

Your Parenting Plan

Defining Yourself as a Parent

Most of us grow up saying things like, "When I'm a parent…" This is usually in response to something our own parents have said or done to us that we felt was unfair. I know I said it many, many times. I am also mature enough now to admit that I spent the first few months of my firstborn's life apologizing to my own mother.

We all have the ideal parent in our minds. That is what helps us define parenting. This ideal parent is made up of many things. Some of these ideas come from our own experiences, what we liked and didn't like as a child. Some of the ideas come from watching other people parent, such as neighbors, friends, and even strangers in public.

Trying to define parenting for yourself and as a couple is an important step in becoming parents. There are many ways to try to find that happy medium for how you will define yourself as parents. My husband and I started by asking ourselves questions about what we wanted to do as parents and then addressed how we were going to accomplish those goals.

By interviewing each other, we found out a lot about our ideas on parenting and child rearing. We found that we had many similar ideas, but we also found some areas where we really differed. It was very good to talk about this, particularly before the baby was born, but it is something that needs to be an ongoing discussion.

Here are some questions to ask yourself and each other about parenting:

- What did your parents do right?
- Are there things you would do differently from your parents?
- Are there parents that you currently admire? What makes them "good" parents?
- What principles do you want to instill in your children? How do you teach those?
- List five important traits of a "good" parent.
- Are there things you said you'd never do? What were they?
- How will you handle anger as a parent?
- What are your thoughts on discipline?
- How would you describe the parenting philosophy of your parents?
- Who is a parent you really look up to? Why?
- What are the skills a good parent needs? Do you have these?

By entertaining these questions, you can start the dialogue. The process of defining yourself as a parent is an ongoing issue. It is not one you can sit down and hash out in one evening, no matter how hard you try.

▶ Flexibility is one of the best things you can have as a parent. Remember that the tree that can sway in the wind bends and doesn't break as fast as the rigid tree. The same is true for parenting. You have to be able to look at the individual, the situation, and all involved. What's right for a two-year-old is not always right for a ten-year-old. Think of your roots as the core beliefs of parenting; these are firmly planted and not shaken by a storm or will.

There are various parenting philosophies. These parenting philosophies are nice starting points for first-time parents, or those looking for helpful advice, though many people don't really identify with any one type of parenting, but rather an eclectic mix of what works for them and what doesn't.

Some parents choose to let their pediatrician rule the roost. They take all their parenting advice from this parenting authority from medical decisions like which shots to get and which medical tests to everyday parenting decisions like what to feed your toddler for breakfast and how to discipline. Most people find that this type of parenting will only get them so far.

Often, as you grow more confident in your parenting, you realize that you have something your pediatrician doesn't have. That would be intimate knowledge of your baby and what is best for him. This is when you may start weaning yourself from the direct orders of your pediatrician as far as daily life advice.

Many of the parenting philosophies work with strict schedules for baby. This may also extend to the whole family as well. There are families who really like knowing that every minute of every day is planned. Most moms I know who have tried this found it stressful to be so rigid.

Of those who stuck with it, they said a more modified version often worked better for them. It is that flexibility issue that many parents need. I found that the idea of routines worked best for us. To me, the difference between a schedule and a routine is the flexibility. This keeps me from freaking out when the kids are a minute late brushing their teeth. I don't have to take that minute or two from storytime. Nor do I have to panic if we read before putting on pajamas.

▶ Many professionals who talk or write about parenting agree that one of the best things you can do for your children is to have a great marriage. While they all differ on how to do this, the basics are the same. By being in a loving relationship, you are the role model for positive relationships, respect for one another, and how affection and love play a part in your daily life. This makes you happy, positive people to be around, which is a good lesson for your children.

Scheduled or Parent-Led Parenting

We have often been told that children should do what their parents tell them to do at all times. This includes not only minding the rules or behaviors but every day tasks like when to eat or sleep. This is also known as **scheduled parenting** or **parent-led parenting**.

Scheduled parenting was popular when we were kids. It was a bit less formal, meaning my mother didn't write down my schedule and post it on our refrigerator. But the theories behind it are that if you provide your baby or small child with a schedule, it will provide him with the comfort of understanding a routine and knowing what comes next.

This routine provides stability. This stability will, in theory, lead to a child who is confident and ready to be a part of society. The schedules usually consist of specific playtimes, mealtimes, alone times, and definitely sleep times. As a stereotype, parents who use scheduled parenting techniques choose cribs, crying-it-out time, and alone time for babies. This is certainly not true of all parents who subscribe to this theory.

Scheduled parenting may also include a form of sleep training known as **crying it out**. Crying it out comes in many different forms. There are many variations on this theme, depending on which specific theory you are following.

There are those who rigidly follow crying-it-out methods. These families believe that your child should sleep through the night at a certain point. Once that point is reached, usually a specific age, then the baby goes to bed in a crib and is not touched again until the morning. So if the baby cries, the baby cries.

Most of these methods are not this strict. They involve comforting your baby in various increments. Some also involved extending the period of time in which the baby can cry by various amounts of time. There are whole books written on this subject. The belief is that the child will learn to self-soothe and therefore sleep better or longer. Other parenting experts warn against this saying that while the child stops crying, it doesn't mean that he has learned to self-soothe.

Many parents describe crying it out as not being a problem. They say that their child responded positively to it and had no issues after a few nights. Other mothers and fathers talk about nightmare evenings spent with inconsolable infants who screamed for hours on end while they, the parents, sat with their hearts in knots. Before you choose any sleep-training method, I would encourage you to read some of the forums on the Internet from both sides of the debate for a good perspective from a cross section of parents in various situations.

Most parents try some form of scheduling. After all, it can be very handy to know that you have some downtime during a nap period and the other benefits that come from being able to plan your day. Some parents need to know exactly, while others are fine with a vague estimate. This will depend largely on your personality.

Flexibility may be the key for you. One of the hardest parts of scheduled parenting is the rigid structure. While some proponents would tell you that it is the rigidity that makes the program work, others would say not to be so crazy that you drive yourself insane.

It is the fear of deviating from the schedule for any reasons that makes most parents feel like a failure at this method. I do not believe that falling off schedule occasionally is harmful. In fact, it can sometimes be beneficial by teaching our children that sometimes life happens and schedules and priorities need to be rearranged.

An example might be that your baby usually takes a nap in the morning at 10 A.M. But this morning your older child woke up with

TOOLS YOU NEED

▶ I would like to recommend that you read Dr. James McKenna's *Sleeping with Your Baby* (2007). This book contains information on how babies sleep and why. This is a great primer for any new parent. But it also discusses in detail how to get your child to sleep in a humane manner. The text is clearly written and easy to understand.

a fever and a sore throat. The pediatrician said to bring in your older child. The problem is that the only time she had available was at 10 A.M. Do you skip seeing the pediatrician? Do you force the issue on time? Or do you try to help your baby nap in a sling at the pediatrician's office?

This may seem like a no-brainer, but there are parents who would reschedule the pediatrician appointment. There is not one perfect answer to every parenting need, which is why it is important enough to say again that flexibility is required in parenting.

Let the Baby Guide You

Having your baby or child guide you as a parent may not sound like a great idea. I can remember being little and promising my mother that when I got to make the parenting decisions, we would all be eating sugary cereals for many meals a day. Thankfully I grew up and my mother never disowned me.

Your baby has a wealth of information for you. This information is specific to him. He knows when he is hungry. He knows when he is overstimulated. And he knows when he has other needs that need to be met. This type of parenting is often referred to as **attachment parenting**.

The key elements in attachment parenting include:

○ Meeting the baby's needs immediately and appropriately.
○ Parents learn to read the needs or **cues** of the baby.
○ Babies are viewed as unique, even when they come in multiples.
○ Physical punishment is not used.
○ Being physically close to your baby often is valued.

The theories behind attachment parenting are that by meeting the needs of the child quickly and appropriately, you teach your child that you are always present to help. You teach them that they are knowledgeable and valuable to you. This supposedly builds the confidence of the baby, which will extend into all avenues of his life as he continues to grow. This comfort allows him the desire and ability to explore his environment.

There are some people who worry that by allowing the baby to say when he is hungry, you are spoiling him. There are also some who believe that even small infants can manipulate you. Attachment parenting responds by saying that meeting your baby's needs are not spoiling. In fact, it is impossible to spoil a child by feeding him, changing him, and loving him.

You need to figure out the cues of your baby. This is done by spending the first few weeks in close proximity to your child. For some parents, this means that they choose to co-sleep with their babies. Others chose to incorporate **baby wearing** instead of co-sleeping or in addition to co-sleeping.

Baby wearing is simply carrying your baby in a soft-sided carrier as opposed to rarely having contact with your baby. It also means a limited amount of time in the stroller, car seat, and other carrying devices that separate parents from their baby.

When you are close to your baby, it is hard not to notice her needs and cues. You can see the early cues of hunger, as opposed to waiting until your baby is starving and crying inconsolably from hunger. You will also see that your baby has her own rhythm to her day. This internal schedule, if you will, has value to you as a parent, because you can use it not only to predict your baby's behaviors and needs, but to meet them as well.

As you see the cues and learn them, you and your baby grow more confident. Your life finds a rhythm and everyone has their

ASK YOUR GUIDE

If I define myself as an attached parent, do I have to co-sleep with my baby?

▶ While many parents who define themselves as attached parents do co-sleep, it is not necessary. While we have co-slept with many of our kids, we had one baby who just slept better alone. Attachment parenting is just that—listening to your baby's cues as we listened to hers. It is also about how you feel and your needs. As long as you are responsive to the needs of the family, you are an attached parent.

needs met accordingly. When this happens, the need to be near your baby does decrease. Attachment parenting does not mean that you are always with your baby all the time.

Meet Yourself in the Middle

Sometimes there is not one clear way that seems like it will work. And to be perfectly honest, it is really hard to tell what type of parent you will be before you have children. Though researching and watching other parents is always beneficial. The truth of the matter is that oftentimes two parents—that is, two people with varied backgrounds and beliefs—rarely see perfectly eye-to-eye on every aspect of parenting. This means that you will have to find a compromise for all aspects on which you don't agree.

Compromise is about finding a middle ground. Compromise is not about winning or losing. Sitting down to discuss ideals with your partner is important to the success of raising your children.

It is also helpful to talk about theories. By this I mean, make up scenarios to decide how you would handle them. Some examples: Your teenage daughter comes home past her curfew. Your toddler bites a neighbor child. Your six-year-old steals a pack of gum from the store.

Hopefully none of these will happen to you, but realistically they will or something else will. By discussing these ahead of time, you get a chance to work together without the pressure and strain of the real deal. You can even laugh and say silly things like my husband's favorite when the kids were young, "I'm not letting my teenage daughter date."

You will make mistakes as parents. You will learn from them, even if it takes you a couple of tries to find the right way for your family. This can be very difficult for a variety of reasons. But parenting is rarely ever an exact science.

Discipline is a four-letter word. It can quickly get you into trouble. Discipline is one of the places where many parents do not immediately agree. This hot topic involves more than punishment, though this is the word we often associate with it. **Discipline** is about setting up boundaries and about following through with upholding those boundaries.

This goes back to the one rule I remember most that my mother said, which was never punish a child in a way that punishes you too. The best example is not to ground your thirteen-year-old daughter for a month if you don't want to spend a month with her moping around. I tend to believe in **natural consequences**.

This means that with the exception of grave danger, I'm going to let my child find out on her own the consequences of her actions. If you break your new toy, you don't have that toy anymore. If you yell at your friends, they don't want to play with you for a while. Afterward, and even sometimes during the conflict, I will step in and point out what's going on.

The danger part comes in when you're saying, "The stove is hot. Don't touch the stove." You see your child reaching for the stove. A burn would be the natural consequence, but this is an inappropriate use for natural consequences. Here you simply try to teach them through role playing and the use of words and gestures, depending on the age of the child.

Handling Parenting Differences

There will be times when you and your spouse or partner do not agree. This might not seem possible, but it is an absolute given. This can be a very trying time for you and your spouse, not to mention your child. So what do you do when you don't agree?

Get a second opinion if you don't agree. By enlisting the opinions of those who know you, you will find that they may be

able to see options you did not see. It may be that these other people have some great insight into your situation. But more likely, it
will merely be the objective sense of not being intimately involved
with what is going on.

Ask those outside of your normal circles if need be. Sometimes
a totally fresh perspective can also be helpful. This is the whole
parenting-by-village belief system. Keeping your mind open to new
ideas and alternatives can help you see many options as a parent,
which prevents you and your partner from being trapped by a
limited view.

Don't do anything. Sometimes the fact that you can't decide
what to do means you should do nothing. Take some time to step
back and let it simmer. Oftentimes a bit of time and perspective will
help clarify the problem in some manner or another, though I will
warn you, this can be very hard to do. I have never made a wrong
decision as a parent by backing off, though I have made plenty of
decisions I would now do differently had I not acted impulsively.
Sometimes even "sleeping on it" is enough to help.

Also take into consideration where you are in your life and
what the decision is concerning. Talking about what you will do to
a child who breaks a curfew is a discussion that is probably best
held as you begin to impose curfews on your child as opposed to
thinking about it as your child starts crawling.

Think ahead and talk it out. My husband and I like to discuss
major issues about parenting, such as sex, drugs, and money, well
before they come up with our children. It's nice to talk a bit and
then shelve it for a while to get that perspective. It also allows us to
be influenced positively and negatively by society and those around
us. But we are also growing and changing as parents as you will.

Remember that when discussing these issues it can get very emotional. Try to speak calmly and clearly. Use "I" statements to describe how you feel as opposed to more attacking language. The good news is that these discussions don't have to be held over the course of an evening or even two evenings. There is plenty of time to continue this discussion, because remember you will both be evolving as parents as your baby grows.

Parenting is not an easy task by any stretch of the imagination. By learning some of the basics of the many different types of methods available, you will be able to learn a good group of tricks to have at your disposal. Being able to be flexible to help your family find the best route for them is the key to successful parenting. The only people you need to answer to are your children.

TOOLS YOU NEED

▶ Find a place to be around other parents. Some communities offer new mother groups, parenting centers, birth networks, etc. No matter what they call them, find a group where you enjoy the other parents and participate. Create for yourself a good sounding board, even if it's just a play group.

Get Linked

Parenting is a process. In finding the right flow for your family, you need to be open to new ideas and old ones too. Here are some more links to my About.com site that offer ways to communicate about being the parents you want to be to your kids.

PARENTING STYLE QUIZ

By answering a few simple questions, you can get a basic idea as to which of the major areas of parenting philosophies you fall into. This is a great place to start your search.

 http://about.com/pregnancy/parentstylequiz

FOR FATHERS ONLY

Dads often need more encouragement to find the parent within. Society is pretty hard on dads and it's important for a dad to find a way to express the paternal instincts that he does have. Here are some ways to stay connected with your family despite societal strains.

 http://about.com/pregnancy/forfathers

PARENTING

Here are some of my favorite parenting sites, which run the gamut from playful ideas on raising a family to more serious topics.

 http://about.com/pregnancy/parentingsites

Appendix A

Glossary

all-in-ones

This is a type of cloth diaper that includes both an inner diaper and a waterproof and protective cover in one diaper. It is frequently abbreviated AIO.

attachment parenting (AP)

Attachment parenting is a parenting philosophy/method that believes in following the lead of your baby and responding appropriately and in a timely fashion to his needs based on the cues that he gives you. Often, parents who identify with attachment parenting will choose to breastfeed, co-sleep, or baby-wear.

axillary temperature

This is the body temperature as taken from the axilla or armpit.

babymoon

This can refer to the period of time immediately following the birth of your baby, like a honeymoon follows a wedding. This is a time when the family closes themselves off to others in a protective mode to get to know their baby and figure out their lives. Some people are now using this term to refer to a last getaway before the baby is born.

baby wearing

This is the concept that you should carry your baby most of the time. It is often done in a cloth or other soft-sided carrier like a sling or a pouch.

battery-operated breast pump

This small pump is used for infrequent pumping of the breasts to remove the breast milk. This breast pump is operated by a battery or even an electrical plug. It is not to be used for everyday pumping, as it will not help you maintain your supply very well.

bilirubin

This is the yellowish chemical breakdown product of hemoglobin in the blood. This is what is measured when your baby has jaundice.

breast pump

This is a series of devices of various shapes and sizes used to pull the milk from your breasts to give to your baby. Which breast pump you choose will depend on your needs

cloth diaper

This is a type of diaper that is made of reusable fabric. Cloth diapers are designed for frequent, multiple washings.

clutch hold

A breastfeeding position in which you hold the baby in the crook of one arm (almost like you would hold a football). The other hand is used to maneuver the breast. So, if your left arm is holding the baby and managing his head, your right hand would hold the left breast. If your baby is very long or large, the baby's legs may go up the back of your bed or chair, or wrap around your back, in this position.

co-bedding

This is the concept that twins and other multiples sleep in the same bed. It is usually discussed in a nursery setting, such as the neonatal intensive care unit (NICU), but it can also be thought of in terms of how your babies sleep together at home. Older, nonmultiple birth siblings can co-bed technically too.

colostrum

This is a protein- and immunity-rich pre-milk substance that is golden in color. It will often leak from the breasts in the last weeks of pregnancy. This important substance is your baby's first meal after birth and stays until the mature milk comes in between three to seven days after the baby is born.

cradle cap

This refers to flaky or scaly patches on your baby's scalp. Typically these patches require no treatment and will clear up on their own within a few months.

cradle hold

This is the most commonly thought-of breastfeeding position. You place the baby's head in the crook of your right arm and your right hand on her bottom or back. You then use your left hand to manipulate or hold the right breast. You switch hands for the opposite side feeding.

cross-cradle hold

This breastfeeding position has you placing the baby's head at the right breast, with your left hand holding the back of the baby's head while supporting his body on your left forearm. You can then use your hand to help maneuver the baby's head. You would use the right hand to make any adjustments as he feeds off the right breast. Switch hands for the opposite side.

crying it out

A sleep-training method that has parents allow their baby to cry for various periods of time in an effort to teach her how to sleep.

cues

These are signals your baby sends that are common or distinct to him. These cues alert those who are observant to his needs. Example cues might be crying or sucking his fist when he's hungry, rubbing at his eyes when he's sleepy. This enables care providers and parents to respond accordingly.

diaper covers

This is placed over the cloth diaper. It is usually waterproof to prevent leaks from the diaper. They may be plain or colorful. They also offer various options, such as Velcro or elastic, to hold them in place.

diaper service

This service brings cloth diapers to your door and picks up the dirty diapers. What they provide may vary from location to location, but it is often used when parents want to use cloth diapers but don't wish to or can't wash the diapers themselves.

diaper doubler

These come in cloth and disposable form, and you use them inside another diaper. This extra piece of soaker makes the diaper more absorbent. Doublers are great for those heavy nighttime wetters and for babies who are a little bit more sensitive to being wet at all. This might buy you more time between nighttime changes. You can also use them for naps.

discipline

There are many official definitions of this word. However, in this sense, it means to teach or share the rules of society with your baby and help him learn self-control by various means, self as a gentle approach.

eczema

This is an itching, flaky skin irritation that can be red and raised. You will not catch it from anyone, nor is your baby contagious. It is most commonly found on the arms, legs, and face, though it can occur nearly anywhere. There are numerous treatments with a variety of benefits and risks; be sure to talk to your pediatrician about maintenance and possible use of medication.

electric breast pump

This is a breast pump that runs on electrical power. Most electric breast pumps are designed for everyday use. They are great for moms who work, those who have a supply that needs maintaining due to a sick infant, and those who choose to pump exclusively. These breast pumps can do single or double pumping to maximize your time.

elimination communication (EC)

This is an infant potty-training method that begins shortly after birth. The parents or care providers watch for signs that the infant needs to urinate or defecate and helps them do so in a receptacle other than a diaper. Some refer to this as the diaper-free method.

express

To draw breast milk from the breast using the hand or a breast pump.

family practitioner

A physician who has studied family medicine in a three-year post–medical school residency. He or she can see the whole family; some also do obstetrics and pediatrics.

fontanel

Commonly known as a "soft spot," this is a space, covered by membrane, between the bones of a baby's skull.

hospital-grade breast pump

This type of breast pump is used to help initiate or maintain your milk supply. It is the best breast pump available and is designed for multiple users (not at the same time). This is frequently used soon after birth when there are nursing difficulties or the baby is having problems nursing because of illness, prematurity, or simply breast issues.

jaundice

A condition marked with a yellowing of the skin or eyes from an excessive amount of bilirubin in the blood. This is a common occurrence for a baby in the first days after birth; it may or may not require medical treatment.

lactation consultant

A professional who has been trained to help breastfeeding women and their families with a variety of normal and problematic breastfeeding scenarios. Look for the International Board Certified Lactation Consultant (IBCLC) designation.

low-grade fever

A fever in your baby, typically under 100.5 degrees Fahrenheit, though this might vary depending on your medical team.

manual breast pumps

This type of breast pump removes milk by using a pump that is triggered by hand motions rather than batteries or electricity.

mastitis

This is an infection of the breast. You may experience fever, pain, and hard spots or streaks on the breast. Your doctor or midwife may prescribe antibiotics for you to take to clear up this condition. It can be caused by not emptying the breasts frequently enough. This does not require that you stop nursing; in fact, nursing often helps with the pain.

meconium stools

These are the first bowel movements a baby has after birth. Meconium lines the intestines of your baby while in the uterus. As your baby nurses, she will begin to switch to normal stooling. Meconium is often described as green and tarlike in consistency.

milia

This condition is also called baby acne. It is when white, pimple-like bumps appear on your baby's face, mostly on the cheeks, chin, and nose. They do not need treatment, and you should avoid popping them. They normally go away within a couple of weeks.

monozygotic twins

This is a set of twins who are born from one egg and one sperm. Monozygotic twins are also known as identical twins.

natural consequences

This would be what happens automatically in response to an action. If I don't eat, I get hungry. If I am not nice to my neighbors, they are not nice to me.

neonatal intensive care unit (NICU)

This is a special unit in a hospital for very sick or premature babies.

neonatologist

This physician has taken a special four-year residency after medical school to care for sick or premature infants in the first few months of life, particularly in an urgent-care setting.

nipple confusion

A baby who has had bottle nipples and breasts may not remember how to nurse on the different types of nipples easily. This can cause breastfeeding difficulties.

nursing strike

A period of time when an otherwise healthy baby refuses to nurse. It is usually temporary.

parent-led parenting

This is a method of parenting where the parents direct all activities according to their schedule. This can be with or without input from the baby's cues.

pediatrician

This physician has studied an extra four years after medical school to specialize in the care of children from birth to 26 years of age, though many pediatricians stop seeing patients when they reach college age.

phototherapy

A treatment for jaundice that uses lights in a blanket or a box to help break down the red blood cells in a baby to reduce the amount of excess bilirubin in his blood and decrease the yellowish tone of his skin to help prevent brain damage.

pocket diapers

These cloth diapers have pockets built in that are used to keep your baby clean.

prefolds

These are nonfitted diapers, meaning that they need to be folded to use within a cover of some sort. They are also known as Chinese prefolds.

scheduled parenting

A structured method of parenting where you parent by the clock and calendar rather than on demand or by the specific needs of the child.

screen time

This is the amount of time any type of screen is being used to entertain or educate a child. Examples include television screens and computer screens.

side-lying hold

A breastfeeding position where mother and baby lie on their sides to nurse.

telecommuting

Attending to work duties from your home by using the computer or telephone without going into an actual office space.

thrush

An overgrowth of yeast in the digestive tract. It can be seen as white patches in the mouth or diaper area.

Developmental Milestones

Babies are awfully cute and cuddly, but one of the best things about being a parent is looking forward to the next stage of development. The trick is to simultaneously enjoy one stage while looking forward to the next.

While babies do develop in roughly the same time frame and in the same order, there are variances. These differences and variances can drive parents wild. Is my baby okay? Is she growing on schedule? Should she be walking by now?

All of these are normal questions. Even an experienced parent has the same questions. It doesn't help that all kids are different. Be sure to ask your pediatrician any questions that you have about developmental milestones. In the meantime, here are some basic milestones for the first year.

Your Amazing Newborn

Physical Development

At birth your baby has a completely developed body, although his head is bigger than the rest of his body. This may take a while to get used to, but your child's body will even out.

The reflexes that he is born with will help guide him physically through the first few months of life. Some are permanent, like breathing, while others are transient like the stepping reflex.

Your baby's pediatrician will let you know if the reflexes are intact and what each of them means. Be sure to ask for a "tour" of your baby's reflexes.

Some babies will have great control over some parts of their body, like the head and neck, while other babies don't. This can take time. Just remember to give your baby some tummy time to allow him to build his strength.

Mental/Emotional Development

New babies will know the voices they have heard in utero. This means yours and your husband's voices are the most familiar. We also know that new babies enjoy touch. Consider holding your baby skin-to-skin on a daily basis; even your husband can do this one.

While newborns do sleep a lot, they also have quiet alert phases. During this time, they are able to watch and take in many things. Remember they see best from "breastfeeding distance"—about

10 inches from your face. Babies are neither blind nor deaf at birth.

First Month

Physical Development

Your baby may now respond more often to the sound of your voice. And sometimes you can watch her stare intently at something as if she's studying it. Continue with the tummy time to help develop the muscles of the head and neck.

Mental/Emotional Development

Your baby still enjoys spending time with you. Babies also love faces. Be sure to let her use some of that staring time to look at you! This is also a great time to practice being silly. You might even get rewarded with small smiles toward the end of this month.

You may notice feedback from your baby in the form of cues. You will soon learn which cues mean what for your baby. You will be able to tell the hungry cry from the bored or wet cry very quickly.

Second Month

Physical Development

Your baby is on a mission. It's usually to bat at something, even though she completely misses.

Your baby can now hold her head up a bit, at least for short periods of time. She still enjoys high-contrast designs like black, white, and red toys, but nothing warms the cockles of your heart like your baby's first coos.

Mental/Emotional Development

You still rock your baby's world and will continue to do so, but now she starts to notice others. This can simply delight secondary caregivers or siblings. Smiles become more deliberate and very obviously have meaning.

Third Month

Physical Development

Your baby is learning to be mobile. This usually means rolling at this stage of the game. You may find that your baby only rolls in one direction—the other will come eventually. Babies of this age also have much more head control; the head is now much more stable and they can hold it up for longer periods of time.

Mental/Emotional Development

Your baby's face lights up when he sees you because he knows your face and your voice. Use this to start playing games with him. Your baby will start making more and more noises. Listen to him as he starts to try to mimic talking by following a pattern of speech.

Fourth Month

Physical Development

Your baby's fourth month is starting to be about the toys. Now that she can see the toys more readily, you find that her interest is piqued. She may bat at toys that are in front of her. Occasionally she may even be able to reach out and grab one, though she can hold on to a toy placed in her hand. She is still working on rolling over, both forward and backward. Some babies even start teething activities this early, though there are few teeth seen.

Mental/Emotional Development

Your baby really responds to you now. The pattern of mimicking speech is much more apparent. He may even try to have a conversation with you. Try mimicking patterns to him in a conversational tone, even if it's all nonsensical. He may even surprise you with an occasional word like "mama," though "dada" usually seems to come first.

Fifth Month

Physical Development

Now that she has mastered rolling over, your baby is ready to move on to bigger and better things. You may notice that she is trying to stand up. Weight bearing on her legs is fine, though I would caution you to avoid tiring her legs out with long periods of time in jumpers, walkers, and exersaucers. Your baby may even start trying to sit up around this time period, but she is often happy to chew on her hands and feet.

Mental/Emotional Development

Bold colors please her in her toys and surroundings. She may start talking to the baby in the mirror as she develops this friendship. I love this age because typically your baby will start to recognize her name and turn to you when called. She is much more aware of her surroundings, although this can sometimes lead to stranger anxiety.

Sixth Month

Physical Development

Your baby has probably nearly mastered sitting without support about now. This new view excites him. As he sees more things, you can watch him try to lunge for objects and toys. This is the start of crawling. Toys are a favorite this month too, particularly in the mouth. This increased oral activity, along with his age, means that you should talk to the pediatrician about adding some solid foods to his diet.

Mental/Emotional Development

Jabbering continues as he continues to rapidly evolve toward talking, including lots of verbalization and making noise with his mouth. More short "words" may appear. Your baby may really enjoy playing with or near others now as his social ability and desire increase.

Seventh Month

Physical Development

She really enjoys sitting up and viewing the world, but watch out! Here she comes. More movement toward crawling is here. She may even have her own brand of scooting or an army-like crawl going on. Another big favorite is banging things together, like two toys or clapping her hands. A few babies may even begin to pull up on steady objects.

Mental/Emotional Development

While she may be sad to see you go, she can now wave good-bye or at least try to. She may wave backward for a while but don't fret, it's just her perspective. You may see more stranger anxiety as she continues to cling to her family, but the good news is that she enjoys the social interactions with those she knows well.

Eighth Month

Physical Development

Most babies can crawl fairly well at this age, even if it looks funny. Some are even experts and moving on to the standing activities of the very young. Another big milestone is passing objects from one hand to the other. The pincer grasp, holding things between the thumb and forefinger, is a new skill for most. The use of small pieces of baby-friendly cereals and other solids may aid this skill in developing.

Mental/Emotional Development

Anxious to let you know what's going on in his mind, your baby has learned to point. He may even cry in frustration. He may point at what he wants, such as food or his favorite toy. He may also point to you to get you to name an object. This is a big step forward in letting you know his wants and needs.

Ninth Month

Physical Development

You will see more of the pincer grasp this month. Your pediatrician will probably ask about this, so try to pay attention to catch her doing it. Self-feeding in general is a great idea, but be prepared for a mess!

Mental/Emotional Development

I love that babies of this age like to kiss themselves in the mirror. Your baby knows his mom from his dad and isn't afraid to say so. Parents usually enjoy this distinction. You may also hear more simple words. Take advantage of this and play more games with the baby.

Tenth Month

Physical Development

Take a stand! At least that's what your baby wants to do, even if it is just for a split second. You will also see some cruising—that is, holding on to the edge of furniture and walking around. Think about offering a sippy cup of water at this point. He can even put objects into a container and remember where they are to take them out—though spilling them out is always more fun.

Mental/Emotional Development

He may become a bit moody in that he is capable of showing moods like happy and sad. Your baby likes to gesture now; although his own version of sign language can make it difficult to figure out what he's up to, eventually you'll get it. He can also really respond to his name. Now you might even catch him telling you no!

Eleventh Month

Physical Development

Clapping is a huge hit around this age. He claps when happy, or when playing a game. He loves the fact that he can control the action and your reaction by such simple moves. He may also be able to stand for a few minutes or even take a few steps at this point. If you haven't started, offer a sippy cup at this point.

Mental/Emotional Development

Your baby enjoys lots of mental games at this stage. Try making a toy disappear, and she loves to search for it. She can mimic this by placing a toy in a bucket. She understands who mama is and who dada is now. Some parents report temper tantrums even this early on.

Twelfth Month

Physical Development

From cruising to a few steps, your baby is definitely upwardly mobile at this point. Running is not far behind! She may also mimic daily activities like writing or talking on the phone.

Mental/Emotional Development

I love this age because finally simple instructions are appropriate. Bring mommy the ball. Don't hit. Say thank you. These are all more easily understood at this point. You may also see more of a clingy nature from your little one; this may be for one parent or both.

Appendix C

Additional Resources

Parenting Resources

Books

Diaper Free! The Gentle Wisdom of Natural Infant Hygiene by Ingrid Bauer

The Everything Father's First Year by Vince Iannelli, M.D.

The Everything Mother's First Year by Robin Elise Weiss, LCCE

The Happiest Baby on the Block by Harvey Karp, M.D.

The Happiest Toddler on the Block by Harvey Karp, M.D.

The Mother of All Baby Books by Ann Douglas

The Mother of All Toddler Books by Ann Douglas

The No-Cry Sleep Solution by Elizabeth Pantley

The No-Cry Sleep Solution for Toddlers and Preschoolers by Elizabeth Pantley

Operating Instructions by Anne Lamont

Sign with Your Baby: How to Communicate with Infants Before They Can Speak by Joseph Garcia

Web Sites

About Fatherhood

Finding a site just for dads isn't difficult. Here's one dad helping you find your way in the maze of parenting.

http://fatherhood.about.com

About Parenting

Parenting center with information about all sorts of parenting topics from adoption and homework help to ages and stages parenting.

http://about.com/parenting

About Pediatrics

Your friendly pediatrician on a Web site! Get answers to questions about lots of parenting topics for children from birth on up.

http://pediatrics.about.com

Ask Dr. Sears

Here you will find parenting advice from Dr. William Sears and his pediatrician sons. It has great quick resources for all things parenting, including lots of information on sleep.

http://askdrsears.com

Attachment Parenting International

This Web site has information on attachment parenting and similar topics.

www.attachmentparenting.org

Keeping Kids Healthy

A site full of wisdom for parents of kids of all ages, it has basic medical and health information designed to help you think.

http://keepingkidshealthy.org

Medline Plus: Parenting

This Web site has the latest in medical research as it applies to parenting.

www.nlm.nih.gov/medlineplus/parenting.html

The New Homemaker

This site is made up of a community of families who put lots of care into everything parenting. Enjoy the musings of the owner, Lynn, a thoughtful mother of two.

http://thenewhomemaker.com

Breastfeeding Resources

Books

Breastfeeding Café by Barbara Behrmann
Breastfeeding Made Simple by Nancy Mohrbacher and Kathleen Kendall-Tackett
How My Breasts Saved the World: Misadventures of a Nursing Mother by Lisa Wood Shapiro
The Nursing Mother's Companion by Kathleen Huggins

The Ultimate Breastfeeding Book of Answers by Dr. Jack Newman and Teresa Pitman

Organizations

International Lactation Consultant Association (ILCA)

1500 Sunday Drive, Suite 102
Raleigh, NC 27607
(919) 861-5577
ILCA certifies lactation consultants. Their Web site has information on finding a board-certified lactation consultant in your area as well as information on becoming a board-certified lactation consultant.

www.ilca.org

La Leche League International

1400 N. Meacham Road
Schaumburg, IL 60173-4808
(847) 519-7730
La Leche League provides information, education, and support for pregnant and breastfeeding women. There are monthly meetings held locally in many cities around the world as well as a wealth of information via publications of various forms. They also have some phone support available. Their Web site has a great deal of information available for pregnant and lactating women in an easy-to-find format, including back issues of their magazines.

www.lalecheleague.org

Web Sites

Breastfeeding Café

A nice Web site to go to, and read or share stories on the beauty and wisdom of breastfeeding. It is also a place where you can share your trials and tribulations and talk to other mothers.

www.breastfeedingcafe.com

Breastfeeding Online

Great information on breastfeeding, from helping you get off to a great start to handling issues that arise and even a super section on dealing with complications. A section to submit your questions is also available.

www.breastfeedingonline.com

KellyMom

KellyMom has lots of advice and simple explanations from Kelly and other moms who have been there.

http://kellymom.com

Postpartum Resources

Books

Eat Well, Lose Weight While Breastfeeding by Eileen Behan

Essential Exercises for the Childbearing Year by Elizabeth Noble

The Everything Pregnancy Fitness Book by Robin Elise Weiss, LCCE

Laughter and Tears by Elisabeth Bing and Libby Coleman

This Isn't What I Expected by Karen Kleiman and Valerie Raskin

Web Sites

Fit Pregnancy

This Web site is based on a magazine of the same name. Here you will find pregnancy-fitness and wellness-related articles.

www.fitpregnancy.com

Postpartum Support International (PSI)

Here you will find information on postpartum depression and mood disorders. There is an awesome self-test here to see how you're feeling after birth.

www.postpartum.net

Walking Guide at About.com

Your walking guide for every avenue of life, which includes the free 10-week "Walk of Life" program.

http://walking.about.com

Managing Multiple Children Resources

Books

Having Twins by Elizabeth Noble

Mothering Multiples by Karen Kerkoff Gromada, IBCLC

When You're Expecting Twins, Triplets, or Quads by Dr. Barbara Luke

Organizations

National Organizations of Mothers of Twins Clubs (NOMOTC)

P.O. Box 700860
Plymouth, MI 48170-0955
(877) 540-2200
Representing over 475 clubs in cities all over the United States, the National Organizations of Mothers of Twins Clubs is the oldest and largest organization serving multiple-birth families today. Locate a club near you, read the latest news on multiple births and find ongoing research projects for multiple sets of children at their Web site.

www.nomotc.org

Web Sites

About Parenting of Multiples

This site starts at pregnancy and takes you through all the stages of physical, mental, and emotional development of multiple children. There is also a gallery of photos of multiple sets of children, polls, and lots of great articles on different aspects of raising multiples.

http://multiples.about.com

Attachment Parenting Multiples

At this Web site, parents of twins, triplets, and higher-order multiples have an active discussion about parenting multiples, including issues concerning breastfeeding and daily life.

http://groups.yahoo.com/group/apmultiples

Pregnancy Loss–Related Organizations

Center for Loss in Multiple Birth (CLIMB)

CLIMB is specifically for people who have experienced a loss that occurred during a multiple pregnancy, whether that loss was one or all of your babies, no matter what gestational age. This helps address the multiples-specific questions that other grief organizations might not be able to answer for you.

www.climb-support.org

SHARE

SHARE is an organization dedicated to helping you grieve the loss of your child, no matter at what point your child died. SHARE has support at heart. They have several resources available from a monthly paper newsletter that is free for the first year to conferences held all over.

http://nationalshareoffice.com

SIDS Alliance

This site offers articles and resources to help parents who are dealing with the loss of an infant from any cause, but especially Sudden Infant Death Syndrome (SIDS).

www.sidsalliance.org

Fertility-Related Resources

Books

The Everything Getting Pregnant Book by Robin Elise Weiss, ICCE-CPE, CD(DONA), LCCE

Taking Charge of Your Fertility by Toni Weschler, MPH

Organizations

American Society for Reproductive Medicine (ASRM)

(formerly The American Fertility Society)

1209 Montgomery Highway

Birmingham, AL 35216-2809

(205) 978-5000

ASRM provides patient and physician information. They also help govern and provide guidance for fertility programs, both in training and in ethical situations. You will find great handouts on various positions from ASRM here; handouts are also available in Spanish.

http://asrm.org

Web Sites

About Infertility Guide

Here you will find information on infertility from diagnosis to high-tech assistance. This site includes a personal touch with lots of opportunities for loving support from others in your situation. It is a great place to look for cycle buddies.

http://infertility.about.com

Couple to Couple League—Natural Family Planning

The Couple to Couple League provides seminars about how to use your body's fertility signals to diagnose your cycle variability and help you achieve or avoid pregnancy with great accuracy. Their Web site includes information on finding local classes.

http://ccli.org

The International Council on Infertility Information Dissemination, Inc. (INCIID)

P.O. Box 6836

Arlington, VA 22206

(703) 379-9178

This is a great site for support purposes and information. They also offer chats with professionals for the layperson on various fertility questions.

http://inciid.org

RESOLVE: The National Infertility Association

7910 Woodmont Ave., Suite 1350

Bethesda, MD 20814

(888) 623-0744

The National Infertility Association is primarily an organization for persons interested in receiving support for various fertility issues. There are some great leadership positions in this organization filled by professionals in the field as well as parents.

http://resolve.org

Society for Assisted Reproductive Technology (SART)

1209 Montgomery Highway

Birmingham, AL 35216

(205) 978-5000, ext. 109

SART collects statistical information that can be used to help you compare the services offered by each fertility clinic. It is leading in its position and should be consulted when trying to decide which fertility program is right for you.

http://sart.org

Just for Fun

Web Sites

The Celebrity Baby Blog

If you think you are living your life under a microscope, check out the celebrities and their babies. Reading this blog really puts my life into perspective.

http://celebrity-babies.com

GameHouse

GameHouse.com has free online games that you can play online or download. These are great in the middle of the night when you can't get back to sleep.

http://gamehouse.com

See Mommy Run

This Web site has a free service dedicated to helping you find a local group of moms to exercise with, typically in a running or walking group.

www.seemommyrun.com

SparkPeople

Here you will find a free online community dedicated to helping you keep a healthier lifestyle. I joined to talk to other moms who were trying to stay fit with a little one in tow and I've really enjoyed it.

http://sparkpeople.com

Pregnancy Resources

Books

About.com Guide to Having a Baby by Robin Elise Weiss, LCCE

The Baby Book by Dr. William Sears

Baby Name Wizard by Laura Wattenberg

The Birth Book by Dr. William Sears

Birthing from Within by Pam England

Blessingways: A Guide to Mother-Centered Baby Showers by Shari Maser

The Happiest Baby on the Block by Harvey Karp, M.D.

Laughter and Tears by Elisabeth Bing

The No-Cry Sleep Solution by Elizabeth Pantley

The Official Lamaze Guide by Judy Lothian, Ph.D., and Charlotte DeVries

The Pregnancy Book by William Sears, M.D., and Martha Sears, R.N., I.B.C.L.C.

Rebounding from Childbirth by Lynn Madsen

The Thinking Woman's Guide to a Better Birth by Henci Goer

VBAC Companion by Diana Korte

Organizations

American Academy of Husband-Coached Childbirth (Bradley Method)

Box 5224

Sherman Oaks, CA 91413-5224

(800) 4-A-BIRTH

The Bradley Method of childbirth includes the use of deep relaxation and breathing with the help of the husband or a partner through the labor process. The classes emphasize prenatal nutrition and exercise, and their influence on a healthy pregnancy.

www.bradleybirth.com

American Academy of Pediatrics (AAP)

141 Northwest Point Blvd.

Elk Grove Village, IL 60007

(847) 434-4000

The American Academy of Pediatrics is the leading authority on children's issues and it is the governing body of pediatricians across America. Their Web site is full of information about babies and children, including the latest policy updates from this body of pediatricians. You will find helpful safety and health information for children of all ages.

www.aap.org

American College of Nurse-Midwives (ACNM)

8403 Colesville Rd., Suite 1550

Silver Spring, MD 20910

(240) 485-1800

The American College of Nurse-Midwives certifies nurse-midwives (CNM) throughout the United States. They focus on the care of low-risk women through pregnancy and birth as well as other time periods of life. Well-woman care is their specialty.

www.midwife.org

American College of Obstetricians and Gynecologists (ACOG)

409 12th St., S.W.

P.O. Box 96920

Washington, DC 20090-6920

(202) 638-5577

The American College of Obstetricians and Gynecologists is the premiere organization for obstetricians and gynecologists. They manage the postmedical school training and certification of this specialty. These physicians are trained in the care of a woman during all the stages of her life.

www.acog.org

Childbirth Connection

(formerly the Maternity Center Association)

281 Park Avenue South, 5th Floor

New York, NY 10010

(212) 777-5000

There is a lot of great consumer advice to be found here, including a new downloadable booklet on cesarean section called "What Every Pregnant Woman Needs to Know About Cesarean Section." There is even a complete pregnancy medical text available for you to read on their Web site.

www.childbirthconnection.org

Citizens for Midwifery (CfM)

P.O. Box 82227

Athens, GA 30608-2227

(888) CfM-4880

On this Web site, you will find information on promoting the midwives' model of care.

www.cfmidwifery.org

Coalition for Improving Maternity Services (CIMS)

P.O. Box 2346

Ponte Vedra Beach, FL 32004

(888) 282-CIMS

The Coalition for Improving Maternity Services has lots of great information on choosing a health-care provider, a place of birth, and information on making decisions for yourself in pregnancy and beyond.

www.motherfriendly.org

DONA International

(Formerly Doulas of North America)

P.O. Box 626

Jasper, IN 47547

(888) 788-DONA

DONA is the leading organization that certifies birth and postpartum doulas. A doula can assist the family before, during, or after birth. Using a doula has been shown to decrease the incidence of many complications of labor and post-

partum, including cesarean section and postpartum depression.

www.dona.org

International Cesarean Awareness Network (ICAN)

1304 Kingsdale Avenue

Redondo Beach, CA 90278

(310) 542-6400

ICAN works toward the prevention of unnecessary cesareans, and the emotional and physical recovery from cesareans.

www.ican-online.org

International Childbirth Education Association (ICEA)

P.O. Box 20048

Minneapolis, MN 55420

(952) 854-8660

ICEA trains childbirth and postpartum educators as well as prenatal fitness instructors and doulas throughout the world. Their Web site offers a search to help you find local instructors.

www.icea.org

Lamaze International

2025 M Street, Suite 800

Washington, DC 20036-3309

(202) 367-1128

Lamaze International is the leading certifying organization for childbirth educators. Promoting normal birth is the core of their philosophy as they train educators worldwide. Their site offers a directory, articles, and other interactive features.

www.lamaze.org

Midwives Alliance of North America (MANA)

375 Rockbridge Road, Suite 172-313
Lilburn, GA 30047
(888) 923-MANA (6262)
This site has information on the midwives' model of care, finding and selecting a midwife in your area, and how to become a certified professional midwife.

www.mana.org

Web Sites

About Pregnancy Guide

Here you will find pregnancy-related articles, a pregnancy calendar, ultrasound photos, community support, a belly gallery, and also pregnancy fitness—related resources.

http://pregnancy.about.com

Birth Activist

This site's tagline is "Bloggin' for better births." You'll find great discussions from well-known birth advocates, parents, and others here.

www.birthactivist.com

Birth Policy

This Web site has interesting information on the politics of birth, including current state and federal legislation to help protect pregnant women and their families.

www.birthpolicy.org

Childbirth.org

This pregnancy Web site is dedicated to helping you maintain a healthy pregnancy. There are many informative articles on all aspects of pregnancy and fun programs, including the boy or girl quiz and a birth-plan creator.

www.childbirth.org

Lamaze Institute for Normal Birth

Here you'll find great information on having a healthy, normal birth. This includes the researched-linked "six cares practices." These six care practices are the cornerstone to a healthy birth.

http://normalbirth.lamaze.org

VBAC

The VBAC Web site has information on all aspects of vaginal birth after cesareans, from personal stories and current research.

http://vbac.com

Index

Live-in help, 230–32
Living room, baby proofing, 156–57
Locks, 153–54
Lotions, 127–28
Lullabies, 76

M

Manual breast pumps, 42
Massage, of baby, 31–32, 76
Mastitis, 52
Matching Moms, 200
Maya Wrap, 176
Medical records, legal right to, 94–95
Medications, for everyday care, 116–18
Milk, storage of, 45–47
Mirror, as toy, 191
Moses baskets, 182–83
Multiples. See Twins
Music, 28–29, 190, 193, 213

N

Nannies, 231–32
Nanny Cam, 159
Naps, 81–82, 83
Neonatal intensive care unit (NICU), breastfeeding and, 44
Neonatologist, 86

Nesting toys, 192
Newman, Dr. Jack, 39
Nipples
    baby's confusion about breast and bottle, 48
    sore, 41
Nose congestion, 111
Nursery, baby proofing of, 158
Nursing strikes, 52
Nutrition, of baby. See Breastfeeding; Feeding
Nutrition, of parents, 82–83

O

Outlet plug covers, 151–52
Outside areas, baby proofing, 157–58

P

Parenting
    books about, 26, 90
    handling unwanted advice about, 14–16
Parenting plan, 237–38
    baby-led parenting, 242–44
    disagreements about, 245–47
    discipline and, 245
    Internet site links, 242, 246, 248

philosophies of parenting and, 237–39
    scheduled or parent-led parenting, 240–42
Parent-led parenting, 240–42
Pediatrician, 85–99
    changing of, 92–95
    choosing of, 85–88
    communicating with, 89–91
    contacting at first sign of illness, 107–8
    Internet site links, 86, 94, 99
    well-baby care and, 91–92
Penis care, 129
Pets, 16–21
Phototherapy, 116
Physical activity, play and, 189
Pillows, 40–41, 182
Play. See also Toys
    importance of, 187–90
    Internet site links, 201
    playgroups and classes, 197–200
    television and, 195–97
Playgroups, 197–200
Portable beds, 180–81
Postpartum depression, 34
Postpartum doula, 13, 14, 39, 83
Potty training, for infants, 65–67

▶ IT'S **About** *INFORMATION DELIVERED IN A REVOLUTIONARY NEW WAY.*

The Internet. Books. Experts. This is how—and where—we get our information today. And now, the best of these resources are available together in a revolutionary new series of how-to guides from **About.com** and Adams Media.

**The About.com Guide to
Acoustic Guitar**
ISBN 10: 1-59869-098-1
ISBN 13: 978-1-59869-098-9

**The About.com Guide to
Baby Care**
ISBN 10: 1-59869-274-7
ISBN 13: 978-1-59869-274-7

**The About.com Guide to
Getting in Shape**
ISBN 10: 1-59869-278-X
ISBN 13: 978-1-59869-278-5

**The About.com Guide to
Having a Baby**
ISBN 10: 1-59869-095-7
ISBN 13: 978-1-59869-095-8

**The About.com Guide to
Job Searching**
ISBN 10: 1-59869-097-3
ISBN 13: 978-1-59869-097-2

**The About.com Guide to
Owning a Dog**
ISBN 10: 1-59869-279-8
ISBN 13: 978-1-59869-279-2

**The About.com Guide to
Shortcut Cooking**
ISBN 10: 1-59869-273-9
ISBN 13: 978-1-59869-273-0

**The About.com Guide to
Southern Cooking**
ISBN 10: 1-59869-096-5
ISBN 13: 978-1-59869-096-5

Available wherever books are sold! Or call us at 1-800-258-0929 or visit us at *www.adamsmedia.com*.